TRAVELER

washington
d.c.

NATIONAL GEOGRAPHIC
TRAVELER

washington
d.c.

by John Thompson
photography by Richard Nowitz

National Geographic
Washington, D.C.

CONTENTS

Pages 2–3: The Jefferson Memorial and cherry blossoms draw crowds on a spring evening.
Left: Colorful kayaks await their turn on the Potomac River beneath the Key Bridge.

TRAVELING WITH EYES OPEN

Alert travelers go with a purpose and leave with a benefit. If you travel responsibly, you can help support wildlife conservation, historic preservation, and cultural enrichment in the places you visit. You can enrich your own travel experience as well.

To be a geo-savvy traveler:

- Recognize that your presence has an impact on the places you visit.

- Spend your time and money in ways that sustain local character. (Besides, it's more interesting that way.)

- Value the destination's natural and cultural heritage.

- Respect the local customs and traditions.

- Express appreciation to local people about things you find interesting and unique to the place: its nature and scenery, music and food, historic villages and buildings.

- Vote with your wallet: Support the people who support the place, patronizing businesses that make an effort to celebrate and protect what's special there. Seek out local shops, restaurants, and inns. Use tour operators who love their home—who love taking care of it and showing it off. Avoid businesses that detract from the character of the place.

- Enrich yourself, taking home memories and stories to tell, knowing that you have contributed to the preservation and enhancement of the destination.

That is the type of travel now called geotourism, defined as "tourism that sustains or enhances the geographical character of a place—its environment, culture, aesthetics, heritage, and the well-being of its residents." To learn more, visit National Geographic's Center for Sustainable Destinations at *nationalgeographic.com/travel/sustainable*.

TRAVELER

washington d.c.

ABOUT THE AUTHOR & THE PHOTOGRAPHER

John Thompson has written or contributed to more than a dozen titles for National Geographic Books. His latest Society publications include *Wildlands of the Upper South* and *America's Western Edge.*

Richard Nowitz was a contract photographer for *National Geographic WORLD* (now *Kids*) magazine and is now a contributing photographer to the National Geographic Image Collection. He has been the principal photographer of more than 20 large-format photo and travel guides; in 1968 he was honored by the Society of American Travel Writers as Travel Photographer of the Year.

Diana Parsell and **Jenny Rough** updated the 2011 edition and contributed many sidebars. Diana Parsell also wrote "Charting Your Trip."

Karen Carmichael updated the 2014 edition.

With contributions by:
Sean Groom, author of "City on the River" feature on pp. 34–35
Thomas Head, former executive wine and food editor of *Washingtonian* magazine, author of the original Travelwise section
David Montgomery, reporter with the *Washington Post* Style section, author of "Washington Today" on pp. 14–19
Barbara A. Noe, author of "It's a Spooky Little Town" feature on pp. 122–123
Mark Rogers, author of "Politics at Work" feature on pp. 58–59
James Yenckel, author of "Famous Denizens of Georgetown" feature on pp. 160–161

Charting Your Trip

Shedding its past reputation as a buttoned-down bureaucratic town, the city of Washington, D.C., buzzes these days with urban life and a cosmopolitan air. Politics still takes center stage. But the fabled monuments, world-class museums, vibrant cultural life, and vast swaths of open parkland make this a city to savor, while the compact layout puts it all within easy reach.

Many people think of Washington, D.C., mostly as the National Mall and the Smithsonian Institution, anchored by the U.S. Capitol at one end and the Lincoln Memorial at the other. But the often overlooked charms of this tiny 68-square-mile (176 sq km) city can best be found in its neighborhoods, each with a distinctive character. **Georgetown** is a favorite for its narrow streets, historic townhomes, and boutiques. **Dupont Circle** and **Adams Morgan** have an eclectic beat, **Capitol Hill** a village ambience. The **14th and U Street** area explodes these days with new restaurants, while the downtown **Penn Quarter** has become a vibrant arts district. Some long-neglected areas are getting a face-lift, thanks to projects like the new Nationals Park baseball stadium near the U.S. Capitol and the hip club scene that's growing up on formerly riot-scarred **H Street.**

What doesn't change is Washington's essential character as the nation's capital and the living embodiment of American democracy. Its symbolic center remains the National Mall. Most visits begin here, with a stroll among the monuments, a trip or two to the Smithsonian Institution (which actually consists of more than a dozen museums both on and off the Mall). It helps that so much of what you'll want to see lies in close proximity to the Mall and downtown. Easy access by the Metro system (*wmata.com*) means you can spend a few hours at a time, then return later for more. Keep in mind when touring on the Mall and Capitol Hill that the buildings are farther apart than they may seem on a map.

If You Have a Week

Washington offers so much that seeing everything would be a challenge even for the most intrepid traveler. But you can pack a lot into a week. Consider an itinerary of museums and sightseeing in the morning, with afternoons open to broader exploration of other places in or beyond town.

The Marine Corps War Memorial shows an iconic World War II moment.

A visit to the **Smithsonian** is mandatory. You'll have to choose, however, which of its museums to see. For a varied taste of the many collections and exhibits, allow a couple of days to explore those clustered around the Mall. **Air and Space, Natural History,** and **American History** draw the biggest crowds, but don't overlook smaller treasures such as the **Freer** and **Sackler Galleries,** with superb displays of Asian objects. The **Hirshhorn** is renowned for its cutting-edge art. Also along the Mall: the vast **National Gallery of Art.** Its two wings are connected underground. Near the Smithsonian museums but not part of them, the **U.S. Holocaust Museum** and the **Newseum** both offer rich educational experiences. The Smithsonian Metro station and several others close by will put you within a block or two of all these sites.

Dusk is the best time to visit the **Lincoln Memorial,** anchoring the Mall's western end. The light grows softer then, and it's quieter once traffic thins and federal workers have all gone home. Steps away from the Lincoln you'll find the black granite **Vietnam Veterans Memorial** and its wall of names especially moving. A hidden gem, with waterfalls and a serene park setting, is the **Franklin Delano Roosevelt Memorial,** tucked away in a glade alongside the **Tidal Basin.**

Start one day with a visit to the **U.S. Capitol** (book a tour in advance since same-day passes are limited), at the Mall's eastern end. You'll enter through the underground Visitor Center, across the street from the **Supreme Court** (no advance tickets; entrance is on a first-come, first-served basis) and a block from the Capitol South Metro station. Nearby and well worth a look inside is the ornate **Jefferson Building** of the **Library of Congress.** Grab lunch several blocks away at a café or bistro around **Eastern Market** and **Barracks Row.**

NOT TO BE MISSED:

The Library of Congress 62–63

Browsing Eastern Market 66

The National Mall, monuments, Smithsonian, and springtime cherry blossoms 69–106

A view of the White House from Lafayette Square 116

Strolling Georgetown 150–154

The Phillips Collection 166–169

Trying ethnic restaurants in lively Adams Morgan 175

Lunch or tea in the gardens at Hillwood Estate 187–188

A visit to Mount Vernon with a stop in Old Town, Alexandria, Virginia 224–226

Visitor Information

Advance planning and reservations are always a good idea, ensuring you don't waste precious time. In the busiest tourist seasons (April through August), when lines can be long, it's often mandatory.

Destination DC *(washington.org)* is a one-site directory of good information. You can request or download the free 128-page Official Visitor's Guide, which is updated twice a year. The **D.C. Tourist Information Center** *(509 9th St., N.W.,*

tel 866/324-7386, dcchamber.org) has free maps and city guides. It's open weekdays from 8:30 a.m. to 5:30 p.m.

If you like discovering hidden points of interest, check out the neighborhood walking tours developed by **Cultural Tourism DC** *(culturaltourismdc.org)*. And for tips on the ever changing restaurant scene and nightlife, browse the online site of *Washingtonian* magazine *(washingtonian.com).*

Come dinnertime, you'll discover that Washington has become a foodie town with a diverse range of choices—from well-priced ethnic restaurants to pricey temples of gastronomy. And do try to take in a play or other performance while you're here. A local favorite are the bold, contemporary stagings of the classics by the **Shakespeare Theater Company,** in the downtown Penn Quarter. The **Kennedy Center,** in the Foggy Bottom neighborhood, offers opera, theater, and ballet as well as free concerts daily at 6 p.m. A heavy influx of young people to Washington in recent years has also given rise to comedy clubs and open-mic events at venues such as the popular café cum bookstores **Busboys & Poets** in Washington, D.C., and Shirlington, Virginia.

If You Have More Time

Plan to reserve one morning or afternoon for a trip to **Mount Vernon,** George Washington's plantation house on the banks of the Potomac River. It's in Virginia, 16 miles (25 km) south of Washington; you can get there by Metro, then bus. For a

---

Pack Your Walking Shoes, or Hop a Bus

Like most world-class cities, Washington is best discovered one step at a time. Indeed, D.C. is a place made for walking. In a 2007 urban study by the Brookings Institution, Washington was named the most walkable city in the United States. At first glance, the city's low structural heights and neoclassical dominance in federal buildings seem to make for a homogenized urban landscape. But upon closer inspection, this compact capital city has a welcoming human scale and a wealth of architectural styles. It's also a refreshingly green city, with thousands of acres of easily accessed federal parkland that is exquisitely landscaped and immune to development.

But even the most devoted on-foot explorer needs to sit back and just look around now and then. The city's fleet of red and gray **DC Circulator buses** (*dccirculator.com*) are just the ticket. They make frequent circuits around the National Mall and along four other routes. It's $1 each time you hop on. You can pay by cash (exact change), Metro's SmartTrip card, or buy unlimited-trip passes online at *commuterdirect.com.*

---

pleasant all-day excursion, combine a visit to Mount Vernon with several hours in colonial-era **Old Town, Alexandria,** halfway between Washington and Mount Vernon. The **Mount Vernon Trail** along the Virginia side of the Potomac gives Washington a great recreational artery for biking, jogging, or strolling. From the section that lies near Rosslyn you'll get awesome views of the D.C. skyline and its famous landmarks. Close by is **Arlington National Cemetery,** easily accessible by Metro.

Back in Washington, D.C., other good ideas for convenient and memorable outings include the **C & O Canal trail,** which runs through Georgetown on its way to Maryland; a summer baseball game at **Nationals Park;** and the popular **National Zoo. Hillwood Estate Museum and Gardens,** with a remarkable collection of Russian art and icons, is in the same Upper Northwest neighborhood as the zoo and has a nice café that serves both lunch and tea (reservations advised).

For an afternoon of shopping head to Georgetown or up **Wisconsin Avenue** to the enclave of swanky shops around Chevy Chase and Mazza Gallerie. And don't

THEY (WHO) SEEK TO ESTABLISH
SYSTEMS OF GOVERNMENT BASED ON
THE REGIMENTATION OF ALL HUMAN
BEINGS BY A HANDFUL OF INDIVIDUAL
RULERS... CALL THIS A NEW ORDER.
IT IS NOT NEW AND IT IS NOT ORDER.

The FDR Memorial also remembers the Depression-era President's lovable dog, Fala.

overlook the city's museum shops when you're downtown; many of them offer distinctive items that make great gifts or souvenirs. The **National Building Museum** has one of the best selections in town.

If you find yourself craving a bit of relief from Washington, consider blocking out a day for a trip to Annapolis or Baltimore. Getting to either place from Washington usually takes less than an hour's drive. But traffic in the metropolitan area can be horrendous, especially during rush hour, so plan accordingly. **Annapolis,** 30 miles (48 km) east of Washington via U.S. 50, is great for rambling. A maze of streets surrounding the **Maryland State House** feature historic homes, high-class antique shops, and a seaside dock of restaurants serving the region's famous crab cakes. **Baltimore,** in revitalizing itself over the last three decades, has managed to preserve a friendly folksiness beneath its urban veneer. You'll find world-class arts, several science museums, and a vibrant **Inner Harbor**—but also bars in **Fells Point** that ring with acoustic guitar music and joints that serve breakfast all day. Get there from Washington by driving north on I-95 or, even better, via an under-an-hour ride on an Amtrak train from **Union Station** in Washington, D.C. ∎

Metro Tips

Washington's subway system is easy to navigate. Plan your routes by visiting *wmata.com*. At the stations, stand to the right on the escalators so that those in a hurry can pass up or down on the left. The farecard machines have step-by-step illustrated instructions. Buy your farecard with a small bill; change is in coins only. Long-term SmarTrip cards can be bought with a credit card and value can be added. You can ask the station manager (usually in the glass kiosk) for help if you have any difficulty.

History & Culture

The gold-leaf eagle has landed—atop
Union Station.
Opposite: "Milestones of Flight," the
main hall at the Smithsonian National
Air and Space Museum

Washington Today

A heady self-confidence is blossoming in Washington, D.C., as the city boldly demonstrates it is a city, not some unclassifiable zone dubbed the District of Columbia—a term that appears in speeches but never in conversation.

To natives and longtime transplants, home is just Dee-Cee, thank you, or Wahrshington in soft Southern-accented tones slightly edged by the oddly Elizabethan flint of dialects around the Chesapeake Bay. Washington never forgets that the government is the reason this once marshy lowland was reclaimed and the federal city was planted at a bend in the Potomac River. Yet the city defiantly transcends its role as a bland backdrop to the grandeur of the monuments, museums, and great American history hereabouts. Those things are why many people come—but not why they stay.

The map looks as if something took a ragged bite out of the once perfect 100-square-mile (259 sq km) diamond-shaped District. That happened in 1846, when Virginia reclaimed its share of the land donated to create the capital. The remaining 68 square miles (176 sq km), originally part of Maryland, make an intimate city of 601,723 people (2010 US Census), though a recent 2013 estimate recorded a population as high as 646,449.

The other physical dimension of the intimate city is up, and in Washington ambition soars higher than architecture. No building stands taller than the Capitol dome; in the densest part of town—the K Street canyon populated by lawyers and lobbyists—offices top out at the 12th floor. This architectural homage to the Capitol means the typical Washington street has one of the biggest skies in urban America. It makes walking a pleasure in a city designed with walkers in mind, with wide avenues and breathtaking sight lines anchored by Pierre-Charles L'Enfant's ceremonial circles. Turn a corner and you might see the upper quarter of the Washington Monument peeking above the modest roofline of a modern office building—a juxtaposition of the monumental capital and the working city that is quintessentially Washington.

The dual nature of the city's soul is reflected in myriad ways as power Washington and workaday Washington mingle serendipitously. Spend time shopping in Georgetown, lunching near Connecticut Avenue, or talking politics on Pennsylvania Avenue,

---

EXPERIENCE:
Take a Bus or Trolley Tour

A good way to begin your visit is with a general tour. It will help you get your bearings, introduce you to places you might not get to on your own, and give you a clue as to where you may want to spend more time later. **Big Bus Tours** (tel 877/332-8689, bigbustours.com), authorized by the National Park Service, has the Patriot Tour, the official tour of the National Mall which also goes to Arlington National Cemetery and the Pentagon. For specialty tours and great views from open-top double-decker buses, check out **DC Tours** (dctours.us). **Old Town Trolley** (tel 202/832-9800, historictours.com) offers two-hour narrated tours.

The Capitol Reflecting Pool mirrors the U.S. Capitol and a statue of Ulysses S. Grant.

and you'll be startled to see motorcycle police appear out of nowhere and block traffic. Next you'll hear the sirens, then comes the speeding motorcade: the President on his way to some engagement, or perhaps some dignitary being whisked across town. Then the police vanish—maestros of that Washington ballet of the blacktop, the rolling blockade.

Washingtonians always know when someone important has moved down the block. Suddenly fit-looking men and women in plain clothes wearing earpieces linger about. In Glover Park, trying to guess which neighbor's house conceals the entrance to a secret FBI tunnel under the old Soviet Embassy has been a favorite parlor game.

Not that the privilege of being the nation's capital isn't sometimes a burden. When that happens, Washington, ever the gracious Southern hostess, can also play the irreverent Northern wag. The lack of a vote in Congress is a sore point. Washingtonians pay $2 billion a year in federal income taxes yet have no say in how the money is spent. Repeated attempts to repeal that have failed. The Constitution dictates that the District cannot be a state, but Congress could grant it a vote in the federal legislature. In 2000, the city's 200th anniversary as the capital, a resident came up with a popular—and populist—new license plate motto: "Taxation Without Representation."

As Washington strides into the future, its aspirations rise in glass and limestone amid the marble totems of its past. Construction cranes hover throughout the downtown like a new kind of Washington monument while layers of scaffolding signal exciting new uses of old spaces:

a buzzing 7th Street corridor, luxury hotel rooms inside the 19th-century Tariff Building, and welcome makeovers of august institutions such as the Smithsonian's American History Museum.

Preservation guidelines are intended to ensure that development travesties don't mar the best of the old; still, there's always a fear that shiny new facades and high rents will doom quirky neighborhood joints. A buttoned-down town like Washington needs as many of these places as it can get. District residents take infinite comfort that Ben's Chili Bowl on U Street continues to purvey the best chili dogs in the free world. Around Ben's, the street that was once known as the "Black Broadway," where native son Duke Ellington played, throbs again with energy beneath the soulful gaze of Ellington himself—painted larger than life on the side of a building *(1209 U St., N.W.).*

District residents take infinite comfort that Ben's Chili Bowl on U Street continues to purvey the best chili dogs in the free world.

Marilyn Monroe is a regular on the busy corner of Calvert Street and Connecticut Avenue.

Postcard Washington is a vision of famous buildings, but the people make the city. Contrary to reputation, this is not a population of transients, a capital of people from someplace else getting ready to leave. When a presidential administration changes, or a new Congress is seated, only a few thousand people arrive to replace the few thousand on their way out.

Most Washingtonians don't work for the government. Many settled here for opportunities in technology, education, public policy, international affairs, and journalism. A large core of native Washingtonians, particularly African-American families, moved here from the South generations ago when jobs in the federal government afforded one of the few avenues of advancement for blacks. Now about 50 percent of the population is black, 43 percent white. The growing Hispanic community is about 10 percent.

In the late 1990s Washingtonians began to hear real estate agents use a surprising word to describe the city: "Hot!" Suburban traffic congestion, falling crime, and an improving economy merged to make city living fashionable again. Decades of population loss subsided, replaced by slight annual gains. The newcomers are busy restoring row houses in once neglected neighborhoods and filling new condo complexes, with the ease of the Metro at their doorstep.

Even longtime Washingtonians still savor monumental Washington. They stand at the top of the Capitol steps and try again to absorb the perfect landscape geometry lesson that is the Mall. They visit their favorite Smithsonian exhibits religiously and take in the latest additions, often after the crowds are gone. They wait to see the Washington Monument at sundown, when the marble turns rose and gold.

But Washingtonians would just as soon leave the Mall and zip out to the National Arboretum in Northeast to study the exquisite bonsai tree exhibition. Or take the kids on an excursion to the remains of the Civil War forts that once ringed the city. Or catch a home baseball game since the national pastime returned to the capital in 2005 after a 34-year hiatus. Or disappear into the wilds of Rock Creek Park, where you can forget you are in a major city. It is places like these—beyond the Mall—where the

Follow the beat at the beautifully landscaped Meridian Park (16th and Euclid Streets).

Who Lives Here

To the people who call it home, Washington isn't just tiny D.C.—but the entire Washington Metropolitan Area, which includes parts of Virginia and Maryland. Total population: 5.6 million. Greater Washington has one of the most affluent, diverse, and educated populations in the United States.

• Some 51 percent of residents 25 and older have a bachelor's degree, 23 percent an advanced degree. D.C. has 50 local colleges and universities.

• The area's median household income is the country's highest: $88,233.

• Diplomatic missions of 174 countries work at embassies in D.C., most of which are near Dupont Circle, Kalorama, and along Massachusetts Avenue—on Embassy Row.

• According to a *Wall Street Journal* survey, Washington tied with Seattle as the No. 1 "youth magnet."

heart of the living city beats in four quadrants. The perfect coda to seeing the Lincoln Memorial is a visit to the Frederick Douglass house in Anacostia. During the Potomac springtime, when the perfume of Southern blooms intoxicates even the most hopeless workaholic, by all means go to see the cherry blossoms suspended like pink breath around the Tidal Basin—but also don't miss the less crowded and still spectacular blossom display at Dumbarton Oaks in Georgetown.

Spanish will get you as far as English in the Adams Morgan neighborhood, where club music blares until 2 a.m. The cuisine in this multicultural part of town runs from Ethiopian and Salvadoran to Vietnamese and Caribbean; there are even dishes from the top of the world at the Himalayan Heritage restaurant. Hop the Metro to the Southwest waterfront and find the latest Pulitzer Prize–winning play at the renovated Arena Stage or the freshest catch from the Chesapeake being hawked on the Maine Avenue docks.

It's in the neighborhoods that Washington comes most clearly into perspective. Make your way up the hill in Anacostia that John Wilkes Booth crossed when escaping after he assassinated Abraham Lincoln, and take in the view from the historic Frederick Douglass house. Or find a perch on the Brookland heights occupied by the Basilica of the National Shrine of the Immaculate Conception. Washington, D.C., spreads out before you—the low downtown skyline slipping into rings of row house neighborhoods stretched along the long lines of L'Enfant's broad boulevards.

And there, too, are the white dome and the obelisk—still grand at this distance, but not so dominating, and part of a larger picture. ■

> **Spanish will get you as far as English in the Adams Morgan neighborhood, where club music blares until 2 a.m.**

History of Washington

George Washington, Pierre-Charles L'Enfant, and the many others involved knew they were engaged in something momentous when they set out to design the capital of the United States in the late 1700s. In an age when preplanned cities of this scale were unheard of, here was a chance to lay out a worldwide center of culture, commerce, learning, and government.

Doing It on Purpose

Seven years had passed since the Revolutionary War when, in July 1790, Congress agreed on the location of a new capital. Until that time, citizens of the new nation had identified primarily with their home state, thinking of themselves as Virginians or New Yorkers rather than Americans. Local ties would continue to command the loyalties of many, but it was clear that establishing the seat of a central government was essential to holding the loosely joined republic together.

One key was to avoid the mistakes of the European empires that had failed the very people who were here now. This was to be a government of the people, so the placement and design of the capital would set the tone for a federal government that aspired to be strong but not domineering. The capital, by extension, must be grand yet welcoming.

The first step in that tall order was to pick an appropriate place. With the 13 Colonies strewn the length of the eastern seaboard, it was logical to locate the capital about halfway down. In a classic display of democratic compromise, Secretary of the Treasury Alexander Hamilton agreed to urge northern states to vote for a southern capital if Virginia Representative James Madison would support federal assumption of state war debts (he did). So despite occupying the approximate midpoint of the coast, Washington was deemed a "Southern" town from the outset, a characterization that had much to do with the fact that Washington lay 60 miles (96 km) south of the Mason-Dixon Line—the Maryland-Pennsylvania border that divides North and South.

As for the precise size and the location of the new city, Congress left President Washington somewhat in the dark. The representatives decreed only that the capital was not to exceed 10 miles square (26 sq km), and that it must be positioned on the Potomac River between the mouth of the Eastern Branch (now called the Anacostia

Smith on the Potomac

Journeying far from Jamestown, Capt. John Smith and his men sailed up the Potomac River in June 1608. It was part of two trips, totaling nearly 3,000 miles (4,800 km), to explore the Chesapeake Bay and surrounding waterways. On the Potomac they went as far as Great Falls, Virginia. From late winter through August, fish such as herring and sturgeon swam upriver. Smith wrote: "Neither better fish, more plenty, not more variety for small fish had any of us ever seen in a place." Along the "Patowmeck" the men saw several villages of Indians—probably Algonquin—on the shore of what is now George Washington Memorial Parkway; one village occupied present-day Theodore Roosevelt Island.

Charles Willson Peale's "George Washington" (1772) portrays the young Virginia colonel.

River) and Conococheague Creek, some 70 miles (112 km) upriver. The rest was up to Washington.

In January of 1791, Washington selected a swatch of land at the highest navigable point on the Potomac River, where it was joined by the Eastern Branch. The site was partly a marriage of convenience: The preexisting river-port towns of Alexandria, Virginia, and Georgetown, Maryland, could easily receive shipments of the lumber and other supplies the city would need to sustain construction.

Laid out in a square carved from Maryland (mostly) and Virginia, the capital was named "City of Washington" to honor America's first President. Surveyor Andrew Ellicott and Benjamin Banneker—his self-taught, freeborn black assistant—delimited a square 10 miles (26 sq km) on a side, with the corners pointing in the cardinal directions. Though President Washington had trained as a surveyor, like any good leader he was quick to recognize those moments when he needed expert advice. For his chief engineer he chose a well-connected young Frenchman who had fought against the British

An undated drawing shows British soldiers gutting the White House with fire during the War of 1812.

during the Revolutionary War and had gone on to design a temporary headquarters for the federal government in New York. The idea of creating an important city out of nothing appealed mightily to the brilliant Pierre-Charles L'Enfant—and apparently daunted him not at all. Angling for the job, he wrote these words to President Washington in 1789: "No nation, perhaps, had ever before the opportunity offered them of deliberately deciding on the spot where their Capital City should be fixed."

L'Enfant got the job. Throughout 1791, he could be seen standing high atop Jenkins Hill (now Capitol Hill) or striding the woods of Tiber Creek (modern-day Constitution Avenue), his surveying instruments in hand, measuring distances and elevations. By contrast, L'Enfant's motivation—a vision of a grand city of broad avenues, monumental government edifices, and stirring vistas—remained invisible to all but himself. "I see the capital city as something more than a place to live and work," he wrote. "I see it as a symbol ... [W]e should plan now with the realization that a great nation is going to rise on this continent ... Right now, we have a chance which no nation has ever given itself ... How can America plan for less than greatness?"

> **Standing a mile apart but joined by Pennsylvania Avenue, the Capitol Building and the President's House formed a barbell.**

L'Enfant Terrible

L'Enfant's extraordinary prescience and pride were voiced at a time when the country's most populous city, Philadelphia, claimed only 28,522 residents. Yet here was L'Enfant, imagining a capital of 800,000 citizens—larger than many of the European cities such as Paris that had served as his models.

As it turned out, L'Enfant was dead-on: At its population peak in 1950, Washington was home to about 802,000 people. (That number is now estimated to be 646,449.)

Standing a mile apart but joined by Pennsylvania Avenue, the Capitol Building and the President's House formed a barbell. This was the core of L'Enfant's design. (The presidential residence would not be officially named the White House until 1901.) Several broad streets would radiate from these two powerhouses, signifying their accessibility. The avenues would unspool at length before ending at circular intersections atop hills, creating views of "magnificent distances."

The Capitol would divide the city into quadrants, while a grid of numbered and lettered streets would be superimposed on the radiating avenues. The Mall, extending about 1 mile (1.6 km) west from the Capitol to the Potomac River, would be a grand esplanade similar to the one L'Enfant had beheld in Marly, near Versailles. The Frenchman foresaw fine baroque houses lining it on either side.

Within a year, L'Enfant had been fired by President Washington for insubordination and refusal to compromise. Still, his plan was largely enacted: Trees and buildings may veil a few hoped-for views of "magnificent distances," yet Dupont and Scott Circles, among others, display the beauty of the original design.

Despite its ambitious origin, the city hardly sprang up overnight. Congressmen arriving for the Inaugural session in 1800 looked out upon a dismal scene. The streets were muddy. Mosquitoes and snakes bred in abundance. Hogs and cattle roamed at will, while the unfinished Capitol and President's House had spawned attendant clusters of huts and shacks resembling refugee villages. One newly minted statesman dubbed this hardship post "a mud-hole equal to the great Serbonian bog."

With no property tax on government buildings, the city relied on real estate speculation for funding. Yet buyers were scarce: By 1800, less than 10 percent of city lots had been sold. Washington grew from 8,208 people by 1810 to 18,826 by 1830, a rate far below the national average. Gazing upon these wide, uncluttered avenues going nowhere, Charles Dickens would dub Washington "the City of Magnificent Intentions."

War Comes to Washington

The War of 1812 proved to be a turning point in the city's fortunes, which mirrored those of the country at large. In August 1814, with the British victory sealed,

redcoats landed in Maryland and marched on Washington, where they torched the Capitol, the President's House, and all federal buildings except the old Blodgett's Hotel, which housed both the Post Office and the Patent Office at the time.

Though slavery would not be outlawed in the city until 1862, by 1830 Washington had more free blacks than slaves.

Afterward, Congress came close to voting that the capital be relocated. But with local bankers promising to help rebuild the city—and galvanized by the strong sense of community in adversity—Washington dug in and bounced back. President Madison repaired to the Octagon House—a friend's nearby residence—Congress moved to the Patent Office (and from there to a temporary building on the site of the present-day Supreme Court), and life went on.

The third of the District lying west and south of the river was ceded back to Virginia in 1846. Not only did the federal government have no need for the land on that side of the Potomac River, but Alexandria—having lost political advantages by its inclusion in the District—had petitioned the state to re-embrace it. This reduced Washington City to a parcel of land covering just 68 square miles (176 sq km).

A time-lapse photograph of Dupont Circle shows that L'Enfant's vision of central circles lives on.

A Second City

History's most bitter irony may be that this bastion of freedom was built on slave labor. Beginning in the 1790s, plantation owners in Maryland and Virginia were paid for the use of their slaves to supplement the meager supply of skilled workers constructing the capital. In a parallel development, the city became a magnet for the disenfranchised. Situated at the northern extreme of the upper South, Washington was a natural gateway for runaway slaves. Though slavery would not be outlawed in the city until 1862, by 1830 Washington had more free blacks than slaves. A "second city"—one composed largely of African Americans—sprang to life within the federal city.

Lacking a permanently entrenched society but rich with a transient mix of foreigners and congressmen, Washington was more tolerant of blacks than were other Southern cities. From 1807 to 1861, more than 15 private black schools flourished in the district.

Occasionally, however, race riots erupted. On the heels of the Nat Turner Rebellion in 1831, the Snow Riot of 1835 was ignited by two unrelated events: A slave allegedly tried to murder the widow of the U.S. Capitol designer, William Thornton, and a white physician was arrested for possession of abolitionist tracts, whose publication or distribution was forbidden in D.C.

Rebuffed from lynching the doctor, a white mob turned its fury on Mr. Beverly Snow, the free black owner of a local restaurant. Snow escaped, but roving bands attacked black churches, schools, restaurants, and tenements for the next week. Before long the city had tightened its black codes—discriminatory laws governing the behavior of free blacks.

"The Peacemakers" (1868) by George P. A. Healy depicts William Sherman, Ulysses S. Grant, President Lincoln, and David Porter discussing peace terms just before the Civil War's end.

In the 1830s and '40s, Congress heard numerous petitions to banish slavery in Washington—the only place over which it exercised total control. Each time, shamefully, Georgetown's Southern-leaning aristocracy joined with the pro-slavery segment of Congress to keep the issue from being seriously debated.

In April 1848, 77 Washington slaves boarded the schooner *Pearl* at a city wharf and tried to escape to freedom down the Potomac River. Captured within a day, the slaves—many of them privileged house servants with only a few years' bondage remaining—were sold off to agents in Louisiana and Georgia. The deep passions stirred by the affair led the House of Representatives to pass a resolution that year calling for an end to the slave trade in Washington.

The resolution was nothing but paper. Slavery itself continued. Free blacks were only marginally better off. Black or white, poor neighborhoods were plagued by violent crime. The seedier areas of town included Swampoodle (now the area north of Massachusetts and New Jersey Avenues) and Murder Bay (today's Federal Triangle). The latter—located between President's Park (the Ellipse) and the fetid Washington City Canal (since covered by Constitution Avenue)—was especially notorious. "Crime, filth, and poverty seem to vie with each other in a career of degradation and death," a police superintendent characterized Murder Bay in 1866. "Whole families ... are crowded into mere apologies for shanties."

Brother Against Brother

Monumental Washington started to take shape in the years leading up to the Civil War. Work began on the Washington Monument in 1848, but within six years funds had dried up, the monument was mired in political controversy, and construction was suspended with the building just 152 feet (46 m) tall. By the time work resumed in 1880, white marble from the original quarry was no longer available; the white marble furnished by the second quarry has weathered differently from the base, yielding the two-tone tower in evidence today.

The distinctive red-sandstone Smithsonian Castle rose beside the Mall in 1855, paving the way for several national museums. A forerunner to the National Theatre was in place on Pennsylvania Avenue by 1835. The Willard and other fine hotels popped up in the neighborhood by the 1850s. Amid the statuary and posh town houses of Lafayette Square, the President's House had settled into a state of manorial dignity, complete with greenhouses, flower gardens, and fruit trees.

Destined to tower above it all, the Capitol's cast-iron dome (replacing its wood dome of 1822) was under way by the Civil War's outbreak in April 1861. Despite an absence of building funds during that conflict, Lincoln ordered the Capitol's construction to go forward as a sign that the Union would endure.

Considered a remote and somewhat sleepy town before the Civil War, Washington now entered the national consciousness as the staging ground for Union forces and the embattled capital of a divided nation. With the Confederate capital of Richmond, Virginia, just 100 miles (160 km) distant, the war's major battles—Fredericksburg, Antietam, Gettysburg—formed an arc within easy striking distance of Washington. The first and second battles of Bull Run, for example, took place just 30 miles (48 km) west of city limits.

To keep the Rebels at bay should they outflank the Union Army, a ring of 68 forts was hastily thrown up around Washington. These installations proved their worth in July 1864, when a large Confederate force led by Gen. Jubal Early dashed through Maryland and reached the city's northern portal of Fort Stevens. Early's assault was repulsed within a day, but it gave the President a vivid taste of combat: Observing the skirmish from the fort's parapet, the 6-foot-4-inch (1.93 m) top-hatted Lincoln made such a tempting target for enemy sharpshooters that a Union officer reprimanded him, "Get down, you damn fool, before you get shot!" The words were out of his mouth before the speaker—Lt. Col. (and future Supreme Court justice) Oliver Wendell Holmes, Jr.—realized he was upbraiding the President.

Washington was eventually overwhelmed—by its own troops. Bone-weary soldiers arrived by ship and rail, thronging the streets, falling asleep on vacant lots and sidewalks. Horse-drawn guns and caissons rutted the muddy streets; livestock grazed on the Mall; a bakery and barracks opened in the Capitol.

The distinctive red-sandstone Smithsonian Castle rose beside the Mall in 1855, paving the way for several national museums.

With more than 4,000 prostitutes in residence, a newspaper reported, the "majority of the women on the streets were openly disreputable." Troops under Gen. Joseph Hooker were such constant patrons of the red-light district southeast of the Treasury Department that the area was dubbed "Hooker's Division."

As battle casualties poured into Washington, the city scrambled to treat as many as 50,000 sick or injured soldiers at once. Practically every church, public building, and large private home in the city was pressed into service as military housing.

Happy Days Again

The population explosion unleashed by the war—during which the city grew from 60,000 to 140,000 inhabitants, including 40,000 former slaves—continued to boom in peacetime. Freedmen's Village in Arlington and Barry Farm in Anacostia received federal aid to house northward-migrating blacks.

With the help of radical Republicans bent on Reconstruction, black Washington enjoyed a sudden (if short-lived) heyday in the late 1860s and early 1870s. Howard University and the nation's first black high school—both staffed by top-notch instructors turning out well-educated graduates—were founded during this period. At the same time, blacks moved into jobs as officials and clerks, launched newspapers and other businesses, and mingled in white society.

Washington had elected its own mayors and aldermen since 1820. With the city in debt and officials apprehensive about the power of the newly granted black vote, Congress scrapped that system in 1871 and replaced it with a territorial government headed by a presidentially appointed governor. The new city government included boards of

Politics as Unusual

If it is true that all politics is local, Washington is no exception. Washingtonians, fueled by the injustice of being deprived of full congressional representation, often obsessively focus on local politics.

Except for a brief flowering of self-governance from 1812 to 1871, Congress and the President long controlled the city government and appointed its officials. In 1970, Washington was finally allowed to send a delegate to the House of Representatives but without major voting authority.

In 1973 civil rights and home rule activists won Washington the right to elect its own mayor and city council. But Congress retained the right to interfere in local government whenever it deemed necessary. That happened in 1995: With district finances in a shambles, Congress created a presidentially appointed D.C. financial control board that took over the city reins for a while.

After the 1998 mayoral election of Anthony Williams, previously the city's chief financial officer, the health of the city improved dramatically and the control board eventually released its grip on Washington.

After Adrian Fenty took office in 2007, he launched an ambitious program of improvements that included major reform of the city's public schools, new recreational facilities, and economic development. He was defeated in re-election by Vincent Gray, whose single term was plagued by hiring and campaign finance scandals. In the April 2014 Democratic primary Gray lost to D.C. council member Muriel Bowser.

public works and health; a nonvoting delegate to Congress; an elected house of delegates; and a President-appointed council, with Frederick Douglass one of three blacks among its 11 members.

President Ulysses S. Grant wanted to hand the governorship of this newborn political entity to his crony Alexander R. "Boss" Shepherd. He backed down when the city's conservative old guard protested his choice, but Shepherd wormed his way into power nonetheless: He was named vice president of public works, a post that allowed him to run the entire city.

"How is our new governor like a sheep?" went a riddle popular at the time.

"He is led by A. Shepherd" was the answer.

By hook but mostly by crook, Boss Shepherd led the way for the next three years. During his reign the city added miles of sewers, water lines, gas lines, sidewalks, and roads, as well as 60,000 trees and more than 1,000 houses and buildings. Most important, Shepherd saw to it that miles upon miles of streets were leveled and paved. Working people adored him for the jobs and civic improvements; blue bloods despised him for raising their taxes.

> **In Washington as in many other American cities, the final quarter of the 19th century was a fin de siècle free-for-all.**

As it turned out, citizens were amply justified in feeling fleeced. Authorized to spend $4 million on the city, Shepherd approved the expenditure of $20 million instead. This put the city in hock but landed Shepherd in a mansion on Farragut Square, two blocks from the White House.

Armed with Grant's tacit approval, Shepherd bullied the city into submission. When the Baltimore & Ohio Railroad delayed removing its tracks from the Capitol grounds, Shepherd loyalists materialized at midnight to rip up the offending ties and rails. He invited critics of such tactics to "git up and git."

Shepherd's undoing was the financial panic of 1873. The next year, Congress dissolved the territorial government and installed three presidentially appointed commissioners. The Organic Act of 1878 abolished home rule for good, giving the three commissioners "near-absolute power." It also set up the system whereby the district receives an annual operating subsidy from the federal government for the costs that the federal presence places on the city. The federal government now employs some 467,000 people, about 14 percent of the region's workforce, and suburban commuters hold many of these jobs.

Into the 20th Century

In Washington as in many other American cities, the final quarter of the 19th century was a fin de siècle free-for-all. Hotels, public buildings, and arriviste villas mushroomed along the city's main avenues. Though industry was confined to a handful of gristmills and breweries in Georgetown and Foggy Bottom, Washington's main employer—the federal government—provided thousands of jobs. In addition to the clerks needed to run the many newly born government agencies, construction workers were in demand to complete the long-delayed Washington Monument (1884), to construct the Library of Congress (1897), and to erect many other buildings that are city landmarks today. The National Zoological Park (1889) and Rock Creek Park (1890) were also created, putting the pleasures of nature within easy reach of downtown museums and monuments.

Even as official Washington flourished, the city was nurturing seeds of discontent. Thousands of poor people had gravitated to the capital, lured by the simple notion that the President's adoptive hometown would welcome them as well. Rarely was that the case. Washington's alleys, home to more than 17,000 residents, were notorious incubators of filth, crime, and disease. Most of these alleys would ultimately be torn down or gentrified, driving the poor underclass from one neighborhood to another.

To help the growing city realize the beauty envisioned by L'Enfant, in 1901 Senator James McMillan proposed a commission that would upgrade the Mall, expand the White House and the park system, and place judicial and congressional office buildings facing the Capitol. McMillan recruited four brilliant designers—architects Charles McKim and Daniel Burnham, landscape architect Frederick Law Olmsted, and sculptor Augustus Saint-Gaudens—whose plans, drawn up free of charge, would be transformed into reality by the U.S. Army Corps of Engineers.

With Burnham leading the way, the city beautification began to take shape. Railroad tracks crisscrossing the Mall were torn out. The Mall was extended to stretch all the way from the Capitol to the site of a planned memorial to Abraham Lincoln at its far west end. Gardens, fountains, and a reflecting pool were slated for the Mall as well. An opulent tram station—Union Station—designed by Burnham himself, rose north of the Capitol.

Not every aspect of the plan was enacted, yet it furnished a blueprint for future growth of the city core. It's fair to say that the McMillan Plan made possible the Mall's current status as a national showpiece.

Struggles for Freedom

During the 1910s, the city's population swelled again as workers flooded in to support America's role in World War I. By decade's end, nearly 450,000 people called Washington home—a 32 percent increase since 1910. The Mall, which had begun to feel like a park, became a vast parking lot for hundreds of new automobiles that suddenly appeared in Washington.

With the proliferation of relief agencies during the Great Depression and President Franklin D. Roosevelt's New Deal, the number of workers on Washington's federal payroll rose from 70,261 in June 1933 to 108,673 in June 1935. Construction added many new facades to the cityscape: the Supreme Court building, the Federal Triangle buildings, the Library of Congress Annex (now called the John Adams Building), the Longworth House Office Building, and nearly 5,000 houses, apartment buildings, and office buildings.

> In 1945, Washington found itself the capital of the most powerful nation on Earth. It had evolved from a small Southern town.

As the city focused it efforts on winning World War II, the early 1940s brought yet another influx of new Washingtonians. Thousands of female office workers and servicemen descended on the city, and many of them stayed on after the war. By 1950, the district's population would peak at just over 800,000.

Once again, the National Mall became a warehouse for the nation's wartime needs. A beehive of "tempos"—temporary government office buildings made of cement and asbestos board—were built along both sides of the Mall, adding to those thrown up during World War I.

Dr. Martin Luther King, Jr., salutes civil rights activists at the August 1963 March on Washington.

In 1945, Washington found itself the capital of the most powerful nation on Earth. It had evolved from a small Southern town. In little more than half a century it had become a world leader. The city seemed to be flexing its new muscles, spearheading a Cold War against communism worldwide. On a local level, however, the story of Washington was increasingly a tale of two cities. More and more, white and black Washingtonians led separate lives in separate parts of town. Throughout the 1940s, D.C.'s schools, parks, playgrounds, restaurants, theaters, and water fountains remained as segregated as those in any Southern town.

Then, in 1954, came the U.S. Supreme Court ruling, in *Brown v. Board of Education*, that "separate but equal education facilities are inherently unequal." The ensuing rapid integration of D.C. public schools served as a model for the nation.

In the late 1950s, blacks outnumbered whites for the first time in Washington history. The far reaches of the city's Northeast and Southeast quadrants had drawn a raft of new residents since World War II, most of them from rural backgrounds. Now, with whites leaving the crowded city for the suburbs, middle-class blacks moved en masse into such upper Northeast neighborhoods as Fort Totten and Brookland. From 1950 to 1975, the city's black population rose from 35 percent to more than 70.

With the appointment of Walter Washington as mayor-commissioner in 1967, black Washington gained a degree of control over its affairs for the first time since the dissolution of the territorial government nearly a hundred years earlier. Congress, however, retained final say over city governance—a power it continues to wield. This has created a troubling and inequitable political quirk: Washingtonians are the only modern Americans who suffer "taxation without representation," as some city vehicle licenses protest. D.C. voters can elect only a nonvoting delegate (as opposed to representatives) to Congress, yet that body has veto power over Washington's laws and budgets—a bone of lingering local contention and resentment.

The People's Parade Ground

The National Mall—the country's unofficial forum—has long been a rallying point for social causes. The women's suffrage movement, for example, demonstrated here in the 1910s; two decades later, thousands of Bonus Marchers descended on the Capitol to demand veterans' benefits, only to be run off by Gen. Douglas MacArthur's cavalry.

On August 28, 1963, more than 200,000 people marched on Washington to demand jobs and freedom for blacks. The event culminated in the rousing "I Have a Dream" speech delivered by Dr. Martin Luther King, Jr., on the steps of the Lincoln Memorial. Television cameras caught the historic moment, which was seen by millions of people across the nation.

This progress was tragically interrupted in April 1968, when Dr. King fell to an assassin's bullet on a motel balcony in Memphis, Tennessee. Around the country, grief erupted in spasms of violence. In Washington, rioting and looting broke out near the intersection of 14th and U Streets in Northwest and spread outward from there. Eventually the conflagration gutted 57 blocks in the heart of the city, crippling the once thriving retail district downtown. Twelve people died and several hundred were injured amid the chaos.

It took 4,000 U.S. Army and National Guard troops three days to restore the peace. But the scars, emotional and physical, lingered for years. Not until the late 1990s did some areas recover. The U Street corridor, for instance, has been spruced up and now draws visitors from all backgrounds.

A Fresh Start

The seeds of the city's rejuvenation had been planted several years before the 1968 riots. In 1961, President John F. Kennedy and his wife, Jackie, initiated improvements to the city core. They applied a mix of historic preservation and urban renewal to Lafayette Square and to the part of Pennsylvania Avenue from the White House to the Capitol.

A few years later, the landscape received another official face-lift, this time from Lady Bird Johnson and her "Beautify America" campaign, which added tulips, daffodils,

A Makeover for the Mall

Laid out in 1791 as part of the master plan for the nation's capital, the Mall, 2 miles (3.2 km) long, was never designed for the level of use it gets today. Every year about 24 million people visit the Mall, including 10 million from overseas. It is the city's most heavily visited area.

In July 2010, the National Park Service released plans for a $700 million makeover. The improvements include new landscaping, paved pathways, and a visitor center for the Vietnam Veterans Memorial.

Improved plumbing for fountains and ponds will conserve water and improve the flow. The Reflecting Pool near the Lincoln Memorial is once again filled with water, after a $34 million rehabilitation project was recently completed. Both the pool and its surrounds were upgraded, with concrete sidewalks on either side replacing gravel paths. The marble D.C. War Memorial has been restored, and the seawalls of the Tidal Basin around the Jefferson Memorial have been stabilized.

A candlelight vigil held at the Lincoln Memorial shortly after the September 11, 2001, terrorist strikes in the United States honors those who died.

and flowering trees and shrubs to the banks of Rock Creek and the Potomac River.

1971 was a pivotal year in the city's growing emphasis on aesthetics. The Mall's temporary structures were finally removed to make way for Constitution Gardens—a 50-acre (20 ha) park north of the Reflecting Pool—and the John F. Kennedy Center for the Performing Arts opened on the Potomac River just off the Theodore Roosevelt Memorial Bridge. Inscribed on a wall of the Kennedy Center are the words of arts patron JFK: "This country cannot afford to be materially rich and spiritually poor."

Yet poverty is still an ugly reality of Washington. As of 2013, per capita income for the District was $74,733, but the income gap between the city's poor and wealthy residents is one of the widest of major U.S. cities.

Poking fun at Washington politics has become a national pastime, yet the city possesses a beauty, grandeur, and cultural richness that can win over even the most hardened cynic. Many Americans have a soft spot for the nation's capital and relish an opportunity to visit. Indeed, a record crowd of 1.5 million flocked to the National Mall on January 20, 2009, to witness Barack Obama being sworn in as the country's President; another one million appeared for his second Inaugural in 2013. ∎

City on the River

Most people don't think of Washington as a riverside city, yet the Potomac is the wildest watercourse running through any major metropolis in the United States. Explore Washington by water, and you'll leave a world of traffic, concrete, and crowds for a realm where turtles bask on logs, an osprey wings low with a fish flashing in its talons, and your only neighbor glides by in a scull.

The Potomac River (nicknamed the Nation's River) has been the heart of Washington since Georgetown was founded as a shipping center in 1751. By the 1790s the harbor was exporting more tobacco than any other port in the country. Later, the Chesapeake & Ohio Canal (whose towpath you can still amble) connected Georgetown to villages inland, fueling both their growth and that of the capital city.

With affluence came effluence: The Potomac was declared unfit for bathing as early as 1894, and even touching the bacteria-laden water was deemed unwise as late as 1971. Political commentator Patrick Buchanan, a native son, used the river's pollution to make a

political statement: "Just as there's garbage that pollutes the Potomac River, there is garbage polluting our culture. We need an Environmental Protection Agency to clean it up."

The 1970s saw a concerted, community-wide effort to clean up the river. Today, the fish are back, the birds have returned, and the water bobs with all manner of recreational craft: canoes, kayaks, rowing shells, sailboats, and—alas—Jet Skis.

At water level, the city takes on a different cast. Near the shore a great blue heron freezes in mid-stride, waiting for a fish. In the safety of mid-river, bass break the surface to feed on hatching bugs. Keen-eyed ospreys peer down from shaggy nests, screaming if you venture too close, while bald eagles soar high above.

EXPERIENCE: Seeing Washington by Water

Many visitors take to the river aboard narrated cruises for sweeping views of the city or sign up for an even more leisurely trip to Mount Vernon. Meal and moonlight cruises are available; schedules vary daily and seasonally. Options include **Capitol River Cruises** (tel 301/460-7447, capitolrivercruises.com); **Washington DC Spirit Cruises** (tel 866/302-2469, spiritcruises.com); and luxury **Odyssey Cruises** (tel 866/306-2469, odysseycruises.com). **Potomac Riverboat Company** (tel 703/684-0580, potomacriverboatco.com) offers cruises as well as a water taxi service that will ferry you to a day of shopping at National Harbor (down the Potomac in Maryland) or an evening baseball game at Nationals Park. For

something quirky, check out **DC Ducks** (tel 855/323-8257, dcducks.com). Passengers are taken past the Mall and museums in a DUKW—an amphibious military personnel carrier used in World War II—and then splash around in the Potomac for a while before heading back to Union Station.

Or spend a few hours quietly skimming the river by canoe, kayak, or rowing shell. Rent from **Thompson Boat Center** (2900 Virginia Ave., N.W., tel 202/333-9543, thompsonboatcenter.com) or **Key Bridge Boathouse** (3500 Water St., N.W., tel 202/337-9642, boatingindc.com .com). **Atlantic Kayak** (tel 703/838-9072, atlantickayak.com) offers rentals as well as instruction and guided tours.

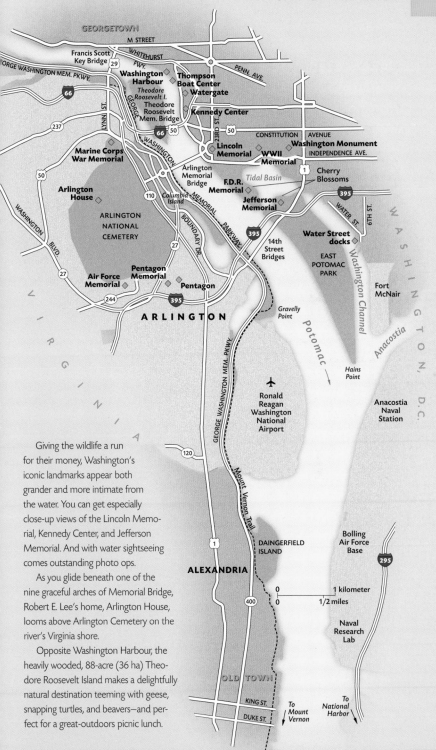

GEORGETOWN

M STREET

WHITEHURST

Francis Scott
Key Bridge   29   FWY.   PENN. AVE.

GEORGE WASHINGTON MEM. PKWY.

66

Washington
Harbour

237   Theodore
Roosevelt I.   Thompson
Boat Center

Watergate

66   50   Theodore
Roosevelt
Mem. Bridge   Kennedy Center

50   50

CONSTITUTION   AVENUE

Washington Monument

Lincoln
Marine Corps
War Memorial   Memorial   WWII
Memorial   INDEPENDENCE AVE.

50   Arlington
Memorial
Bridge   1   Cherry
Blossoms

Arlington
House   F.D.R.
Memorial   Tidal Basin

110   Columbia
Island   Jefferson
Memorial   395

ARLINGTON
NATIONAL
CEMETERY   WATER ST.   6TH ST.

27   395   14th
Street
Bridges   Water Street
docks

Pentagon
Memorial   EAST
POTOMAC
PARK

27   Air Force
Memorial   Pentagon   Fort
McNair

244   395

A R L I N G T O N   Gravelly
Point   Anacostia
Naval
Station

V I R G I N I A   Hains
Point

✈
Ronald
Reagan
Washington
National
Airport

120

Giving the wildlife a run
for their money, Washington's
iconic landmarks appear both
grander and more intimate from
the water. You can get especially
close-up views of the Lincoln Memorial, Kennedy Center, and Jefferson
Memorial. And with water sightseeing
comes outstanding photo ops.

As you glide beneath one of the
nine graceful arches of Memorial Bridge,
Robert E. Lee's home, Arlington House,
looms above Arlington Cemetery on the
river's Virginia shore.

Opposite Washington Harbour, the
heavily wooded, 88-acre (36 ha) Theodore Roosevelt Island makes a delightfully
natural destination teeming with geese,
snapping turtles, and beavers—and perfect for a great-outdoors picnic lunch.

DAINGERFIELD
ISLAND   Bolling
Air Force
Base

295

1   ALEXANDRIA

0   1 kilometer
0   1/2 miles

Naval
Research
Lab

400

OLD TOWN

KING ST.

DUKE ST.   To
Mount
Vernon   To
National
Harbor

P O T O M A C

W A S H I N G T O N ,   D. C.

Washington Channel

Anacostia

George Washington Mem. Pkwy.

Mount Vernon Trail

LYNN ST.

WASHINGTON BLVD.

BOUNDARY DR.

MEMORIAL   PARKWAY

3RD ST.

The Arts

Despite being the birthplace of many gifted musicians and actors—among them John Philip Sousa, Duke Ellington, Helen Hayes, and Pearl Bailey—an artistic community of note did not really coalesce here until 1971, when the John F. Kennedy Center for the Performing Arts welcomed its first music and theater patrons. Today, Washington is a leading center of the arts worldwide.

Classical Music

One of the nation's finest orchestral companies, the National Symphony Orchestra (NSO) was officially incorporated in 1931. At the opening of the Kennedy Center 40 years later, the NSO premiered Leonard Bernstein's "Mass," a work commissioned for the occasion. The orchestra now has a busy year-round season that includes local performances in the Kennedy Center Concert Hall, tours in this country and abroad, televised Independence Day and Memorial Day concerts on the West Lawn of the U.S. Capitol, and programs for visiting heads of state and music festivals.

Branching out in recent years, the NSO has expanded its programs to include more contemporary music as well as classical favorites. After 12 years under Leonard Slatkin, the orchestra tapped Christoph Eschenbach to infuse new energy as music director.

From a regional company struggling to make its name in 1956, the Washington Opera has evolved into a world-class organization playing to sellout audiences in the Opera House at the Kennedy Center: It now stages up to eight operas a year. The opera is under the artistic direction of Francesca Zambello, whose theatrical honors include three Olivier Awards. A commitment to staging new American operas and epic-scale productions, bringing out lesser known important works, and nurturing young talent keeps this company in the mainstream of the opera world.

Music lovers in Washington can find a concert any night of the week, whether performed by a D.C.-based or visiting group. The Kennedy Center has hosted renowned companies from around the world, including the Berlin Philharmonic Orchestra, the Metropolitan Opera, and La Scala, while the Millennium Stage program brings free daily performances of all sorts of musical genres to the Kennedy Center's Grand Foyer.

Just north of Washington, near the Grosvenor Metro stop, the Music Center at Strathmore features the Baltimore Symphony Orchestra, the National Philharmonic, and other arts performance groups. A converted mansion and an 11-acre (4.4 ha) setting make for pleasant surroundings. In the heart of the city, Lisner Auditorium at George Washington University is a comfortable 1,490-seat hall, and other area universities feature music by local and guest artists. Downtown churches and museums often schedule musical events: Concerts at the National Gallery of Art, the Phillips Collection, and the Library of Congress can be wonderfully intimate occasions. The 670-seat auditorium at the National

> **Music lovers in Washington can find a concert any night of the week, whether performed by a D.C.-based or visiting group.**

A ballerina performs the Washington Ballet's *Carmen* at the Kennedy Center.

D.C. native and jazz maestro Duke Ellington gazes from a painting on sale at Eastern Market.

Academy of Sciences, with its excellent acoustics, occasionally offers free concerts, often of new music. Another small venue, the Folger Shakespeare Library, presents medieval, Renaissance, and baroque music in an Elizabethan setting.

Many music aficionados consider the District of Columbia to be the nation's capital of choral music. The Choral Arts Society of Washington, under artistic director and maestro Scott Tucker, regularly performs in concert with the National Symphony Orchestra and touring orchestras.

Popular Music

Washington has historically excelled at military band music. The U.S. Marine Band received a great boost in 1868 when a local 13-year-old boy signed up as an apprentice. His name was John Philip Sousa, and within 12 years he would assume leadership of the band. Dismayed by the band's outdated and poorly arranged music, Sousa sent off to Europe for scores by Wagner, Berlioz, and other modern composers of the day. He also began writing music of his own. Demanding excellence from others as well as from himself, Sousa drilled the band into shape. Many members quit within a year, but those who stayed became a well-honed and disciplined unit. In 1892 Sousa formed his own band and toured the United States and abroad. His tuneful lifetime outpouring ultimately included 140 original military marches, among them "The Washington Post" march (1889) and "The Stars and Stripes Forever" (1896).

Heart-poundingly patriotic performances of the illustrious U.S. Marine Band and other military combos are staged free of charge on summer evenings at the Sylvan Theater (on the grounds of the Washington Monument) and on the West Terrace of the Capitol. Alternatively, you might enjoy an evening tattoo at the Marine Barracks on Capitol Hill.

Another local musician who made good was jazz legend Edward Kennedy "Duke" Ellington. Born at 1217 22nd Street in 1899 and raised in the Shaw neighborhood,

Ellington studied classical music with a neighbor who taught music at Dunbar High School. At 24 he headed off to New York City—and thence into the Big Band and Jazz Hall of Fame. Washington jazz has enjoyed a devoted following ever since. After the Howard Theatre opened at 7th and T Streets in 1910, it marqueed such standouts as W. C. Handy, Fletcher Henderson, Bessie Smith, and Count Basie. Duke Ellington and Pearl Bailey were among the local talents who debuted at the Howard. Another star-studded black showcase, the 1922 Lincoln Theater on U Street closed for a short while but reopened as a movie theater in the 1970s; renovated in 1994, the 1,250-seat theater today features a mixture of concerts, dance recitals, plays, and movies.

Blues Alley in Georgetown has long worn the crown as the best place in town to catch big-name jazz acts. This comfortable den has low ceilings, high cover charges, and a serious and sophisticated clientele. Other reliable spots for hearing live jazz include Columbia Station in Adams Morgan and Bohemian Caverns in the Shaw neighborhood. On U Street, Twins Jazz adds Ethiopian food to the mix, while nearby Dahlak dishes up Eritrean fare during free jazz jam sessions on Sunday evenings, welcoming any musicians who want to join in. The National Gallery of Art offers free jazz Friday evenings in the summer. The Kennedy Center and other venues also host a range of jazz performers.

Blues Alley in Georgetown has long worn the crown as the best place in town to catch big-name jazz acts.

An endless number of options exist for rock and other popular music. These range from headliner concerts at the 20,000-seat Verizon Center downtown to eclectic local acts (and some up-and-coming national ones) at popular hangouts such as the 9:30 Club on V Street and the Black Cat on 14th Street. On the east side of Rock Creek Park, Carter Barron Amphitheatre is a fun summer weekend place for pop, rock, blues, and jazz, much of it free. Acoustic folk and bluegrass have also carved out solid niches in the Washington area; the Birchmere in Alexandria, which nurtured Grammy-winner Mary Chapin Carpenter and bluegrass pioneers The Seldom Scene, is the top choice.

Theater

Home to dozens of active theaters, the Washington metro area can boast more playhouses than any city besides New York. Most prominent is the Kennedy Center, with two large theaters: The 1,100-seat Eisenhower Theater is a plush venue for touring productions of dramas and comedies, while the adjacent 2,350-seat Opera House presents musicals and performances of the Washington Ballet and other dance troupes.

A theater has operated continuously on the Pennsylvania Avenue site of the National Theatre, rebuilt in the early 1920s, since 1835. In 1845 fire destroyed the building during a performance of *Beauty and the Beast*—the first of five such conflagrations in the theater's history. Until 1873, blacks were confined to the balcony; after that they were not admitted at all. Finally, in 1948, local civil rights activists campaigned to desegregate the National.

John Wilkes Booth, Jenny Lind, Helen Hayes, John Barrymore, Sarah Bernhardt, Vivien Leigh, and Katharine Hepburn have all trod the boards of the National, which has premiered such groundbreaking productions as *West Side Story* and *M. Butterfly*. It continues its tradition of offering big glittery Broadway and pre-Broadway productions.

Half a block away on 13th Street, the Warner Theatre opened in 1924 as a silent-movie palace and vaudeville stage. From 1945 to the late 1960s, it presented movies only. It then deteriorated, as did much of downtown Washington, but stayed alive with a menu of porn films and rock concerts. After closing for three years, the Warner reopened in 1992 with its rococo finery intact. It now offers a mix of musical performances and live comedy.

About three blocks east of the Warner, on 10th Street, is the city's most famous theater. Ford's Theatre had been in business for only four years when, in 1865, it became notorious as the scene of Lincoln's assassination. Restored to its 1860s appearance, it now offers plays and musicals as well as spring and summer walking tours led by actors playing characters from Civil War Washington.

> Ford's Theatre had been in business for only four years when, in 1865, it became notorious as the scene of Lincoln's assassination.

Probably the city's best program of serious and innovative drama is offered at Arena Stage, on the waterfront in Southwest Washington. Since its 1950 founding, Arena has pioneered the resident theater movement. Arena Stage also owns the distinction of being the first playhouse outside New York City to win a Tony Award. James Earl Jones, Ned Beatty, Jane Alexander, and other notable actors cut their teeth here. After a major face-lift, Arena moved back to its historic spaces in fall 2010, with new state-of-the-art capabilities in three separate theaters.

After 20 praiseworthy years in its original home at the Folger Shakespeare Library on Capitol Hill, the Shakespeare Theatre Company moved downtown in 1992 to a larger, 451-seat theater in the Lansburgh on 7th Street. In 2007, the much acclaimed company expanded its facilities further to include the 775-seat Sidney Harman Hall at 6th and F Streets. The group also stages a summer Shakespeare play presented free to the public.

EXPERIENCE: Engage the City's Intellectual Life

Think about it. With a well-educated and culturally savvy population, Washington supports an abundance of activities for the curious-minded. Many events are free, but advance tickets may be required.

For 40 years, patrons have turned out in large numbers for lectures and other programs organized by **Smithsonian Associates** (smithsonianassociates.org). **"National Geographic Live"** (nationalgeographic.com/events) features presentations by leading explorers, scientists, photographers, and performers.

Literary types may want to plan a visit that coincides with the **National Book Festival** (loc.gov/bookfest); it attracts thousands of people to the Mall every fall for appearances by numerous authors. For readings and book signings year-round—often by nationally known figures—check the events calendars of **Politics and Prose** bookstore (tel 202/ 364-1919, politics-prose.com) and **Barnes & Noble** downtown (tel 202/347-0176, barnesandnoble.com). Civic affairs and progressive politics top the bill at **Busboys & Poets** (tel 202/387-7638, busboysandpoets .com). **E Street Cinema** (555 11th St., N.W., landmarktheatres.com) screens independent and foreign-language films, documentaries, and classic revivals.

All the city's museums and cultural institutions offer special events. At the **National Archives** (see pp. 142–143), for example, you can see free historic films, hear a historian read excerpts from a new book on the Civil War, or attend a seminar on researching your family's history.

Known for its bold and eclectic contemporary plays, Studio Theatre at 14th and P Streets in the Logan Circle neighborhood has claimed many Helen Hayes awards in its three decades of existence. These homegrown awards for theatrical excellence recognize the formative contributions to local drama of Hayes, a Washington native who first appeared on a D.C. stage at the age of six and later won an Academy Award for her portrayal of the title character in 1932's *The Sin of Madelon Claudet.*

Definitive productions of Stephen Sondheim shows, such as *Sweeney Todd,* and other lively works are the hallmark of the Signature Theatre group. After 17 successful years operating in a converted auto garage, the group moved to a new theater in suburban Arlington's Shirlington Village.

Drawing strong material from political proceedings on Capitol Hill, comedy is growing more popular around town. The Capitol Steps, founded by congressional staffers, offer witty, well-polished songs and skits every Friday and Saturday night at the Ronald Reagan Building on Pennsylvania Avenue. The Connecticut Avenue comedy club DC Improv features headliners as well as promising locals doing traditional stand-up.

Fine Arts

In a city of monumental buildings and larger-than-life statuary created by some of the nation's finest architects and sculptors, D.C. art has tended to be powerful and realistic, depicting powerful people and real events. With a preponderance of these pieces being commissioned—and with many of them requiring committee approval—it's a wonder the city holds so many truly fine works of art.

The U.S. Capitol, for example, is a trove of officially sanctioned art. Its chief muralist, Italian artist Constantino Brumidi (1805–1880), was known as the Michelangelo of the

Experience a little night magic at Wolf Trap, about 16 miles (25 km) west of downtown Washington.

Capitol; his 1865 "Apotheosis of George Washington" graces the ceiling of the Rotunda. Acclaimed artist John Trumbull (1756–1843) painted the eight large historical scenes hanging in the Rotunda.

Much of the city's great painting and sculpture is housed in established museums: the National Gallery of Art, the Corcoran Gallery of Art, the Phillips Collection. Significant works of art created on-site in Washington have tended to be in portraiture and outdoor sculpture.

Early painting in Washington was documentary as well as aesthetic: Public figures, it was agreed, should have their portraits painted for posterity. Thus locals such as George Washington and James Madison sat for eminent portrait painter Gilbert Stuart (1755–1828), who lived in Philadelphia and Boston. Another leading portrait painter of the time, Charles Willson Peale (1741–1827), completed seven life paintings of George Washington, as well as portraits of Benjamin Franklin, Thomas Jefferson, and John Adams. His son Rembrandt Peale (1778–1860) parlayed his family connections into a precocious start in portrait painting: At age 17 he produced a life portrait of George Washington. The younger Peale studied under his father, whose neoclassical style exerted a strong influence; Rembrandt Peale's 1805 portrait of Jefferson, now owned by the New-York Historical Society, is considered his masterpiece—and our best likeness of the third President.

The White House, too, has a Rembrandt Peale oil of Jefferson, as well as other fine portraits. The Reception Rooms of the Department of State hold several portraits by the Peales, Stuart, and Thomas Sully (1783–1872). Other places to look for early Washington faces include the National Portrait Gallery and the National Gallery of Art.

What did the city look like in its infancy? Thanks to the efforts of several minor artists, we have a fairly good idea. Sketches by surveyors and architects show the lay of the land around the Capitol, the White House, and other government buildings as they were going up. Views of Washington by painter George Jacob Beck depict the Georgetown waterfront in the 1790s as a Constable-style landscape, where a country lane stands sprinkled with little houses.

City views by August Kollner in the 1830s show a Potomac busy with sailboats and the new steamboats. The latter owed their existence to engineer and painter Robert Fulton (1765–1815), who in 1807 invented the first commercially successful steamboat; in the early 1800s Fulton had stayed with friends who owned a country estate that would become the Kalorama neighborhood, and he painted its pastoral scenes.

An 1832 lithograph of the west front of the Capitol by Hudson River artist Thomas Doughty (1793–1856) shows the important building in a decidedly bucolic setting; the wooded hills and cultivated fields around Jenkins Hill (now Capitol Hill) make the government structure seem almost comically out of place. Washington's rural aspect would continue to be emphasized as late as the 1880s in the sketches and drawings of isolated cabins by DeLancey W. Gill (1859–1940), an illustrator for the Smithsonian Institution's Bureau of American Ethnology. Perhaps these were in wistful lament for a town changing into a city?

An artists' salon blossomed in Washington at the turn of the 20th century. It met at the studio-home of painter and playwright Alice Pike Barney (1857–1931), at 2306 Massachusetts Avenue, next to what is now the Turkish Embassy. Overlooking Sheridan Circle, Barney's Studio House became the venue for poetry readings, plays, art shows, and other creative undertakings of the sort now associated with a multitude of Dupont addresses. Barney helped establish the Sylvan Theatre on the Mall. Both George Bernard Shaw and Alice Roosevelt Longworth sat for portraits in oil by her hand.

Nowadays many of the homes of the rich and au courant are graced by abstract art turned out by Washington Color School artists, who rose to prominence in the 1960s. Gene Davis (1920–1985), known for his boldly striped canvases, worked as a White House correspondent during the Truman years before settling down to abstract art. Sam Gilliam (1933–) stepped into the limelight with his "drape paintings" in the late 1960s—stained, unframed canvases thrown over sawhorses and furniture, hung from ceiling beams, or draped on walls. The *Washington Post* described a 1999 show of his glass-enclosed collages of acrylic on birch plywood as "cubist African kimono

Music Under the Stars

From Sheryl Crow to Al Jarreau, *Mama Mia!* to "Prairie Home Companion," enjoy top performers of all genres at Wolf Trap National Park *(wolftrap .org)*, off the Dulles Toll Road or Route 7 in Virginia. The open-air amphitheater with covered stage, built on a sloping meadow, holds 4,000; many patrons prefer cheaper lawn seating and picnicking with friends. Two restored barns offer opera in the summer, other programs in off-summer months. There's round-trip bus service from the West Falls Church Metro station.

sculptures." Gilliam's work has been commissioned for the Washington Convention Center and Ronald Reagan National Airport. He has also been honored with solo exhibitions at the Corcoran Gallery of Art and other showcases.

Literature

In more than two centuries as the nation's capital, Washington has inspired many writers to capture this power spot in prose or verse. Washington novels often aspire to capitalize on their setting by taking on the city's major industry: politics. The first classic "Washington novel"—an insider's look at the political machinations of the federal government—was probably *The Gilded Age*, an 1873 satire of political and financial shenanigans co-authored by Mark Twain and newspaper editor Charles Dudley Warner. It was followed in 1880 by *Democracy, an American Novel,* a mysterious and anonymously written exposé that became wildly popular for blowing the lid off corruption in the Grant Administration. Not until the author's death in 1918 would it be revealed that *Democracy* had been written by Henry Adams.

For history enthusiasts, Margaret Leech's *Reveille in Washington,* which won the Pulitzer Prize in 1942, offers an intimate portrait of the city during the Civil War. Many people regard it as the best book ever written about D.C. Allen Drury's *Advice and Consent* (1959) broke new ground for its startling portrayal of backroom politics.

The late Gore Vidal, the erudite author of *Washington, D.C.: A Novel* (1967) and more than 25 other books, spent much of his childhood inhaling politics at the Rock Creek Park home of his grandfather, Thomas P. Gore, a populist senator from Oklahoma. Vidal's most popular work, *Lincoln* (1984), painted a balanced and humane portrait of a President who had been only canonized until then. Vidal's novel *1876* puts recent political history into perspective. In that year, Republican Rutherford B. Hayes stole the election from Democrat Samuel J. Tilden, who had won the popular vote; one of the states whose election returns were contested was Florida.

> **Washington novels often aspire to capitalize on their setting by taking on the city's major industry: politics.**

Edward P. Jones, who grew up in Washington and still lives here, may be the city's modern laureate. He won the Pulitzer Prize in 2004 for his novel *The Known World,* based on free black people who owned slaves. He has published many stories with characters inspired by daily life in Washington. Another author, Marita Golden, found a rich setting for her novel *Long Distance Life* in the city's Columbia Heights neighborhood.

For a hilarious tale set in Washington during 1976, when the country was celebrating its Bicentennial, read Porter Shreve's *When the White House Was Ours.* Published in 2008, it chronicles a family's attempt to create an alternative school in the nation's capital—modeled loosely on the author's own family.

Amid the flurry of political books emanating from Washington, some well-known pundits about town, like public television's Jim Lehrer and *Washington Post* columnist David Ignatius, turn their attention instead to other genres, such as Westerns, mysteries, and political thrillers. Local authors continue to turn out lots of books on historical figures and events. Recent examples include Scott Berg's book on D.C.'s

Stories in Stone

Filled with monumental architecture and heroic statuary, Washington sometimes transcends words. The pediment of the Supreme Court's west facade, for example, shows Liberty holding the scales of justice. The scene on the pediment of the National Archives uses winged horses, rams, and papyrus flowers as classical symbols of aspiration.

As you walk around Washington, you'll encounter more equestrian statues than you'd see in any other North American city. These sculptures—most of them depicting military men astride horses in various stances—came into vogue in the late 19th century, when the nation's compulsion to honor its Civil War heroes dovetailed with the rapid growth of its capital city. As for equine symbolism, by the way, it's a myth that a horse with one hoof raised denotes its rider was wounded in battle; nor is it true that two hooves in the air suggests the rider died in battle.

Befitting its wartime role as the Federal capital, Washington bristles with Union generals in bronze. Only one Confederate officer is so honored: Even then, the statue of Brig. Gen. Albert Pike *(3rd & D Sts.)* recognizes his service not as a soldier but as a Mason. Otherwise you'll have to cross the river to Alexandria, Virginia, to find the nearest Confederate statue—the Rebel soldier who stands at Prince and South Washington Streets in Old Town, head downcast, arms crossed, and back turned resolutely on the North.

Washington's late 19th-century renaissance in statuary also coincided with America's emergence as an environment favorable to artists. A nation of growing affluence and power demanded artists to document its glory. As a result, many world-renowned sculptors have work on display in Washington. One of them is Augustus Saint-Gaudens (1848–1907), a Dublin-born artist who grew up in New York City. His 1890 Adams Memorial, commissioned by author Henry Adams to honor his wife, Clover, is one of the most beautiful, moving, and remote pieces of sculpture in Washington: The cast-bronze grave marker is in a grove of

A 19-foot-high (5.8 m) marble statue of Lincoln dominates the Lincoln Memorial.

Japanese yews in Rock Creek Cemetery.

The most famous sculpture in Washington, if not the entire country, is Daniel Chester French's 1922 marble figure of Lincoln, who sits in brooding majesty 19 feet high (5.7 m) inside the rectangular marble Lincoln Memorial at the east end of the Memorial Bridge. Lincoln clenches his left hand to show strength and resolve; his right lies open to signal compassion.

What does it take to get memorialized in the nation's capital? First, you must form a citizens' group to petition Congress. A vote must then be taken, a sculptor commissioned, an approval granted by the Commission of Fine Arts, and funds raised. Only a fraction of proposals make the long journey from paper to stone.

For a guide to more than 400 of the city's outdoor sculptures, take a look at James M. Goode's *Outdoor Sculpture of Washington, D.C.* (Smithsonian Institution Press, 1974).

Kramer Books & Afterwords Café is a literary landmark just north of Dupont Circle.

visionary planner Pierre-Charles L'Enfant (*Grand Avenues,* 2008), Kirsten Downey's thorough biography of Frances Perkins (*Woman Behind the New Deal,* 2009), and David Taylor's look at the WPA Writers' Project during the Great Depression (*Soul of a People,* 2009).

Reporters have used journalism as a springboard to literary fame. Bob Woodward and Carl Bernstein are the best known. The 1976 film version of their book *All the President's Men* has become a classic. Another newspaperman turned literary lion, Ward Just has written several acclaimed works with a Washington-centric focus. His novel *Echo House* (1997) presents a portrait of D.C. government over eight decades and three generations.

Poets, too, have been central in the city's literary life. Walt Whitman, who helped care for Union soldiers in Washington during the Civil War, wrote one of his greatest poems here: the moving elegy to Lincoln, "When Lilacs Last in the Dooryard Bloom'd." Ironically, 1865 was the same year Whitman was fired from his job as a clerk in the Indian Bureau. The charge: writing offensive poetry.

Poetry has a strong presence in Washington in part because U.S. poet laureates are based at the Library of Congress. The latest, Natasha Trethewey, follows eminent poets such as Philip Levine, Kay Ryan, Charles Simic, and Ted Kooser.

Architecture

Conceived as a grand capital, Washington has attained a unifying look about its core. One of the main proponents of a neoclassical-style capital was architect-philosopher-statesman Thomas Jefferson. The great buildings and monuments, harking back to ancient Greek and Roman models, were designed to impress with their massiveness and their references to earlier democracies. Weighty columns of marble and pediments embellished with allegorical scenes are the general rule for these early (and many later) federal buildings.

Precious few 18th-century buildings remain. The White House and the Capitol were started in the early 1790s, but both were burned in 1814—and both have undergone many alterations and renovations since they were rebuilt. The Capitol recalls the Pantheon in Rome, begun in 27 B.C. as a temple for worshiping the gods. A less grandiose style was chosen for the executive mansion: Its Georgian format was popular in many manor houses of the day, among them Mount Vernon, Woodlawn, and Gunston Hall, all in Virginia. All three estates feature porticoes, cornices, steep roofs pierced by several chimneys, and almost perfect symmetry.

The federal style flourished in tandem with Washington's growth in the 19th century. Alexandria and Georgetown, already well established, built scores of elegant brick town houses and row houses for prosperous local merchants. Residences from the early 1800s tend to be unadorned, while those built after the Civil War betray unmistakable Victoriana: They sport rosettes, urns, swags, and decorative ironwork. The finest examples of the federal style in Washington are the 1800 Octagon (1799 New York Ave., N.W.) and the 1816 Tudor Place (1644 31st St., N.W.). The latter, despite its name, blends neoclassical and federal elements. Conceived as private homes by Capitol designer William Thornton, both are now national historic landmarks.

Other building styles began to appear later in the 1800s, but architects risked opprobrium if they strayed too far from the city's neoclassicism. Completed in 1887, the handsome redbrick Pension Building (now the National Building Museum) has a breathtakingly cavernous interior. It was nearly razed in the 1960s.

Next to the West Wing of the White House, the Eisenhower Executive Office Building—the world's largest office building at the time of its 1888 construction—was ridiculed and likewise threatened with demolition. Harry S. Truman, for one, called it the "greatest monstrosity in America." But the gilded age building, with its mansard roofs and hundreds of window pediments and columns, is now recognized as an outstanding American example of French Second Empire–style architecture.

Daring and exuberant, the Old Post Office (1899) was likewise slated for obliteration until it was saved in the late 1970s and converted into a retail-office complex. Real estate mogul Donald Trump is now transforming the castlelike building, with its prime location on Pennsylvania Avenue, into a luxury hotel.

Popular in the first half of the 20th century, the beaux arts style, with its use of

Arts in the Park

Established in 1891 as the Chautauqua movement swept America, **Glen Echo Park** *(glenechopark.org)* provided an open-air setting for speakers, preachers, and entertainers. It later became an amusement park, and today features arts and crafts activities and a restored 1921 carousel. Most popular, however, are the social dances in the historic Spanish Ballroom and Bumper Car Pavilion. Waltz, swing, salsa, square, contra—the styles vary, with live music and classes of all levels offered. You'll mingle with people of all ages and levels of experience. The website has directions to the park, which is in Maryland, 12 miles (19 km) from D.C.

Since its 1988 restoration, Union Station has been a shopping, dining, and partying hub.

columns and other classical elements, meshed well in Washington. Union Station (1908) by Daniel Burnham and John Russell Pope's National Archives (1935) and National Gallery of Art (1941) are grand without ostentation.

Many downtown buildings were razed in the mid-20th century and replaced with concrete cubes, a few of them noteworthy. Though boxy, Edward Durell Stone's National Geographic Society 17th Street building (1964) and Kennedy Center (1971) have an interplay of columns and white stone well suited to Washington.

Other architectural styles have made their way onto Washington streets, but even these bear details of their forerunners. Architect I. M. Pei's radically modernist East Building (1978) of the National Gallery of Art, for instance, is faced with the same pink marble as the neoclassical West Building (1941).

Washington's sense of openness derives largely from an absence of skyscrapers. In general, no city building is allowed to rise more than 20 feet (6 m) higher than the width of the street on which it stands. In the end, this rule is what helps keep Washington, D.C., refreshingly timeless. ∎

On Washington's most prominent hill: grand marble halls of law, justice, and knowledge—plus inviting parks, markets, and gardens

Capitol Hill

Look up: The Capitol Rotunda ceiling gleams like the heavens.

Capitol Hill

"A pedestal waiting for a monument" city planner Pierre-Charles L'Enfant called the swell of land then known as Jenkins Hill, on the city's southeastern side. Today beautiful monuments grace this hill, including the Capitol and the Supreme Court. Humanizing the grandeur of marble buildings and plazas are tree-lined residential streets. The heart of Washington, Capitol Hill is a good place to begin your tour.

Spruced-up historic row houses cluster in the desirable Capitol Hill neighborhood.

For nearly a century, the Capitol was the only government building on "the hill." To the east spread an orderly neighborhood of brick row houses. But by the end of the 19th century, the Library of Congress's Jefferson Building had risen across from the Capitol, followed shortly by architect Daniel H. Burnham's imposing Union Station and adjacent City Post Office.

The early 1900s saw construction of the Cannon Building (1908) and Russell Building (1909), the first House and Senate office buildings. In the 1930s, the Supreme Court, the Folger Shakespeare Library, and the Adams Building of the Library of Congress added more density to Capitol Hill.

Plan on getting some exercise—the area was designed on a grand scale. Walking gives you a chance to savor the magnificent architecture from various points. As you walk, bear in mind that these buildings are historical museums and working halls of democracy. Touring them gives you a sense of the great enterprise upon which the Founding Fathers embarked.

By the mid-20th century, much of the residential area was in decline as middle-class families abandoned the city for the suburbs. Then in the 1970s, urban pioneers, lured by low real estate values and the convenient location, began moving in and revitalizing the area. With Eastern Market (*7th & C Sts., S.E.*) as an anchor, Capitol Hill became a vibrant neighborhood once again. Today, commercial development is spreading rapidly from Eastern Market to Barracks Row on 8th Street, which offers a selection of small shops and a wide range of restaurants. To learn more about this fascinating neighborhood, follow the poster-size signs along the designated Heritage Trail. The first sign is at the Eastern Market Metro station plaza (*7th St. & Pennsylvania Ave., S.E.*). ∎

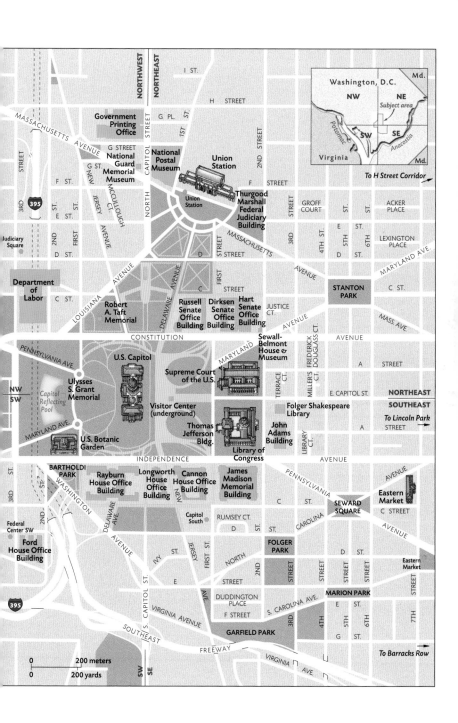

NORTHWEST
NORTHEAST

I ST.

H STREET

Government
Printing
Office

G PL.

G STREET

National
Guard
Memorial
Museum

National
Postal
Museum

Union
Station

Union
Station

Thurgood
Marshall
Federal
Judiciary
Building

GROFF
COURT

ACKER
PLACE

Judiciary
Square

MASSACHUSETTS AVENUE

MCCULLOUGH CT.

NEW JERSEY AVENUE

NORTH CAPITOL STREET

1ST STREET

2ND STREET

LEXINGTON
PLACE

MARYLAND AVE.

STANTON
PARK

MASS. AVE.

Department
of
Labor

LOUISIANA AVENUE

DELAWARE AVENUE

Robert
A. Taft
Memorial

Russell
Senate
Office
Building

Dirksen
Senate
Office
Building

Hart
Senate
Office
Building

JUSTICE
CT.

FREDERICK DOUGLASS CT.

AVENUE

CONSTITUTION

AVENUE

U.S. Capitol

Ulysses
S. Grant
Memorial

Capitol
Reflecting
Pool

Supreme Court
of the U.S.

Sewall-
Belmont
House &
Museum

TERRACE CT.

MILLER'S CT.

E. CAPITOL ST.

NORTHEAST
SOUTHEAST

To Lincoln Park

Visitor Center
(underground)

Thomas
Jefferson
Bldg.

Folger Shakespeare
Library

John
Adams
Building

LIBRARY CT.

U.S. Botanic
Garden

Library of
Congress

INDEPENDENCE

AVENUE

BARTHOLDI
PARK

Rayburn
House Office
Building

Longworth
House
Office
Building

Cannon
House Office
Building

James
Madison
Memorial
Building

PENNSYLVANIA

SEWARD
SQUARE

Eastern
Market

Federal
Center SW

Ford
House Office
Building

DELAWARE AVE.

WASHINGTON

Capitol
South

RUMSEY CT.

CAROLINA

Eastern
Market

FOLGER
PARK

IVY ST.

JERSEY ST.

FIRST ST.

NORTH STREET

2ND STREET

MARION PARK

DUDDINGTON
PLACE

S. CAROLINA AVE.

CAPITOL ST.

VIRGINIA AVENUE

F STREET

GARFIELD PARK

SOUTHEAST

FREEWAY

VIRGINIA AVE.

To Barracks Row

0   200 meters
0   200 yards

Washington, D.C.

NW   NE

Subject area

SW   SE

Virginia

Potomac

Anacostia

Md.

Md.

To H Street Corridor

U.S. Capitol

One of the most recognized landmarks in the world, the white marble U.S. Capitol, rising at the National Mall's east end, defines the center of Washington. South, East, and North Capitol Streets and the Mall radiate outward in the cardinal directions, dividing the city into quadrants. In this vaulted location, Presidents are inaugurated, national issues debated, and new laws made.

Paintings by John Trumbull (1756–1843), gracing the echoing cavern of the Capitol's imposing Rotunda, depict pivotal moments in the American Revolution.

U.S. Capitol

🅼 Map p. 51

✉ Capitol Hill, bet. Independence & Constitution Aves.

☎ 202/593-1762

🚇 Metro: Capitol South, Union Station; Bus: 32–36, 39, 96–97, P6, Circulator

visitthecapitol.gov

Evolution

The Capitol you see today looks almost nothing like its original conception. Some half dozen major designers and architects put their visions and efforts into the final image. The egos of architects, engineers, and congressmen often clashed; funding grew scarce at times; and disputes drove major players into resigning their positions.

The city's planner, Pierre-Charles L'Enfant, stubbornly refused to come up with an architectural plan for the Capitol,

declaring that he had it "in his head." His dismissal in 1792 led to a national competition to design the building. The 16 known entries were so poor that the contest had to be extended. An amateur architect named William Thornton finally came up with a winning design—a Pantheon-like dome flanked by symmetrical wings for the Senate and the House. George Washington laid the cornerstone in 1793.

Though greatly modifying and extending the design over the years, later architects generally followed the basic layout. They also incorporated the Corinthian pilasters, seven-bay portico, balustrade, and other neoclassical details Thornton had envisioned.

In 1800 the government moved from Philadelphia to Washington, and President John Adams addressed the Congress in the Capitol's brick-and-sandstone north wing, the only completed part of the building. During these early years, Thornton resigned, and two out of the three other architects were fired over their attempted design alterations. Fortunately, in 1803 the government hired the brilliant British architect Benjamin Henry Latrobe, and his collaboration with President Thomas Jefferson, himself an amateur architect, made for substantial progress.

Then in August 1814, British troops marched on Washington, and torched many buildings, including the Capitol. The fire destroyed much of the building's interior, though the walls remained standing.

For the next few years, Latrobe worked at restoring the damage. Cost overruns and a dispute about vaulting the ceilings of the House and Senate Chambers finally led to his resignation. Boston architect Charles Bulfinch stepped in. He served until 1830, completing the building with a copper-covered wooden dome and an east portico.

By 1850, an expanding Congress had outgrown its chambers, necessitating the addition of grand wings to the original building. The Capitol expansion project was still under way when the

EXPERIENCE: Watching Congress in Action

If you're looking to see a bit of the long and complicated process of lawmaking, you can visit the **House** or **Senate Gallery** when either body is in session. Tour passes are required and can be obtained through your senator or representative on the Capitol Visitor Center's website (*visitthecapitol.gov*). Passes for international visitors are also available online or at the appointment desks on the upper level of the visitor center. Some congressional offices offer staff-led tours to constituent groups of up to 15 people. Check the website for contact details as well as policies on security and etiquette.

Because of heavy demand, you should reserve well in advance. Congress is usually in recess during August and fall elections, and the visitor center is closed on Sundays and major holidays. Plan to arrive at least 45 minutes before your scheduled tour; take the confirmation number you'll receive by e-mail with you.

If you just want to view the visitor center exhibits or have lunch at the restaurant, tickets are not required.

Capitol Views

One of the earliest travel books about America was written by Frances Trollope, mother of English writer Anthony Trollope and herself a prolific novelist. In her popular *Domestic Manners of the Americans* (1832), which she wrote after spending three years in the fledgling United States, she found much to disparage. But she was impressed by the Capitol: "None of us, I believe, expected to see so imposing a structure on that side of the Atlantic. I am ill at describing buildings, but the beauty and majesty of the American capitol might defy an abler pen than mine to do it justice. It stands so finely too, high, and alone ... The view from the capitol commands the city and many miles around, and it is itself an object of imposing beauty to the whole country adjoining."

Civil War broke out. Construction went on, culminating in the addition of the current cast-iron dome, which replaced a leaky, wooden predecessor.

On December 2, 1863, the magnificent nine-million-pound (4,082 tonne) dome, rising from a circular portico, was crowned with "Freedom," the 19.5-foot-tall (6 m) bronze figure of a woman dressed in flowing robes. The original plan was that she would wear a liberty cap, something worn by freed slaves in ancient Greece. Secretary of War Jefferson Davis—president of the Confederacy by the time the statue was placed atop the Capitol—objected, saying the cap was "inappropriate to a people who were born free." A helmet with eagle feathers was substituted. Renowned landscape architect Frederick Law Olmsted designed and landscaped the grounds in the late 1880s to early 1890s.

Congress again outgrew the building in the early 1900s, scattering to the nearby Senate and House office buildings. An addition in 1958–1962 added 32 feet (9.7 m) to the east front.

Touring the Capitol

A new Capitol Visitor Center on the building's east front now serves as the gateway for all tours. Book in advance (*visit thecapitol.gov*) or, if you are an American citizen, through the offices of your senator or representative. Or call the Office of Visitor Services (*tel 202/226-8000*). A limited number of same-day passes are issued at the information desk on the Capitol's lower level. Visitor hours are 8:30 a.m.–4:30 p.m. Monday–Saturday. Begin your tour with the 13-minute film explaining the role of Congress. In the exhibition hall, an 11-foot-high (3.3 m) touchable model shows a cross section of the Capitol dome at one-twentieth the size. Original documents and artifacts tell the story of the Capitol and the U.S. Congress.

Among the sites you will see on the tour, the **Rotunda** soars 180 feet (55 m) to a round ceiling fresco, "The Apotheosis of Washington" (1865), by Italian-American artist Constantino Brumidi. A berobed George Washington stares down from on high, surrounded by a swirl of clouds and figures that represent the 13 Colonies and American democracy. Encircling the Rotunda, a 300-foot-long (91 m) frieze depicts more than 400 years of American history, from Columbus to the Wright brothers. The four huge scenes from the American Revolution were painted by Washington's aide-de-camp John Trumbull. A small white marble stone marks the center of the Rotunda's floor, where noted Americans such as Abraham Lincoln and John F. Kennedy have lain in state.

South of the Rotunda, the **National Statuary Hall** is where the House of Representatives met from 1807 to 1857. In 1864 Congress first invited each state to send statues of two prominent citizens. Some have been moved elsewhere. Among the notables are Henry Clay (Kentucky), Daniel Webster (New Hampshire), Robert E. Lee (Virginia), and King Kamehameha I (Hawaii).

North of the Rotunda is the **Old Senate Chamber,** which served the Senate at various times in the 1800s. Here such famous men as Clay, Webster, and John C. Calhoun hotly debated the issues of slavery and economics prior to the Civil War. Today the Senate uses this chamber for closed-door conferences, including a 1999 session on the impeachment trial of President Bill Clinton.

On the first floor, directly beneath the Rotunda, is the **Crypt.** George and Martha Washington were to be entombed here, but family members objected, so the two remain at Mount Vernon, in Virginia. Ringing the room, 40 Doric sandstone columns help support the Rotunda. Gutzon Borglum, the sculptor who carved Mount Rushmore, created the marble head of Lincoln displayed here. The statue's missing left ear symbolizes the

In the Capitol stands a plaster version of the large bronze "Freedom" that famously tops the building's dome.

slain President's incomplete life.

North of the Crypt, through the small Senate Rotunda and to the right, stands the **Old Supreme Court Chamber.** The Senate originally met in this vaulted room designed by Latrobe; the Supreme Court used it from 1810 to 1860.

In the early 1970s, restorers armed with mid-19th-century descriptions set out to return the chamber to its earlier appearance. Half of the furnishings here, including justices' desks and chairs, are original.

On the first floor of the north wing, the colorful Brumidi Corridors boast a wealth of frescoes and other paintings by Constantino Brumidi, who worked in the Capitol for 25 years in the late 1800s. Sometimes called the Michelangelo of the Capitol, Brumidi based his designs for the corridors on the Raphael loggia in the Vatican, where he had done some restoration work. The historical scenes and heroes, along with depictions of flora and fauna in trompe l'oeil frames, provide a rich summary of early America.

Senate Chamber

The heart of American democracy, the U.S. Capitol is also the geographic center of Washington; the city's four quadrants radiate from the middle of the building.

U.S. Capitol

West Front

Later paintings include scenes of the first moon landing and a tribute to the crew that died in the 1986 explosion of the *Challenger* space shuttle.

On the other side of the Crypt, in the south wing, are the **First Floor House Corridors** containing more statuary as well as murals by contemporary American artist Allyn Cox. Among the scenes depicted are the Capitol in flames in 1814 and wounded Union soldiers lying in a makeshift hospital in the Rotunda.

The **Congressional Chambers** are in the Capitol's wings (the House south, the Senate north). The 435 House representatives are not assigned specific seats, though Democrats traditionally sit to the Speaker's right, Republicans to the left. The same arrangement holds for the more stately Senate, but here desks are based on seniority. ■

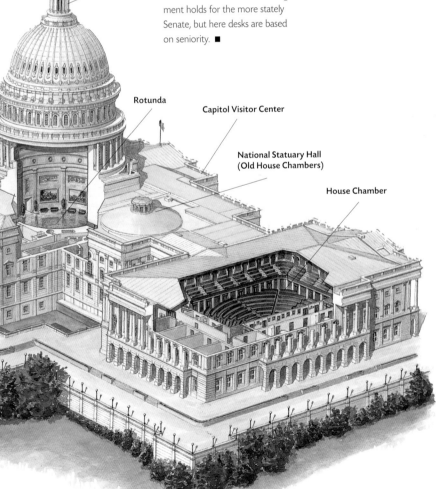

When a white light shines in the dome, Congress is in session.

Rotunda

Capitol Visitor Center

National Statuary Hall (Old House Chambers)

House Chamber

Politics at Work

Regardless of the outcome of a bill, the process is interesting and illuminating to watch. You will get to observe how the blueprint for government, the Constitution of the United States of America—hashed out in a steamy room centuries ago—is applied to issues today. Seeing how constitutional democracy plays out can't help but take you back to the early days of the still young United States.

"Senate Hearing" by William Gropper (1897–1977) satirizes gasbag lawmakers. Indeed, discord, as understood by James Madison, was built into our constitutional democracy to give voice to many.

In the summer of 1787, following the successful rebellion of the 13 Colonies against England and the loosely structured "Confederation" period, 55 leaders from the newly independent states met in Philadelphia's State House (now Independence Hall) to revise the Articles of Confederation, the country's first constitution.

Trying to strike a delicate balance between sufficient government power to rule a nation yet allow adequate liberty for its citizens, the delegates decided to toss the Articles and create a new document. The result: the

Constitution of the United States of America. This constitution could not become the law of the land by fiat, so the founders asked that it be ratified by the people of the 13 independent states. There were many heated state conventions, some producing violence, others producing eloquent words, that have helped Supreme Court justices determine the meaning of this concise plan for the government we have today—living up to its preamble: "We the People of the United States ..."

From the beginning Congress met to air differences and reach hard fought compromises. The reason the capital is in Washington, for instance, is because of the Compromise of 1790, in which northern congressmen and senators got their southern counterparts to approve funding our first national debt in return for placing the nation's capital in the south on the Potomac River, not far from George Washington's home.

From the First Congress came the traditions of national debt and logrolling. And anyone who has tuned into C-SPAN knows that political debate and compromise continue to be integral ingredients in making laws.

While the work done on the House or Senate floor is well publicized, much of the real work of Congress goes on behind the scenes in committees and subcommittees, which meet on most days when the legislature is in session. If you visit you might be able to watch as the Environmental Protection Agency administrator is grilled about pollution enforcement, attend confirmation hearings for a newly nominated federal judge, or listen as the future of space exploration is debated.

If a bill is good and has powerful friends on the committee, it will be recommended to the House or Senate for debate and vote. Of the thousands of bills introduced every year, only a small percentage make it to the

INSIDER TIP:

Whenever I pass the Capitol, D.C.'s most iconic and magisterial building, I feel the presence of a force that sets the agenda, like it or not, of the country. The Capitol is so approachable—its visitor center is the gateway to the nation's story.

—KEITH BELLOWS
National Geographic Traveler
magazine editor in chief

floor of the House or Senate to be voted on.

If passed, the bill is then sent to the other chamber, referred to committee, and so on. If the bill makes it through the tortured path to passage in that chamber, then a "Conference" committee is set up to settle differences between the two bills. The Senate and House vote again on the revised bill, and if that compromise bill passes, it goes to the President for signature—or veto.

And so a landmark document of the Western world gets put through its paces and shows its strengths one more time.

EXPERIENCE: Following the Lawmaking Process

An exciting part of visiting "official" Washington is getting a peek inside the political process. But even if you have a chance to observe Congress in session, it's not always clear exactly what's going on, or what the end result might be. Briefing yourself on the day's agenda and what bills are under consideration can help you make better sense of it all. The Library of Congress offers a comprehensive online source of legislative information. The old "Thomas" website (named for Thomas Jefferson) has now been revamped as **congress.gov.** The site provides the full text, related details, and status of all bills in the current Congress, as well as those dating back to 1973. You can browse legislation by sponsor, for example, to find out what your senator or representative has been doing. Streaming video follows any floor proceedings that may be under way. Look under "Current Legislative Activities" to find out what's hot.

If a bill has been enacted into law, you can read the full text on the website. For a quick tutorial on the process of lawmaking, click on "The Legislative Process" at the top of the page.

Supreme Court

This imposing neoclassical building opposite the Capitol makes a simple yet powerful statement with its wide marble stairway and its lofty portico rising on 32 Corinthian columns. An architrave just below the pediment bears the inscription "Equal Justice Under Law."

The Supreme Court's four-word pediment inscription is an echo of Justice John Marshall Harlan's famous dissenting opinion in 1896 in *Plessy* v. *Ferguson:* "In view of the Constitution, in the eye of the law, there is in this country no superior, dominant, ruling class of citizens. There is no caste here ... [A]ll citizens are equal before the law."

Here the nation's highest tribunal arbitrates cases involving the Constitution or the nation's laws. In this court of final appeal, decisions have been handed down that have profoundly influenced the country. In 2000 the Court showed its muscle again by effectively settling the controversial U.S. presidential race.

Surprisingly, the Supreme Court did not have its own building until 1935. Before then it sat in various places within the Capitol. In 1929, Chief Justice William Howard Taft, the only U.S. President (1909–1913) to serve on the Court (1921–1930), urged Congress to authorize the erection of a Supreme Court building. The formal edifice designed by Cass Gilbert was constructed with 27,400 pieces of marble. Every feature lends a sense of gravity and dignity, from the 6.5-ton (5.8 tonne) bronze doors to the seated marble giants out front—"Contemplation of Justice" (left) and "Guardian of Law" (right).

Touring the Court

You enter through one of the doors that flank the building's

A stone's throw from the Capitol, the neoclassical Supreme Court, with its courtyard of marble, was completed in 1935.

main staircase and lead to the **Great Hall** and its long line of busts depicting former chief justices. At the end of the hall lies the actual courtroom.

When the court is not in session you can visit the chamber and learn about court procedure by attending a lecture given on the half hour. In the nation's most important courtroom stand the chairs of the nine justices, their height varying according to how tall the justice is (so they all appear the same height when seated). Along the sides of the room rise 24 veined marble columns, above which sculpted marble panels depict such lawgivers as Moses, Confucius, and Napoleon.

When the court is in session (*Mon.–Wed. Oct.–April*), you can listen to oral arguments by lining up on the plaza in front of the building. Seating begins at 9:30 a.m., and you must go through two security checkpoints. Some cases attract crowds, with people even sleeping outside the court to ensure a place inside. You may have a better chance with the other line—for those who just want to hear a three-minute sample of the case.

More than 10,000 petitions asking the Supreme Court to overturn a lower-court ruling arrive annually. Only about 100 make it to the argument stage. Each side is given 30 minutes to argue its case; the justices then write their opinions.

From the Great Hall, go down a flight of stairs to the small theater on the **Ground Floor;** a 24-minute film details

the workings of the Court and includes interviews with current justices. The floor also has several exhibits. On the south side the Warren Court (1953–1969), presided over by Chief Justice Earl Warren, still sits in session in a stone and aluminum sculpture. The Warren Court's progressive opinions included the outlawing of school segregation.

At the floor's east end is a statue of the great fourth Chief Justice, John Marshall, who served 1801–1835. He is considered responsible for our system of constitutional law, including the doctrine of judicial review (*Marbury v. Madison,* 1803), by which the Court can declare acts of Congress unconstitutional. Follow signs for a view of two marble-and-bronze spiral staircases; the ascending ovals make the five-story building appear twice as tall as it really is. ■

Supreme Court

- Map p. 51
- 1st & E. Capitol Sts., N.E.
- 202/479-3000 or 202/479-3211
- Closed Sat.–Sun.
- Metro: Capitol South, Union Station; Bus: 96–97, A11, Circulator

supremecourt.gov

Milestones for Women

When Justice Elena Kagan, the former dean of Harvard Law School, joined the Supreme Court in August 2010, it marked the first time that three women sat on the High Court at the same time. The chief justice—currently John G. Roberts—and eight associate justices, nominated by the President and confirmed by a majority vote in the Senate, are appointed for life terms. To date, only four of the 112 Supreme Court justices have been women. The first, Sandra Day O'Connor, was nominated by President Reagan; she retired in 2006. Ruth Bader Ginsburg joined the Court in 1993 after being nominated by President Clinton. President Obama nominated Sonia M. Sotomayor, the first Hispanic on the Court; he also nominated Kagan.

Library of Congress

The world's largest library, the Library of Congress contains what many people regard as the most beautiful space in Washington: the Great Hall in the Thomas Jefferson Building. It dazzles with an abundance of murals, mosaics, sculptures, and architectural flourishes in Italian Renaissance style. The circular Main Reading Room with concentric rows of polished wood research desks is also splendid. Get the full dramatic effect from the elevated Visitors' Gallery.

The central desk is where books are requested for use in the Main Reading Room.

Library of Congress

- Map p. 51
- 1st St. & Independence Ave., S.E.
- 202/707-8000 or 202/707-5000
- Closed Sun. & major holidays
- Metro: Capitol South; Bus: 32–36, A11, Circulator

loc.gov

The Jefferson Building, which opened in 1897, is the main building of three on Capitol Hill that anchor the Library. The original Library, started in 1800 as a reference collection for Congress, was housed in the U.S. Capitol. After the British burned the Capitol in 1814, destroying the books, Thomas Jefferson sold his large and eclectic personal library—of 6,487 volumes—to Congress to reestablish the Library of Congress.

A second devastating blow came in 1851 when fire destroyed two-thirds of the Jefferson collection. The Library has searched worldwide for copies of the books; only 282 are yet to be replaced. Thomas Jefferson's library (re-created) now is on public display in the Jefferson Building.

Today the Library holds a mind-boggling array of items, totaling more than 155 million;

nearly 1.7 million visitors consulted materials on-site in 2012. *(Access to the reading rooms requires a "reader card," available in the Madison Building.)* Besides books, the available items include manuscripts, maps, posters, photographs, sheet music, prints and drawings, films, and other audiovisual materials. An ever growing amount of the Library's collections can be accessed online. The Library also joined UNESCO's efforts to make available via the World Digital Library *(wdl.org)* many of the world's greatest writing and art treasures held by national libraries and archives.

Among its many functions, the Library registers copyrights for published works and prepares legal research reports for Congress. The **Young Readers Center** in the Jefferson Building presents book information specifically targeted to families.

on much of what you'll see.

Several galleries have exhibits on American history and culture. "Exploring the Early Americas," for example, displays the 1507 Waldseemüller World Map, the first to use the word "America." Other exhibits have showcased comedy

Miles of Books

Contrary to what many people believe, the Library of Congress does not have copies of every published book. That was the practice in the early years, when the flood of acquired materials included two copies of each copyrighted work in the country (which led to the need for construction of the Thomas Jefferson Building). Today the Library reviews and retains materials on an individual basis, adding about 11,000 items every day. It has several overseas offices to obtain foreign works deemed important to scholars; some 470 languages are represented in the collections.

INSIDER TIP:

A stunning overview of the Jefferson Building's Main Reading Room is featured in the 1976 film *All the President's Men.*

—DIANA PARSELL
National Geographic writer

Touring the Library

You can take an organized tour of the **Jefferson Building** or pick up a self-guided tour brochure at the visitor desk, near the ground-level entrance. Touch-activated screens provide details

materials from a Bob Hope collection, political cartoons, and artifacts of musical legends George and Ira Gershwin. Not to be missed on the entrance level: the Gutenberg Bible, the first book printed using movable metal type, and the Giant Bible of Mainz, both from the mid-1450s.

Proceed one level up to the **Great Hall,** reminiscent of a Mediterranean palazzo. Note the intricate mosaics and the overhead paintings honoring music, poetry, astronomy, and other disciplines. Stairs lead to a mezzanine with overhead views of the **Main Reading Room.** ∎

Folger Shakespeare Library

A unique treasure, the library holds the world's largest collection of William Shakespeare's works. Originating from a gift by Henry Clay Folger, the library opened in 1932 and now houses 320,000 books and manuscripts, and 90,000 paintings, drawings, prints, and photographs—plus many musical instruments, costumes, and films.

Folger Shake-speare Library

⛰ Map p. 51

✉ 201 E. Capitol St., S.E., bet. 2nd & 3rd Sts., S.E.

☎ 202/544-4600

🚇 Metro: Capitol South, Union Station; Bus: 32–36, 96–97, Circulator

folger.edu

In 1879 a lecture on the Bard by Ralph Waldo Emerson fired the interest of Folger, then a 22-year-old student at Amherst College. A decade later, he bought his first Shakespeare folio. With money he made as president of the Standard Oil Company of New York, he went on to buy thousands of rare books, manuscripts, and paintings. In the early 1900s, he began casting about for a site to build a library; he chose one adjacent to the Library of Congress (see pp. 62–63). But just after the cornerstone was laid, in 1930, he died; his wife, Emily, saw the project to completion.

The bold lines of this art deco–inspired neoclassical marble building make it a fitting presence among its neighbors. Nine bas-reliefs on the north side depict scenes from the Bard's plays. On the east lawn lies an **Elizabethan flower and herb garden.**

For more details, take one of the daily tours, which start at the docent's desk. Or wander on your own through the wood-paneled 30-foot-high (9.1 m) **Great Hall,** which displays a copy of the Bard's first folio and changing exhibits from the collection. You may peer into the Tudor-style **Paster Reading Room** *(closed Sun.),* where a stained-glass window depicting the "Seven Ages of Man" *(As You Like It)* adorns the west end. A Shakespeare bust is on the east wall. The room is open to scholars and graduate students for research.

At the Folger's east end, the **Elizabethan Theatre** is an intimate spot for the Bard's plays. The oak columns and tiered balconies add to the atmosphere of a Renaissance courtyard. ∎

The Folger's Reading Room evokes an Elizabethan great hall.

U.S. Botanic Garden

If you're surprised to suddenly find yourself in the thick of a tropical rain forest or surrounded by a soothing oasis in metropolitan Washington, D.C., then you've stumbled onto the U.S. Botanic Garden, an oasis of green in the shadow of the U.S. Capitol.

Congress established this garden in 1820 for the collection, growing, and distribution of important plants. The historic greenhouse, built in 1933, was renovated in 2001. Today, some 4,000 plants are on view at any one time in the glass-paneled **Conservatory,** with ten garden rooms. You can stroll through the various areas devoted to desert, tropical, and Hawaii flora, and explore exhibits on

For a good view of the Conservatory, head across Independence Avenue to the U.S. Botanic Garden's Bartholdi Park.

INSIDER TIP:

Inside, see carnivorous plants (thrilling for kids) from spring through fall, and an enthralling Christmas-season miniature train set.

—KEITH BELLOWS
National Geographic Traveler
magazine editor in chief

medicinal and economically useful plants, primeval vegetation, and plant exploration, among others.

Don't miss climbing the stairs to the overhanging walkway in the large tropical atrium. In the orchid house, you can stroll through the outstanding collection of orchids and other unusual epiphytes.

The 3-acre (1.2 ha) **National Garden,** adjacent to the

Conservatory, has plants native to the mid-Atlantic region, as well as a butterfly garden, rose garden, and the First Ladies Water Garden.

Across Independence Avenue is the garden's beautifully planted pocket-size **Bartholdi Park,** a favorite of the locals. Frédéric-Auguste Bartholdi, who created the Statue of Liberty, sculpted the park's 30-foot-high (9 m) cast-iron fountain for the Centennial Exposition of 1876 in Philadelphia—the first world's fair. The sculpture's upper basin is borne by three upright sea nymphs, as water jets from the mouths of stylized fish and turtles. ■

U.S. Botanic Garden

⚑ Map p. 51
✉ 100 Maryland Ave., S.W.
☎ 202/225-8333
🚇 Metro: Federal Center; Bus: 32–36, A11, Circulator

usbg.gov

Eastern Market & Barracks Row

Farm stand, flea market, community center—historic Eastern Market is the heart and soul of Capitol Hill's residential area as well as a popular destination for residents from all across the city who love the ambience, and crab cakes at Market Lunch. Neighboring Barracks Row, Washington's oldest commercial corridor, is undergoing a revitalization that's steadily attracting many new dining and retail establishments.

Eastern Market is where the locals go for food and flowers.

Eastern Market

- ⛰ Map p. 51
- ✉ 225 7th St., S.E.
- ☎ 202/698-5253
- 🕐 Closed Mon.
- 🚇 Metro: Eastern Market

easternmarket-dc.org

Barracks Row

- ⛰ Map p. 51
- ✉ 8th St., S.E.
- 🚇 Metro: Eastern Market

barracksrow.org

The first **Eastern Market** was one of three public markets Pierre L'Enfant included in his design for the city. The present redbrick building opened in 1873. After it was heavily damaged by fire in 2007, the market was carefully restored and reopened in 2009.

Weekends draw crowds as patrons flood the South Hall food stalls for groceries or a bite to eat. At **Market Lunch,** in business for more than three decades, customers tolerate long lines for a taste of the renowned crab cakes and, on Saturday mornings, blueberry buckwheat pancakes. A popular flea market fills the adjacent sidewalks.

The surrounding neighborhood buzzes with new shops and bistros. Across the street from Eastern Market, **Acqua Al 2** *(212 7th St., S.E., tel 202/525-4375)* serves authentic Tuscan cuisine. Pop into the charmingly cluttered **Capitol Hill Books** *(657 C St., S.E., tel 202/544-1621)* to find the perfect mystery novel to read while sipping a honey latte at **Peregrine Espresso** *(660 Pennsylvania Ave., S.E., tel 202/629-4381).*

Barracks Row gets its name from the U.S. Marine Corps Barracks that anchor one end of the corridor. Thomas Jefferson and other Episcopalians attended services at **Christ Church** *(620 G St., S.E.),* and composer John Philip Sousa took music lessons at a house on 8th Street. The area got a burst of cool with the opening of **The Fridge** *(516 1/2 8th St., S.E., rear alley, tel 202/664-4151),* an eclectic arts community that displays public street art, stages live performances from slam poetry to electronic music festivals, and hosts weekly art workshops. ∎

Nationals Park Baseball Stadium

Four decades after the team called the Senators left town, professional baseball returned to Washington in 2005. Nationals Park, which opened in 2008 within sight of the U.S. Capitol, was located near the Anacostia River to spur area development. A full lineup of entertainment and beyond-the-usual food concessions (come hungry) has made a day at the park a popular local outing no matter how the home team performs.

The look of the new ballpark was inspired by architect I. M. Pei's East Wing of the National Gallery of Art (see p. 86). An odd right-angled jog into the right center field was borrowed from the now demolished Griffith Stadium, where the Senators used to play. For many of the seats you can walk inside and take your place on the same level as the sidewalk; the field is 24 feet (7.3 m) below street level.

The design incorporates "green" elements such as high-efficiency lighting, recycled building materials, reflective roof materials, and a storm water management system that reduces runoff into the Anacostia. Tours are available on nongame days.

The favorite moment comes in the middle of the fourth inning, when a group of 10-foot-tall (3 m) giant-headed Presidents—George Washington, Thomas Jefferson, Abraham Lincoln, Theodore Roosevelt, and William Howard Taft—run a clumsy, antics-filled race across center field to home plate.

Among the way-beyond-franks fare are falafel sandwiches, Jamaican BBQ, and a wide selection of microbrew beers. ■

Nationals Park
- Map p. 195
- 1500 South Capitol St., S.E.
- 888/632-6287
- Metro: Navy Yard-Ballpark; Bus: A9, P6, V7–V9, Circulator

washington.nationals.mlb.com

EXPERIENCE: Catch a Game

Washingtonians love their sporting events. Until an unpopular shift of team ownership several years ago, the **Washington Redskins** (redskins.com) were known to have one of the most fiercely loyal fan bases in all of professional football; many families have passed along prized season tickets for several generations. The team plays at **FedEx Field** in Landover, Maryland, accessible by Metro and shuttle bus.

The streets around **Verizon Center** in Penn Quarter (see pp. 134–139) roar with energy on nights when the **Capitals** (capitals.nhl.com) meet another hockey team on the ice. Thanks to his thunderous style of play and his scoring exploits, spectators can't get enough of Russian import Alex Ovechkin, a three-time NHL Most Valuable Player.

In the decade since they arrived in town, the **Nationals** have become one of the most exciting teams in Major League Baseball. Superstar players and a new stadium make Nationals games a hot ticket.

Always popular, basketball has an even bigger profile since the basketball-playing President Obama took office in 2009. Check out the **Washington Wizards** (nba.com/wizards) at Verizon Center.

More Places to Visit on Capitol Hill

National Guard Memorial Museum

This small but engrossing museum at the National Guard Memorial uses memorabilia, light and sound effects, and narratives to chronicle the experiences of citizen soldiers who have served America at home and abroad for nearly four centuries. The displays

The National Postal Museum displays great American moments in miniature.

and programs are especially poignant given the Guard's role in homeland security and war in the Middle East following the September 11, 2001, attacks. *ngef.org*  Map p. 51 ✉ 1 Massachusetts Ave., N.W. ☎ 888/226-4287 🕐 Closed Sat.–Sun. 🚇 Metro: Union Station

National Postal Museum

The building that formerly housed the Washington City Post Office makes an elegant home for this interesting museum, near Union Station, which is part of the Smithsonian Institution complex. The galleries explore topics such as the history of mail delivery, stamp collecting, and the art of correspondence. Among the artifacts on display in the 90-foot-high (27 m) atrium are

prop planes and a railway car, modes of mail conveyance in the past. Hour-long guided tours for groups are available by calling in advance. *postalmuseum.si.edu* 🅰 Map p. 51 ✉ 2 Massachusetts Ave., N.E. ☎ 202/633-5555 🚇 Metro: Union Station; Bus: Circulator

Sewall-Belmont House & Museum

Robert Sewall built this two-story brick house in 1799–1800. In the 20th century, Alva Belmont helped purchase it for the National Woman's Party, headquartered here since 1929. Various collections document the movement to gain political rights for women. Midday tours are available Thursday through Saturday. *sewallbelmont.org* 🅰 Map p. 51 ✉ 144 Constitution Ave., N.E. ☎ 202/546-1210 🕐 Closed Mon.–Tues. 🚇 Metro: Union Station, Capitol South

INSIDER TIP:

With its grand space and elaborate architectural details, Union Station makes a case for the romance of rail travel.

—AMY ALIPIO
National Geographic Traveler
magazine associate editor

Union Station

Completed in 1908 and beautifully restored in the 1980s, this grand beaux arts–style building is worth visiting just for its architecture. Faced in white Vermont granite, the station's huge Romanesque arches give way to a triumphal, echoing Main Hall where 36 larger-than-life Roman legionnaires preside on the gallery level. A barrel-vaulted ceiling with gold-leaf coffers soars 96 feet (29 m) above the station's bustle. Today there are shops and restaurants. *unionstationdc.com* 🅰 Map p. 51 ✉ 50 Massachusetts Ave., N.E. ☎ 202/289-1908 🚇 Metro: Union Station

Must-see museums and monuments, to be sure, but also lots
of fun, games, picnicking, strolling, people-watching, and relaxing

National Mall

Summer's annual Smithsonian
Folklife Festival on the Mall is all
about the energy of global cultures.

National Mall

Lined and dotted with the most significant group of museums and monuments in the country, the National Mall is a long avenue of green grass edged by shade trees. You could spend a week (more, to tell you the truth) enjoying this world-famous tourist mecca.

One day hundreds of colorful kites fly near the Washington Monument, on another a crowd waves banners, and on yet another the Mall is just a peaceful stretch of green. From the U.S. Capitol to the Lincoln Memorial, America's grand promenade extends for more than 2 miles (3.2 km), sandwiched between Constitution and Independence

Avenues. Walkers, joggers, soccer players, and Frisbee throwers (and their dogs) regularly take to the inviting lawns.

Pierre-Charles L'Enfant's city plan of 1791 included a "vast esplanade" lined with grand residences. But by the end of the 1800s, the Mall was a place of coal piles, sheds, tracks, and a railroad station. In 1901 the MacMillan

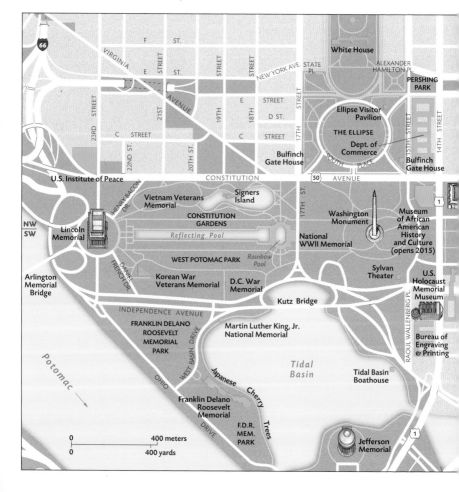

Commission recommended reviving L'Enfant's plan. Tracks and debris were removed. With the addition of the Lincoln Memorial, the Mall stretched west to the Potomac River.

By the late 1980s, the Mall held nine Smithsonian museums and two National Gallery of Art buildings. In 2004 the National Museum of the American Indian and the World War II Memorial opened, and 2011 saw the openings of the Martin Luther King, Jr. Memorial, on the Tidal Basin, and the U.S. Institute of Peace, off the Mall's northwest corner. The new National Museum of African-American History and Culture is being built just east of the Washington Monument and is due to open in 2015. ■

NOT TO BE MISSED:

James McNeill Whistler's Peacock Room in the Freer Gallery   72

The National Museum of Natural History's human origins exhibit   94

Julia Child's kitchen at the National Museum of American History   98

The wall of names at the Vietnam Veterans Memorial   101–102

Viewing the Mall from the steps of the Lincoln Memorial   102

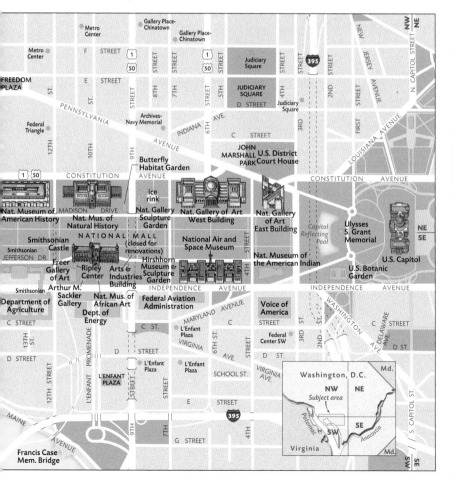

Freer Gallery of Art

Dating from the fourth millennium B.C. to modern times, the objects in the Freer make a comprehensive sweep of Asian art. The collection, donated by Detroit businessman Charles Lang Freer (1856–1919), is considered among the finest in the world. It is complemented by 19th- and 20th-century American pieces, including many works by James McNeill Whistler.

Whistler painted the Freer's sumptuous Peacock Room as though it were a huge lacquer box.

Freer Gallery of Art

🅰 Map pp. 70–71
✉ Jefferson Dr. & 12th St., S.W.
☎ 202/633-4880
🖼 Metro: Smithsonian; Bus: 32–36, 52

asia.si.edu

Opened in 1923, the Italian Renaissance–style building has a pink granite exterior and polished white marble floors. Its galleries surround a hallway where large windows look out onto a refreshing inner courtyard. The lighting and exhibit space combine to lend a refined, contemplative atmosphere.

Of the 19 galleries, 16 are devoted to Asian art, including Indian sculpture, Japanese lacquerware, Chinese paintings, Korean and Vietnamese ceramics, and Islamic metalware. The Freer, which does not lend out its objects, rotates works from its 25,865-piece collection.

American treasures include the exquisite **Peacock Room,** which is a must-see. James M. Whistler painted the room for a wealthy London shipowner. Recently restored to its original elegance, the room features antique gilded leather walls, a metal ceiling painted in a feather pattern, and a painting known as "The Princess in the Land of Porcelain." The opposite wall has a painting of two peacocks, a reference to a quarrel between Whistler and his patron over the fee. Freer bought the room intact from a London dealer and installed it in his Detroit home; it was moved to Washington in 1919.

The Freer connects to the Arthur M. Sackler Gallery (see page opposite), another trove of Asian treasures. ■

Arthur M. Sackler Gallery

Housed almost entirely below the ground, this 1987 museum has at its core the Asian collection of research physician and medical publisher Arthur M. Sackler. Among its treasures are Chinese bronzes and jades, Persian manuscripts, ancient Iranian silver, and works from Tibet and Japan. The museum exhibits items from its growing permanent collection as well as from other collections in the United States and elsewhere.

Visiting the Freer (see page opposite) and the Sackler, which are administered jointly, gives you a comprehensive overview of Asian art. The Sackler's **first level**—belowground—contains artfully arranged works from a variety of cultures. Many rooms feature artfully arranged objects in plexiglass cases, with subtle lighting and just enough information to keep you interested but not overwhelmed. A recent exhibition, "Kiyochika: Master of the Night," showcased dozens of wood-block prints by the artist Kobayashi Kiyochika that elegantly conveyed Tokyo's transformation into a modern city in the 1870s.

In the **Arts of China galleries,** also on the first level, the Ancient Chinese Art section displays 12th- to 13th-century B.C. jade knives crafted by artisans with meticulous care and great skill. Another section, the Arts of Six Dynasties and Tang in China, holds Tang dynasty tomb guardians adorned with brilliant horns and flames. The guardians look as fierce as they must have 13 centuries ago.

The **second level** of the gallery is composed mainly of administrative offices. Be sure to visit the **third level** of the Sackler, where a rotating ceramics gallery, most recently highlighting items from Vietnam and Thailand, is complimented by a small pool and bubbling fountains.

From the third level, visitors can make their way to the S. Dillon Ripley Center, which features temporary exhibits. ■

Arthur M. Sackler Gallery

🅰 Map pp. 70–71
✉ 1050 Independence Ave., S.W.
☎ 202/633-4880
Ⓜ Metro: Smithsonian; Bus: 32–36, 52

asia.si.edu

The Smithsonian: All the Museums

African Art Museum
Air and Space Museum
Udvar-Hazy Center (Va.)
African-American History and Culture Museum
American Art Museum and its Renwick Gallery
American History Museum
American Indian Museum, Heye Center (NYC)
Anacostia Community Museum
Cooper-Hewitt (NYC)
Freer Gallery of Art and Arthur M. Sackler Gallery
Hirshhorn Museum & Sculpture Garden
National Zoo
Natural History Museum
Portrait Gallery
Postal Museum
Smithsonian Institution Building, the Castle
Arts and Industries Building (closed for renovation)

National Museum of African Art

This museum, with more than 9,000 pieces, traces its roots to a town house on Capitol Hill once owned by Frederick Douglass, a former slave who became a noted abolitionist. In 1964 Warren M. Robbins founded the Museum of African Art there as a private educational institution that mainly displayed some Douglass memorabilia. But that was just the beginning.

National Museum of African Art

- 🅜 Map pp. 70–71
- ✉ 950 Independence Ave., S.W.
- ☎ 202/633-4600
- 🚇 Metro: Smithsonian, L'Enfant Plaza; Bus: 32–36, 52

africa.si.edu

The museum's early holdings also included a collection of 19th-century paintings by African-American artists, but for exhibitions of African works Robbins had to rely on loaned objects.

In 1979 the museum became part of the Smithsonian Institution. Three years later it was officially renamed the National Museum of African Art, and in 1987 the steadily growing institution moved to its present location on the Mall. Its permanent collection has grown to represent 900 cultures across the continent and a vast range of materials and art forms—textiles, sculpture, pottery, paintings, jewelry, masks, musical instruments, furniture, tools, and religious and household objects. Together they show the degree to which art permeates African culture. Changing exhibitions highlight treasures from the museum's collection along with pieces from public and private collections.

The displays are designed to illuminate the high aesthetic and technical craftsmanship in African art. They show, for example, how Africans often fashion all kinds of materials—from simple household utensils to ceremonial objects to monumental sculptures honoring the living and the dead—in ways meant to embody expressions of an "ideal" that reflects standards of beauty, moral behavior, leadership, intelligence, and fertility. Contemporary traditional ceramics show the dexterity and artistry of the continent's master potters—mainly women.

The ongoing "African Vision" exhibition features highlights from the Walt Disney Company's donation of 525 outstanding pieces, from a collection assembled by real estate developer Paul Tishman and his wife, Ruth. Many of the items, which represent most of Africa's major artistic traditions, are unique and rare works from throughout sub-Saharan Africa.

The museum also houses the Warren M. Robbins Library and offers cultural programs. Its **Eliot Elisofon Photographic Archives,** named for the famous *Life* magazine photographer, has an expanding collection of some 350,000 items, ranging from photo prints and transparencies to slides and film footage. ∎

A Democratic Republic of the Congo mask evokes power.

Hirshhorn Museum & Sculpture Garden

A striking touch of modernity on the Mall, the Hirshhorn houses the Smithsonian's pre-eminent works of international modern and contemporary art. The museum opened in 1974, after American entrepreneur and philanthropist Joseph H. Hirshhorn (1899–1981) donated his art collection to the Smithsonian. A drum-shaped building three stories high, this eye-catching landmark has a bi-level sculpture garden and plaza of nearly 4 acres (1.6 ha).

The Hirshhorn's circular courtyard often serves as a setting for receptions.

Architect Gordon Bunshaft designed the museum to have outdoor spaces that encourage intimate, contemplative viewing of the artworks. The Hirshhorn has a permanent collection of more than 11,500 works by leading artists from the late 19th century to the present. Paintings, mixed-media pieces, photography, works on paper, videos, and films are among the holdings, along with an outstanding modern sculpture collection that's regarded as one of the most comprehensive in the world. A piece that is hard to miss is Roy Lichtenstein's towering "Brushstroke" (1996), installed on the plaza. Among the 60 pieces in the sculpture garden are traditional figures by artists such as Auguste Rodin and Aristide Maillol, biomorphic

Hirshhorn Museum & Sculpture Garden

⬛ Map pp. 70–71

✉ Independence Ave. & 7th St., S.W.

☎ 202/633-1000

🖥 Metro: L'Enfant Plaza; Bus: 32–36, 52

hirshhorn.si.edu

figures by Henry Moore and Barbara Hepworth, and abstract and kinetic works by Alexander Calder and Mark di Suvero.

Other major artists represented in the museum's wide-ranging collection of paintings and sculpture include Willem de Kooning, Alberto Giacometti, Jackson Pollock, Pablo Picasso, Clyfford Still, Gerhard Richter, Ana Mendieta, Georgia O'Keeffe, Ernesto Neto, Hiroshi Sugimoto, Lorna Simpson, Robert Lazzarini, Ann Hamilton, Yoko Ono, and many others.

In an effort to continually expand its holdings and showcase modern works, the Hirshhorn works closely with today's artists. To present pieces from its col-

What Was Here Before?

Prior to the Hirshhorn, this piece of the Mall was occupied by the U.S. Army Medical Museum—now the National Museum of Health & Medicine (see p. 192)—from 1887 to 1968. The museum was established during the Civil War to help advance medical treatment. More than 25,000 specimens of diseased or wounded flesh and bones were kept here, and morbidly fascinated visitors could see preserved gunshot wounds, and disfigured and diseased organs. Over the years the tastes of the public changed, and the museum relocated to the Walter Reed Army Medical Center until its recent move to 2500 Linden Lane, Silver Spring, Maryland.

lection in fresh, new ways, the museum introduced a program series, titled **Ways of Seeing,** in which working artists, filmmakers, and other creative thinkers are invited to organize exhibitions

INSIDER TIP:

Bringing life to the lawn right next to the Hirshhorn is sculptor Juan Muñoz's dazzling "Last Conversation Piece." The five figures suggest both whimsy and intensity.

—SHEILA BUCKMASTER
National Geographic Traveler
magazine editor at large

using objects from the museum's holdings. In one such installation, for example, artist John Baldessari incorporated paintings by Milton Avery, Philip Guston, and Thomas Eakins, photographs by Eakins, and sculpture by Emily Kaufman.

A series titled **Directions** explores new work by emerging and established artists, while the **Black Box** series presents recent film and video works.

Other programs include "Meet the Artist" lectures, gallery talks, and art-related activities for teens. Several times a year the Hirshhorn hosts "After Hours" events that offer inviting social environments in which to enjoy the exhibits.

In addition, a renowned film program—one of the first in the United States to focus on independent cinema—presents narrative and experimental features, documentaries, shorts, and presentations by directors and others in the museum's 272-seat auditorium. ∎

National Air and Space Museum

The excitement of aeronautical and spaceflight technology has made the National Air and Space Museum one of the most visited museums on the planet. Every year millions of people roam its flagship building on the Mall, where the exhibits feature only 10 percent of the Smithsonian's aviation and space collection. Many of the remaining artifacts are on display at the museum's annex, the Steven F. Udvar-Hazy Center in suburban Virginia (see pp. 222–223).

With the greenery of the Mall as backdrop, airplanes fill the National Air and Space Museum.

The Smithsonian's involvement in air and space goes back to 1857, when it began using balloons to collect weather data. Later, during the Civil War, the first secretary of the Smithsonian, Joseph Henry, won President Abraham Lincoln's support for making military observations from balloons. The third secretary, Samuel Pierpont Langley (1887–1906), was an astronomer and airplane pioneer. He experimented successfully with large, powered model aircraft on the Potomac in the 1890s, but the first actual man-powered controlled flight was made by the Wright brothers in 1903.

During the first half of the 20th century, the Smithsonian participated in and funded major rocket research and astrophysical

National Air and Space Museum

Map pp. 70–71

Independence Ave. & 7th St., S.W.

202/633-2214

Metro: L'Enfant Plaza; Bus: 32–36, 54, A9

nasm.si.edu

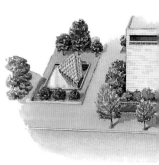

Sea-Air
Operations

WWII
Aviation

Flight
simulators

Golden Age
of Flight

observation projects. In 1971, Apollo astronaut Michael Collins was appointed director of the new National Air and Space Museum, and construction began the next year. The new museum opened to the public in 1976.

Visiting

With so much to see at this museum and such large distances to cover, it's best to map out your visit, especially if you're with children or others who tire easily (see floor plan this page). In a half-day visit, it's best to choose one of two tactics: Either aim for a quick overview of the entire museum or take a close look at just a few galleries. Moving around in this popular museum can be a challenge during peak visiting times because of the huge crowds, so pace yourself—and agree on a place to meet others in your party if you get separated.

If you want to see any of the shows in the IMAX theater or the Planetarium, it's a good idea to purchase the tickets at the start of your visit, because tickets often sell out. Then tour the galleries that interest you until the show starts. At lunchtime, you can grab a bite to eat at the museum's large, airy cafeteria.

In terms of layout, airplanes and aviation are in the building's west end, while rockets and spaceflight are in the east end. Almost all the artifacts on display are the real thing, though in some cases backups, test vehicles, or authentic reproductions are shown instead. Labels indicate the difference.

First Floor

Just inside the Mall entrance, the **Milestones of Flight** gallery highlights aviation's "greatest hits," with artifacts such as the *Spirit of*

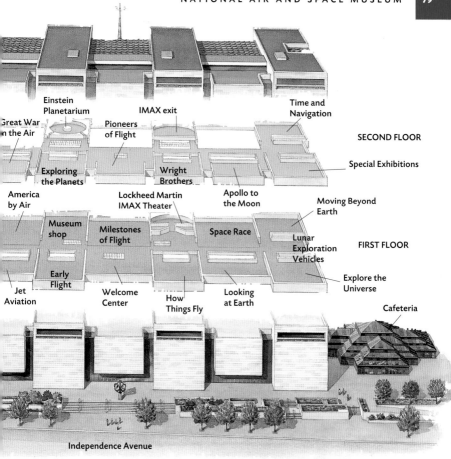

Einstein
Planetarium

IMAX exit

Time and
Navigation

Great War
in the Air

Pioneers
of Flight

SECOND FLOOR

Exploring
the Planets

Wright
Brothers

Special Exhibitions

America
by Air

Lockheed Martin
IMAX Theater

Apollo to
the Moon

Moving Beyond
Earth

Museum
shop

Milestones
of Flight

Space Race

Lunar
Exploration
Vehicles

FIRST FLOOR

Early
Flight

Explore the
Universe

Jet
Aviation

Welcome
Center

How
Things Fly

Looking
at Earth

Cafeteria

Independence Avenue

St. Louis, in which Charles Lindbergh made the first solo nonstop flight across the Atlantic in May 1927, and John Glenn's Mercury Friendship 7 capsule. Using a $30 million donation from Boeing, the gallery will be utterly revamped in time for the museum's 40th anniversary in 2016, adding such icons as the enormous Apollo Lunar Module and the model of the U.S.S. *Enterprise* from *Star Trek.*

Proceeding to the right, you'll come to the museum's popular gift shop and toy store. Beyond that is the **America by Air** gallery, with attractions that include a giant nose cone section from a Boeing 747 and interactive programs. For more participatory displays, head to the gallery next door, which features flight simulators.

Across the hall, in the far corner gallery, is the exhibit **Golden Age of Flight.** Scratchy recordings of old torch songs set the tone for this exhibit of the glamour days of aviation in the period between the two World Wars. A small theater features historic film footage, including information about the life of famed pilot Jimmy Doolittle.

In the adjacent **Jet Aviation** gallery, you'll take a leap forward in time to focus on the development of jet technology. Included in this display is a German WWII fighter, the infamous Messerschmitt Me 262.

Then wander next door to the **Early Flight** gallery to experience the time when flight was still a novelty. Among the featured artifacts are the world's first military plane, the 1909 Wright Military Flyer, and an 1894 Lilienthal glider with bat-like ribbed wings.

INSIDER TIP:

Charles Lindbergh's *Spirit of St. Louis* is an obvious Air and Space must-see; Amelia Earhart's bright red plane is a fine surprise.

—DANIEL R. WESTERGREN
National Geographic Traveler
magazine director of photography

As you cross the hall, making your way past the Welcome Center entrance on the Independence Avenue side, take some time to study the two impressive murals. Robert T. McCall's 1976 "The Space Mural: A Cosmic View" traces space history from the Big Bang to lunar exploration and beyond. On the opposite wall, Eric Sloan's mural "Earthflight Environment" (1976) shows a Western landscape beneath a sky filled with the various kinds of weather elements

pilots must fly through.

A favorite among children, the **How Things Fly** gallery, adjacent to the Welcome Center, has 50 hands-on exhibits with gadgets that explain principles such as lift, drag, air pressure, and wave action.

Next door, the **Looking at Earth** gallery shows how views of the planet obtained from the sky through Landsat and other means aid our understanding of Earth. Several of the surrounding galleries continue the space theme. Hard-to-miss artifacts on display include a giant black-and-white V-2 rocket in the two-story **Space Race** gallery and a shiny lunar module featured in the **Lunar Exploration Vehicles** gallery.

The nearby **Moving Beyond Earth** gallery puts people "in orbit" with drifting views of the Earth from space and on a fly-around tour of the space station. Artifacts include first space tourist Dennis Tito's space suit, which points to a future of commercial spaceflights.

Directly across the hall, past the lunar exhibit, **Explore the Universe** showcases some of the many tools that astronomers have used over the centuries to study the universe. Also on this level of the museum, between the Space Race and Milestones of Flight galleries, is the **Lockheed Martin IMAX Theater** (*$$–$$$*). Its several films, including the long-running classic "To Fly!"—a thrilling film not to be missed—are projected on a screen that is a whopping five stories high.

EXPERIENCE: Joining the Revelry on the Mall

During the warm months of the year, there's bound to be something special happening on the National Mall just about any time you might be visiting. Some activities are targeted to particular groups—such as D.C. Yoga Week (April–May) and the Black Family Reunion (September)—but most cater to the general public and a wide range of interests.

Summer is the busiest time, and no Mall event has a bigger bang than the annual **Fourth of July** celebration (*nps.gov/foju*). The spectacular display of fireworks will have you "oohing" and "ahhing" at the colorful streamers of light bursting around the silhouetted monuments. Some spectators start arriving on the lawn as early as 10 a.m. to claim choice places (everyone must enter the grounds through a security checkpoint). Starting at midday, an Independence Day parade of fife and drum corps, drill teams, guest bands, and national dignitaries wends its way down Constitution Avenue, from 7th to 17th Streets.

Around the same time, the two-week-long **Smithsonian Folklife Festival** (late June–early July; *festival .si.edu*) also draws crowds. Each year the festival spotlights the cultural traditions of several nations, regions, ethnic groups, and occupations. The packed program of events includes presentations by musicians, artists, storytellers, and dancers, along with traditional foods and crafts.

A popular springtime event is the **Smithsonian Kite Festival,** when butterflies, dragons with long tails, and an array of colorful geometrical shapes dot the sky above the Mall. The event features kite-flying competitions and workshops on kite-making.

In summer, what could be better than movies under the stars? Plan to take a blanket and picnic to enjoy **Screen on the Green** (*tel 877/262-5866, hbo.com/screenonthegreen*). The popular July–August series often features favorite Hollywood classics.

If you are out for an evening stroll on the Mall, you may catch a free **military band concert** (*schedules on websites of the military branches*) held regularly Memorial Day through Labor Day. The Army, Navy, Air Force, and Marine Corps have traditional military bands and specialty groups such as jazz ensembles and string quartets; venues include the Lincoln Memorial and the U.S. Capitol lawn.

On the Fourth of July, the Mall crackles with pyrotechnic action.

Second Floor

Escalators in the Milestones of Flight gallery carry you to the museum's second floor, where you can visit the **Einstein Planetarium** *($$)* and view multimedia presentations in the domed theater.

Across the hall from the planetarium, a full-scale model of a Mars rover is on display in the **Exploring the Planets** gallery, along with spacecraft, telescopes, and other tools used to explore and acquire an understanding of the universe. The displays in this gallery, designed to be basic enough for children to enjoy and understand, include highlights of recent planetary discoveries.

Also in the west end of the second floor are several galleries that focus on various aspects of aviation during the two World Wars: the **Sea-Air Operations** gallery, which includes a simulated aircraft carrier; **World War II Aviation;** and **Legend, Memory, and the Great War in the Air,** which offers an unromanticized view of aerial combat during World War I.

Once you leave this end of the second floor and head in the other direction, you'll come to the **Pioneers of Flight** gallery, which is devoted to individual feats in aviation history. Among the famous aircraft here is Amelia Earhart's Lockheed Vega, in which she became the first woman to fly solo across the Atlantic in 1932.

Celebrated Aviator Charles Lindbergh

Perhaps more than any other aviator, Charles Lindbergh (1902–1974) captured the public's heart. Son of a Minnesota congressman, he spent some early years in Washington, D.C. Later he attended a Wisconsin college but dropped out to enroll in a Nebraska flying school. For a few years he was a stunt flyer and an airmail pilot. Then he competed for a $25,000 prize offered to the first person to fly from New York to Paris nonstop.

On May 20, 1927, the aviator took off in the *Spirit of St. Louis,* named for the city where he received financial backing. Because the large fuel tank partially blocked his view, Lindbergh relied on a periscope or tilted the plane to see forward. He flew for 33.5 exhausting hours before landing at Le Bourget Field near Paris and receiving a warm welcome by a cheering crowd of 100,000.

Back in Washington, Lindbergh stayed a few days at the Patterson House on Dupont Circle with President Coolidge, who lived there while the White House was being renovated. Later that year the U.S. Congress awarded him a Medal of Honor. The following year he gave his plane to the Smithsonian, where it is prominently displayed.

In 1929, Lindbergh wed Anne Morrow, and together they made several flights to chart airline routes. When their son was kidnapped and killed in 1932, the unending publicity drove them abroad. Lindbergh advocated neutrality at the outbreak of World War II, leading to criticism by President Roosevelt, yet he quietly served as an aircraft consultant and flew on combat missions over the Pacific. He described his famous transatlantic flight in thrilling detail in *We* (1927) and *The Spirit of St. Louis* (1953), the latter winning a Pulitzer Prize.

The 1975 Apollo-Soyuz mission (Apollo left, Soyuz right) was the first U.S.-Soviet manned spaceflight.

Next door, the **Wright Brothers & the Invention of the Aerial Age** offers an eye-level view of the famous wood-and-fabric Wright Flyer that was flown at Kitty Hawk, North Carolina, in 1903, marking the dawn of modern aviation. This gallery was established in 2003, during the centennial celebration of that momentous event.

Apollo to the Moon, the adjacent gallery, examines the heady years of manned spaceflight, and in particular the challenges of putting humans on the moon. Featured artifacts range from food, clothing, and personal items of astronauts such as Neil Armstrong, Buzz Aldrin, and Gene Cernan to a sample of moon dust. Just outside the gallery stands a mock-up of Skylab, which you can enter to find out how everyday activities were performed aboard the international space station, which was launched in 1973.

The gallery across the hall in the far corner, **Time and Navigation,** explores the crucial role of accurate timekeeping in helping us to find our way. Exhibits represent revolutions in timekeeping over three centuries, ranging from the 1775 Ramsden dividing engine, which divided a circle into degrees of arc, to an inertial navigation system used to steer submarines such as the U.S.S. *Alabama.*

To view another of the National Air and Space Museum's popular exhibits, you'll have to return to the first floor and step outside, through the Mall entrance. There, **Voyage: A Journey Through Our Solar System** depicts the solar system—at one-ten-billionth of its actual size—in an arrangement that depicts the relative sizes of the planets and the great distances between them. The planets are represented by porcelain balls mounted atop stainless steel posts; the sun is about the size of a large grapefruit; Earth is the size of the head of a pin. The installation runs along the Mall, extending all the way from the Air and Space Museum to the front of the Smithsonian Castle. ■

National Museum of the American Indian

Striking in its architecture, which was inspired by the rocky mesa cliffs of the American Southwest, the National Museum of the American Indian opened in September 2004 after 15 years of planning. It gives the nation a vibrant center for Native American events and educational programs as well as a showcase for outstanding Indian art and artifacts.

The museum got its start at the turn of the 20th century when a wealthy New York banker, George Gustav Heye, needed a place to house the objects he had obtained from North and South American native cultures in a buying frenzy from 1903 to 1954—an astonishing collection of almost a million pieces spanning 10,000 years. He established a museum in what is now the restored Alexander Hamilton U.S. Custom House in lower Manhattan, New York.

In 1989, Heye's collection was transferred to the Smithsonian Institution. Among the artifacts were human remains that had to be repatriated and buried in native grounds. As the Smithsonian's Native American collection swelled to some 400,000 objects, a campaign began to build a major museum for Indian art and culture. The original location in New York City is now a branch of this 4.25-acre (1.7 ha) museum on the Mall, along with a 200,000-square-foot (18,580 sq m) Cultural Resources Center in Suitland, Maryland, where a large bulk of the collection is preserved.

The museum's collection of Native American artifacts is one of the most extensive in the world, with about 825,000 items that represent more than 12,000 years and more than 1,200 indigenous cultures throughout the Americas. Its Photographic Archive holds about 324,000 images dating from the 1860s to the present,

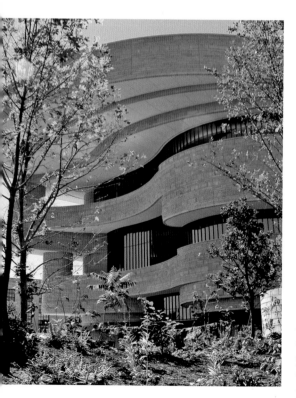

The museum's undulating curves and deep window ledges suggest the work of wind and water.

while the 12,000-item Media Archive includes film and audio-visual collections ranging from phonograph discs to 35mm film and digital video.

Among the museum's treasures are intricate carvings and masks from Pacific Northwest coastal tribes; embellished hides and feather bonnets from North American Plains Indians; pottery and basketry from the Southwest; 18th-century pieces from the Great Lakes area; and early Navajo weavings. Artifacts from Mexico, Central and South America, and the Caribbean include jade carved by the Olmec and Maya and Amazonian feather works.

Visiting

As you wander about the five-story museum, observe the many symbolic references to the cultures it honors. The curvy outside façade of Kasota limestone was made to appear like an ancient slab of stratified stone. Crystal prisms embedded in the south-facing wall create "light shows" when reflecting the midday sun, while the main doors bear native sun symbols.

Inside is a central space called the **Potomac,** a Piscataway word for a place "where the goods are brought in." The overhead dome, 120 feet high (36.5 m) and 120 feet wide, has an oculus offering views of the sky and celestial bodies. On the floor is a circle of red sandstone and rings of black and red granite that map the solstices and equinoxes. A wall of copper bands woven to suggest baskets and textiles encircles the room.

A theater on the ground floor features storytelling, music, and dance. An exhibit in the Potomac area spotlights boatbuilding traditions of native peoples.

Take an elevator to the exhibition areas on the upper levels. The 120-seat **Lewali Theater** on the fourth floor offers an orientation program explaining the themes and messages of the exhibits.

INSIDER TIP:

Driving by the monuments at night is a D.C. delight. The Museum of the American Indian also makes for a fine nighttime spectacle of shadow and light.

—JUSTIN KAVANAGH
National Geographic
Travel Books editor

The museum has three ongoing exhibits. **Our Universes: Traditional Knowledge Shapes Our World** looks at the primary role of cosmology in the myths and lives of native peoples, and their reverence for the spiritual relationship between mankind and the natural world. The exhibit **Our Lives: Contemporary Life and Identities** examines how Native Americans preserve and define their identities in the 21st century. **Return to a Native Place: Algonquian Peoples of the Chesapeake** features displays that highlight events affecting the Nanticoke, Powhatan, and Piscataway tribes. ■

National Museum of the American Indian

⬛ Map pp. 70–71
✉ 4th St. & Independence Ave., S.W.
☎ 202/633-1000
🚇 Metro: L'Enfant Plaza; Bus: 30, 32–36

americanindian .si.edu

National Gallery of Art

One of the country's top art museums, the National Gallery of Art holds a comprehensive collection of Western masterpieces. The West Building exhibits European painting and sculpture from the 13th to 19th centuries; American art; and prints, drawings, photography, and decorative arts. The East Building contains modern and contemporary art. Both buildings also present temporary exhibits.

Rising between the East and West Buildings, tetrahedrons are skylights for the concourse below.

National Gallery of Art

 Map pp. 70–71

✉ Constitution Ave. bet. 3rd & 9th Sts., N.W.

☎ 202/737-4215

🚇 Metro: Archives, Smithsonian; Bus: 32–36, 54, A9, V8

nga.gov

In the 1920s, financier and Secretary of the Treasury Andrew Mellon began planning to establish a museum in Washington. In 1931 he completed a purchase of 21 paintings from Russia's Hermitage Museum, including Raphael's "Alba Madonna." Mellon died in 1937, the same year that construction began for the new museum designed by John Russell Pope and funded by the A. W. Mellon Educational and Charitable Trust. In March 1941, President Roosevelt presided over a dedication ceremony attended by nearly 9,000 guests.

The holdings grew rapidly, thanks to many generous donations, and in the late 1960s, architect I. M. Pei was hired to create a plan for a new building to accommodate the collection. Opened in 1978, the glass-fronted East Building had to fit a trapezoidal site and mesh with the neoclassical West Building. An underground concourse connects the two buildings.

Under phased renovation plans, various galleries in the two buildings close temporarily and some works may be moved to different locations in the museum, so check the website before your visit if there's a particular masterpiece you want to see.

Also check for special exhibitions and new acquisitions. In recent years 22 new galleries were added on the ground floor of the West Building, featuring 900 works of art such as sculpture masterpieces from the Middle Ages, antique Roman coins, and porcelain vases from the Ming and Qing dynasties. The galleries for photographs and works on paper opened in 2004.

West Building

All entrances other than on the Mall put you on the ground floor. One level up is the **main floor,** where European art from the 13th to 19th centuries and American painting and sculpture from colonial times to the early 20th century are displayed. The spectacular **Rotunda,** ringed by Tuscan marble pillars, rises to a high oculus above a central fountain graced by a statue of Mercury. The dome is strongly reminiscent of John Russell Pope's other great Washington structure, the Jefferson Memorial.

Extending from either side of the Rotunda, the **West Sculpture Hall** contains works in bronze, while the **East Sculpture Hall** has works in marble. Each hall ends in a garden court, where free concerts are often held. Several cafés and coffee bars throughout the National Gallery offer light fare.

The museum's hushed halls and courts are surrounded by galleries that are numbered 1 to 93 and generally proceed in chronological order, with nationalities grouped together.

Vermeer's Legacy of Light & Beauty

Art aficionados and experts alike are invariably struck by the paintings of the Dutch artist Johannes Vermeer (1632–1637), particularly his style and his gift of contrasting light and dark. The National Gallery has the honor to possess four of the world's 35 known Vermeer paintings.

"Girl with a Pearl Earring," held by the Mauritshuis gallery in the Hague, Netherlands, is regarded as Vermeer's ultimate masterpiece and lies at the heart of a fictionalized novel of the same name written by Tracy Chevalier (later made into a movie directed by Peter Webber).

Of the canvases credited to Vermeer, the famous tear-shaped pearl was featured in eight of them, including "A Lady Writing" and "Girl with the Red Hat," both displayed at the National Gallery of Art. Was the same woman the model for multiple paintings? No one knows for sure, but it's a favorite topic of conversation.

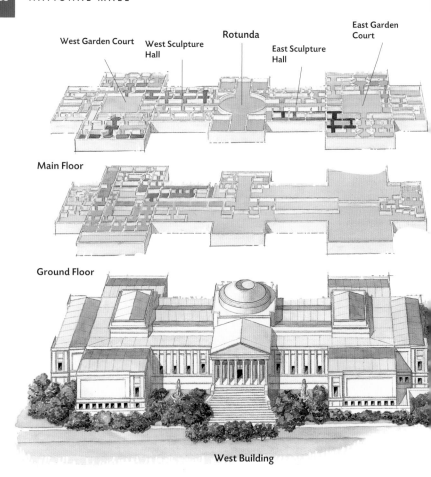

West Garden Court

West Sculpture Hall

Rotunda

East Sculpture Hall

East Garden Court

Main Floor

Ground Floor

West Building

Galleries 1–13 hold **13th- to 16th-century Italian paintings.** Representing the early Florentine and central Italian Renaissance, these works range from Byzantine iconography to the beginnings of the high Renaissance. Master-pieces include Giotto's "Madonna and Child" (ca 1320–1330); Fra Filippo Lippi's "Adoration of the Magi" (ca 1445); Leonardo da Vinci's "Ginevra de' Benci" (1474); and Botticelli's "Giuliano de' Medici" (ca 1478).

You'll find **16th-century Italian and Spanish works** in Galleries 17–28. Here is art from the northern Italian Renaissance, distinguished by allegorical and religious scenes within a colorful, sensual, pastoral setting. Especially outstanding are paintings by the Venetian master Tiziano Vecelli, or Titian, whose "Venus with a Mirror" (1555) is vibrant with life. Raphael's "Alba Madonna" (1510) hangs here, as do works by Tintoretto, one of the great Venetian painters. Pause in Gallery 26 for Bernardino Luini's "Fresco Cycle," with the "Story of Procris and Cephalus" (1520–1522). America's only Italian Renaissance fresco series recounts

West Building Galleries

- 13th- to 16th-century Italian
- 16th-century Italian and Spanish
- 17th- and 18th-century Italian, Spanish, and French
- 15th- to 16th-century Netherlands and German
- 17th-century Dutch and Flemish
- 18th- and 19th-century Spanish
- 18th- and early 19th-century French

- 19th-century French
- British
- American
- Special Exhibitions
- Drawings from the Armand Hammer Collection
- Non-Exhibition Space
- Sculpture

National Gallery of Art

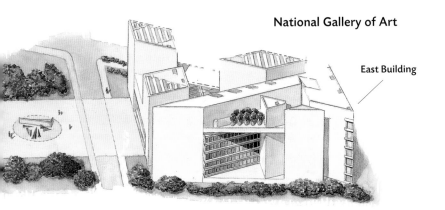

East Building

a myth in nine pastoral scenes around a villa-like room with mosaic tiles from third-century Tunisia. Gallery 28 has works by the Spanish painter El Greco.

Galleries 29–34 and 36–37 display **17th and 18th-century Italian, Spanish, and French baroque paintings.** Among the artists are Canaletto, a Venetian master known for his views of Venice, and Tiepelo, another Venetian, who painted in a colorful style. Look for Georges de la Tour's "The Repentant Magdalene" (1640) and Procaccin's sensuous "Ecstasy of the Magadalen" (ca 1620).

In Galleries 35, 35A, and 38–41A, **15th and 16th-century Netherlands and German** painters include Albrecht Dürer and Matthias Grunewald, whose few works, mostly religious, such as "The Crucifixion" (ca 1520), were enough to secure his reputation as one of the greats of his time.

Among the most popular areas of the museum, Galleries 42–51 feature **17th-century Flemish and Dutch paintings**. The large collection of Van Dyck portraits is among the finest in the world. Here also is Rubens's monumental "Daniel in the Lions' Den." Dutch realism can be found in portraits by Frans Hals, landscapes by Jacob van Ruisdael, and still lifes by Ambrosius Bosschaert. Great treasures on display include the luminous paintings of Johannes Vermeer (among them "Girl with the Red Hat") and the forceful images of Rembrandt van Rijn, including his brooding "Self-Portrait" of 1659 and "The Mill," with its chiaroscuro effects.

In the east side of the rotunda, Gallery 52 contains **18th- and 19th-century Spanish paintings,** notably by Francisco de Goya. **French art from the 18th and early 19th centuries** lines the

INSIDER TIP:

Leo Villareal's "Multiverse" (2008), installed along the concourse walkway between the East and West Buildings is a hypnotic play of light and movement.

—KAREN CARMICHAEL
National Geographic writer

walls of Galleries 53–56, much of it in a florid style depicting light-hearted sophistication in French society. Among the treasures are Antoine Watteau's "Italian Comedians" (1720), Boucher's "Madame Bergeret" (1746), and Fragonard's "A Young Girl Reading" (1776).

British works fill Galleries 57–59, 61, and 63. Represented here are Hogarth, Reynolds, Gainsborough, Constable, and Turner. The landscapes of Constable and

the seascapes of Turner are well worth noting. **American paintings** are on view in Galleries 60A–B, 62, and 64–71. Gilbert Stuart's portraits of early U.S. Presidents vie for attention with the big mid-19th-century landscapes of Bierstadt, Cole, and Church. Other works are by Homer, Whistler, Bellows, Cropsey, Ryder, and Sargent. Galleries 72–79 are reserved for **special exhibitions.**

Impressionist and other 19th-century French painting is on exhibit in Galleries 80–93. These rooms are filled with the light and color of leading exponents Renoir and Monet, and the idiosyncratic styles of Cézanne and van Gogh. Also on display are Parisian nightlife scenes by Degas and Toulouse-Lautrec. Among the great works are Renoir's "Girl with a Watering Can" (1876), Manet's "The Railway" (1873), and Monet's "Woman with a Parasol—Madame Monet and her Son" (1875).

The ground floor showcases **photography and sculpture,** as well as **prints and drawings** by luminaries such as Michelangelo, Leonardo, Manet, and Cézanne. From here you can reach the East Building via a belowground concourse under 4th Street, N.W.

East Building

The walls and angles of the East Building (or East Wing) are marvels in themselves. The building itself consists of two triangular shapes, covered in some 16,200 pink marble panels; a three-year repair project, completed in 2014, removed and reinstalled each panel with new supports.

Extensive renovations underway are constructing 12,260 square feet (1,139 sq m) of art exhibition space within the building's current footprint. Expected to open in spring 2016, the new spaces include an outdoor sculpture terrace overlooking Pennsylvania Avenue flanked by two skylit Tower Galleries, which will display primarily modern art from the museum's permanent collection. During the renovations, the East Building atrium and concourse walkway will remain open. The renowned mobile "Untitled" (1976) by Alexander Calder and Andy Goldsworthy's "Roof" (2004–2005) are still on view in the atrium, along with other sculptures, including Richard Long's "Whitechapel Slate Circle" (1981), which hasn't been on view since 1998, and the recently donated "Five Cones" (1990–1992) by Ursula von Rydingsvard.

Sculpture Garden

Opened in 1999, the 6-acre (2.4 ha) sculpture garden is across 7th Street, N.W., from the West Building. Its 17 works include "Puellae" (1992), featuring 30 headless, shriveled, 3-foot-tall (1 m) girls—Polish-born sculptor Magdalena Abakanowicz's chilling depiction of a Holocaust story. You can't miss Louise Bourgeois's 9-foot-tall (2.7 m) "Spider" (1997), part of a series exploring childhood memory and loss. Another large piece, "Aurora" (1992–1993) by Mark Di Suvero, illustrates elegance and balance on a massive scale.

An attractive glass-sided café in the garden serves refreshments

Experts speculate that Jan van Eyck's "Annunciation" (1434–1436) was likely the left wing of a triptych.

and offers free "Jazz in the Garden" concerts on Friday evenings from Memorial Day to Labor Day. Nearby is a fountain that becomes an ice-skating rink from November to March. ■

National Museum of Natural History

Dinosaur fossils, sparkling gems, mammals, an insect zoo, and rare Native American artifacts—these are the kinds of things that make this such a popular museum. The Smithsonian's National Museum of Natural History explores in wondrous detail the natural world and our place in it. Housed in a green-domed beaux arts building from 1910, this was the third Smithsonian building, erected to hold the institution's bursting collection.

Millions of people have viewed the African elephant on display in the Rotunda since 1959.

National Museum of Natural History

  Map pp. 70–71

✉ 10th St. & Constitution Ave., N.W.

☎ 202/633-1000

🚇 Metro: Federal Triangle, Smithsonian; Bus: 32–36, 52–54

mnh.si.edu

Fascination with the natural world never goes out of style. More than 90 percent of the Smithsonian's entire collection of artifacts, specimens, and works of art belongs to this museum alone. That's more than 127 million individual specimens and artifacts.

Researchers from around the world use the collection—much of it stored off-site—to carry out various systematic studies. Just think of all the millions of beetles, butterflies, mosquitoes, sponges, mollusks, mineralogical samples, birds' eggs, and microscopic organisms stored in drawers and on shelves.

Visiting

You can easily spend a day wandering through the museum, getting sidetracked from whatever it was you had set out to see. If you have only a few hours, pinpoint a couple exhibits and plot your route (maps are available at information desks at both entrances).

Entering from the Constitution Avenue side puts you on the **ground floor,** which has a **highlights** exhibit, a sampler of the treasures awaiting you within. Before you head up to the two other exhibit floors, walk to the back of this floor, past the Atrium Café and Museum Shop, to the **Birds of D.C.** exhibit. Many people miss this compendium of taxidermied eastern birds (native and migratory) on display since the 1920s. Along with bald and golden eagles, swans, and yellow warblers, the extinct Carolina parakeet and passenger pigeon are represented.

The museum features a number of special exhibitions. A long-running exhibit on the second floor, **Eternal Life in Ancient Egypt,** focuses on Egyptian burial ritual and cosmology. Visitors can learn how scientists use computer scans to study mummies without unwrapping them, and view alabaster tomb vessels and a vivid blue beaded necklace that was wrapped around a mummy's neck.

The museum's former dinosaur and fossil halls closed in 2014 to undergo an extensive five-year renovation. The halls had last been updated 30 years ago, and some exhibits, like the 90-foot-long (27 m) **Diplodocus dinosaur skeleton,** hadn't been moved in more than 80 years. The modernization, due to be completed in 2019, will create more than 31,000 square feet (2,880 sq m) of exhibition space showcasing the museum's unparalleled collection of 46 million fossils. The centerpiece will be a nearly complete 66.5 million-year-old *Tyrannosaurus rex* skeleton called the Nation's *T. rex,* which was unearthed in Montana in 1990.

While the renovations are under way, visitors can still view dinosaur fossils in **The Last American Dinosaurs: Discovering a Lost World.** The new exhibition explores the ecosystem of 66 million years ago and tracks the final days of dinosaurs found in North Dakota before a devastating asteroid impact forever changed their world. The Nation's *T. rex* is on view in the Rex Room.

First Floor

If you enter the museum from the Mall side, you'll step into the grand **Rotunda,** one of the city's great interior spaces. The eight-sided Rotunda rises to a dome

125 feet (38 m) from the floor; columned galleries offer splendid views of the space from above. But the sight in the middle of the Rotunda is what grabs most people's attention: Standing 13 feet 2 inches (4 m) at the shoulder, the **African elephant** weighed 12 tons (10.8 tonnes) when it was killed in 1954. It is the largest mounted specimen of Earth's

largest land animal, and its grassy savanna display has sound effects and other mounted animals.

You may want to begin your visit in the building's recently restored west wing, which features an exciting new attraction: the **Kenneth E. Behring Family Hall of Mammals.** The 25,000-square-foot (2,322 sq m) permanent exhibition, which tells the story of mammal evolution through adaptation to changing habitats, features 274 taxidermied specimens artfully posed in a variety of environments—from polar to desert, dry to humid. Interactive features enhance the displays by explaining aspects of the remarkable diversity of mammals. A short film traces mammal evolution.

A complementary exhibit, the new **Hall of Human Origins,** a $20 million, 15,000-square-foot (1,393 sq m) display, tells the story of human evolution. Among the skulls and fossils is the only Neanderthal skeleton in the U.S. The exhibit, spanning six million years, includes forensically reconstructed faces of prehistoric relatives. Other exhibits on this floor explore various cultures. The **African Voices** exhibit offers world-beat music and touch terminals.

Between the two galleries is the **Sant Ocean Hall,** the museum's largest exhibit. Extraordinary in scope, the hall presents 674 marine specimens and models, including a replica of a 45-foot-long (13.7 m) North Atlantic

A model of a salt crystal, enlarged nearly 1.5 billion times, bedazzles museum visitors.

right whale and a giant squid.

Next door is the **Q?rius** (pronounced "curious") lab, designed for teens and tweens. In the interactive and experimental learning space, students can chat with scientists and interact with thousands of authentic specimens. **The Q?rius Jr. Discovery Room** lets kids nine and under get hands-on with real museum artifacts such as fossils, skulls, shells, and minerals.

On the west side of the museum, a 400-seat **IMAX theater** ($$) shows 2-D and 3-D films on a screen six stories high—the largest in the D.C. area.

Second Floor

On the second floor, many people head for the **Janet Annenberg Hooker Hall of Geology, Gems, and Minerals.** Here you can learn how a meteorite impact may have wiped out the dinosaurs, build a virtual volcano, touch a piece of limestone scarred by Ice Age glaciers, view a mock-up vertical mine shaft, and watch a film on plate tectonics.

You will want to ogle the dazzling **National Gem Collection,** starring the 45.52-carat Hope Diamond, the largest blue diamond in the world. Other outstanding riches include a thousand-diamond diadem given by Napoleon I to his wife Empress Marie Louise; a pair of Marie Antoinette's earrings; and the world's largest perfect quartz sphere, a magically clear 107-pound (48.5 kg) globe from China. Just beyond lies a hall of sparkling crystals in a myriad of colors, shapes, and sizes.

One of the hall's newest

James Smithson

The man who originally endowed the Smithsonian Institution and gave it his name, English scientist James Smithson (1765–1829), never actually visited the United States. Passionate about chemistry, mineralogy, and geology, he dedicated himself to the advancement of science, at times even risking his life while gathering observations. He directed that a large portion of his estate—$12 million in today's dollars—be used to create an "Establishment for the increase and diffusion of knowledge" in Washington. Why he left his fortune to the United States is a mystery. His remains are interred in a crypt in the Smithsonian Castle, thanks to Alexander Graham Bell, who had them brought here from Italy, where Smithson died.

---

acquisitions is the Carmen Lúcia Ruby, a stunning 23.1-carat Burmese ruby set in a platinum ring with diamonds. The exceedingly rare gem, one of the largest and finest rubies in the world, was mined from the fabled Mogok region of Burma in the 1930s.

Walk on to the **Hall of Bones and Reptiles,** where you can see mammal skeletons varying in size from the pocket mouse to the huge, extinct Steller's sea cow.

The adjoining **O. Orkin Insect Zoo** is a storehouse of delights for anyone who appreciates the most abundant animals on Earth. Live exhibits, animated by buzzing and chirping sounds, give this display an edge. Watch live bees, water striders, darkling beetles, centipedes, tarantulas, and whip scorpions go about their daily lives. Also at work are unfailingly industrious leaf-cutter ants. ■

National Museum of American History

The Smithsonian Institution, with 19 separate museums and galleries, has been called "the nation's attic," and the National Museum of American History is particularly rich in treasures that document American history and culture. At any one time, only about 3 to 5 percent of the three million artifacts in the museum's collection are on display.

A museum visitor takes to the podium and delivers an impromptu Inaugural Address.

National Museum of American History

 Map pp. 70–71

 14th St. & Constitution Ave., N.W.

☎ 202/633-1000

 Metro: Federal Triangle, Smithsonian; Bus: 52, 13F–G, X1

americanhistory .si.edu

When it opened in 1964, the building was called the National Museum of History and Technology. That name was changed in 1980 to reflect the museum's changing focus.

In recent years, the museum has been redesigning its exhibits to present various artifacts in the context of broad themes relevant to U.S. life from colonial to modern times. The museum closed down in late 2006 for major renovations. It reopened in November 2008 with a new state-of-the-art

gallery at the center of the museum, safeguarding one of the country's most beloved artifacts: the original Star-Spangled Banner, which inspired the poem that became the national anthem.

The museum continues to transform with a major project to renew its 120,000-square-foot (11,150 sq m) west exhibition wing. Included in the plans are new galleries, an education center, and interior public plazas and space for performances. A new panoramic window will provide a sweeping

At the Museum of American History, you can actually get very close to the original Star-Spangled Banner. Thoroughly thrilling!

—JEANNETTE KIMMEL
National Geographic Traveler
magazine editorial business manager

view of the Washington Monument and the National Mall. The museum's center core and east wing remain open, and several popular exhibits have been moved to accommodate the renovations, including the **Dolls' House.** The five-story-tall miniature house with 23 rooms and 1,354 tiny items, from furniture to linens to toys, is now located on the first floor

Some of the other most popular artifacts at the museum are Dorothy's ruby slippers from *The Wizard of Oz;* President Lincoln's top hat; a compass used by Lewis and Clark during their journey across the Louisiana Territory; the Woolworth lunch counter from Greensboro, North Carolina, where four African-American students staged a nearly six-month-long sit-in to protest segregation (see sidebar right); Thomas Jefferson's Bible; and Kermit the Frog from *Sesame Street.*

Visiting

If you enter the museum from Constitution Avenue, you'll be on the first floor; the Mall entrance puts you on the second floor, where there's a **Welcome Center.** Maps and information are available at both entrances. The museum has stores on all three main floors, and food services on the lower level.

First Floor

A large exhibition, **America on the Move,** anchors the Hall of Transportation and Technology. More than 300 vehicles and other artifacts are showcased in period settings that offer a chronological look at how transportation has shaped America. The journey takes you, for example, along 40 feet (12 m) of Route 66's pavement in Oklahoma and aboard a commuter car of a Chicago "L" train in the 1950s. Be sure to check the impressive **John Bull locomotive.** The oldest operable self-propelled locomotive and striking symbol of the industrial revolution, it was built

Historic Protest

On February 1, 1960, four male African-American college students sat down at the "whites only" lunch counter at F. W. Woolworth's in Greensboro, North Carolina, and politely asked for service. They were refused. When asked to leave they remained in their seats. Their peaceful sit-in ignited a movement: Hundreds of students, residents, civil rights organizers, and church members joined the protest.

In the two months that followed, sit-ins occurred in 54 cities in nine states. By late July 1960, the Woolworth's lunch counter had been desegregated. You can see part of the original counter on the second floor of the National Museum of American History's east wing.

"What So Proudly We Hail'd"

The 30-by-34-foot (9 x 10 m) flag known as the Star-Spangled Banner is fragile despite its size. Woven loosely to fly on a 90-foot (27 m) flagpole, its expected life span was only two years. Flying over Fort McHenry, it incurred much damage. When the British attacked Baltimore in 1814, amateur poet Francis Scott Key was on a ship in the Chesapeake Bay. Moved by the sight of the enormous flag still flying in "the dawn's early light" after a 25-hour bombardment, he scribbled the words that became the lyrics for a popular patriotic song; Congress made it the national anthem in 1931. As part of conservation efforts, specialists at the Smithsonian recently removed a cloth backing (and 1.7 million stitches) added decades ago for support. Photo images documented the original flag's condition close up, guiding work to ensure the flag's survival for future generations.

in England and brought to America in 1831 for use on one of the first public U.S. railroads, which carried passengers from Philadelphia and New York City.

On the Water traces the history of the country's maritime trade and transportation, which fueled national growth and the development of major cities by connecting people and places across the continent.

The star attraction of the new exhibition **FOOD: Transforming the American Table 1950–2000** is Julia Child's kitchen. Museum staff catalogued and packed 1,200 items from the late chef's custom-designed home kitchen in Cambridge, Massachusetts, where many of her TV shows were taped. They then reassembled everything in the museum. Objects in the 14-by-20-foot (4 x 6 m) kitchen include Child's cookbooks, utensils, kitchen sink, and six-burner commercial range.

Second Floor

The **Star-Spangled Banner Gallery** supports the museum's important mission of preserving the Star-Spangled Banner (see sidebar above). The exhibit evokes the conditions under which Francis Scott Key saw the flag flying during wartime, on the morning of September 14, 1814.

Within These Walls conveys the history of a house at 16 Elm Street in Ipswich, Massachusetts, and looks at the everyday life of five of the many families who occupied it from the mid-1760s through 1945. Historically important activities the house "witnessed" include American colonists working to spark a revolution, African Americans struggling for freedom, community activists organizing an end to slavery, immigrants striving to build new lives, and a grandmother and her grandson serving on the home front during World War II.

Among the other special artifacts on display on this floor is a famous marble statue of George Washington, which was commissioned by the U.S. government in 1932 and sculpted by Horatio Greenough. He had in mind as a model for his design Phidias's "Olympian Zeus."

Third Floor

A major multimedia exhibition, **The Price of Freedom: Americans at War,** looks at how the United States has shaped its destiny, protected its values, and maintained its leadership in world affairs through engagement in wars, from the colonial era to the present. The featured objects include a rare Revolutionary War uniform, furniture used during the surrender ceremony that ended the Civil War, a restored Huey helicopter that was used in the Vietnam War, and the uniform worn by Gen. Colin Powell during Operation Desert Storm.

A separate exhibit, **Gunboat Philadelphia,** illustrates events in October 1776 when American troops with only a ragtag collection of boats faced an advancing line of ships of the British Navy on Lake Champlain in New York. The Americans, under the command of Benedict Arnold, were forced to retreat, but not before they fought the British to a standstill. The American vessel *Philadelphia,* a small gunboat, sank during the battle, but was retrieved from the lake in 1935 and has been part of the museum's holdings since 1964.

Formerly located on the second floor, the lovely **First Ladies** exhibition has been moved to the Rose Gallery in the central section on the third floor. Displayed are more than two dozen original gowns worn to presidential inaugurations, including those worn by Frances Cleveland, Lou Hoover, Jacqueline Kennedy, and Michelle Obama.

The American Presidency: A Glorious Burden highlights aspects of presidential leadership and life in the White House. More than 900 artifacts, images, and interactive stations tell the story. ■

A portrait primer on American Presidents presents a time line of command.

Walk Around the Monuments

The western end of the Mall, where you'll find the city's most significant monuments and memorials, is a delightful place for walking. A 3-mile (4.8 km) loop taking you past a half dozen major memorials makes for a wonderful morning or afternoon; benches along the way offer rest stops. About two blocks from the start is the Smithsonian Metro station.

A wreath adorns the black granite wall of names at the Vietnam Veterans Memorial.

Begin at the **Washington Monument ❶**, off 15th Street between Constitution and Independence Avenues. Set on a slight rise, this 555-foot (169 m) marble obelisk is surrounded by flags from every state in the nation. Begun in 1848, the monument rose slowly but steadily for five years to 152 feet (46 m); then funding ran out and building ceased for almost 25 years. Look about a third of the way up to see where the work stopped: The more recent marble is darker.

From the Washington Monument grounds you can see the Lincoln Memorial to the west and the Jefferson Memorial across the Tidal Basin, but your next destination is hidden among the trees of **Constitution Gardens,** a memorial to the founders of this nation. Walk down the hill, cross 17th Street, and take the sinuous trail through lovely landscaping just north of the **Reflecting Pool.**

NOT TO BE MISSED:

World War II Memorial • Vietnam Veterans Memorial • Lincoln Memorial • Jefferson Memorial

On the pool's east end is the **National World War II Memorial ❷**. Thousands of veterans were on hand for the Memorial Day 2004 dedication of the $174 million, privately funded memorial, which has drawn criticism for its massive design amid the Mall's more graceful monuments. Around a fountain are two facing arcs of granite columns, each bearing two bronze wreaths; the 56 pillars represent U.S. states and territories during the war and the District of Columbia. The columns are anchored by a pair of 43-foot-high (13 m) arches—one for the war's Atlantic theater and one for the Pacific. Two dozen bronze panels depict scenes from the war, and a Freedom Wall with 4,000 gold stars honors the 400,000 Americans who were killed during World War II. On **Signers Island,** a memorial honors the 56 signers of the Declaration of Independence.

Just west, architect Maya Lin's stunning **Vietnam Veterans Memorial ❸** presents a moving contrast to the classical-style monuments all about. A tremendous black-granite wedge, bermed into the earth instead of standing above it, is inscribed with the names of all the 58,209 Americans who died or were

---

Top of the Town

On August 23, 2011, Washington, D.C., was rocked by a 5.8-magnitude earthquake. The tremors damaged several city landmarks, including the Washington Monument. Closed for 32 months while more than 150 cracks in its structure were repaired, the monument finally reopened in May 2014.

Go early for free same-day admission and a trip to the top of the obelisk. The kiosk opens at 8:30 a.m. and tickets go fast. Or reserve in advance through the National Park Service's reservation page (recreation.gov).

Inside, the elevator shoots to the 500-foot-high (152 m) viewing level in 70 seconds. On the leisurely ride down, you'll see the 195 commemorative stones inside the monument.

- 🅰 See also area map pp. 70–71
- ▶ Washington Monument
- 🕒 2 hours
- ↔ 3 miles (4.8 km)
- ▶ Jefferson Memorial

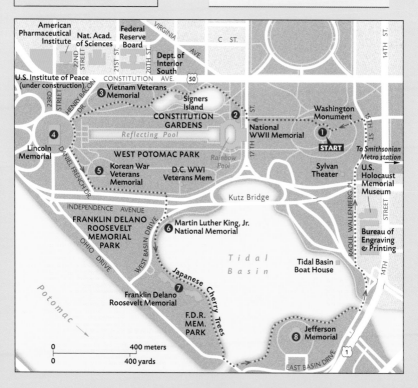

missing in action in the Vietnam War. Polished to a reflective sheen, the walls of the wedge seem to project life as much as honor death. As you walk the path beside the memorial, the names of the dead increase dramatically as the walls reach their high point at 10.1 feet (3 m). The nearby bronze group of three soldiers, by Washington sculptor Frederick Hart, adds a dose of gritty realism. Dedicated in 1982, the memorial was supplemented in 1993 by another bronze group, the **Vietnam Women's Memorial.**

Continue on to the magnificent **Lincoln Memorial ❹,** built from 1914 to 1922 to honor Abraham Lincoln, President during the Civil War. The 36 Doric columns represent the number of states at the time of Lincoln's death. Inside, facing the Mall, the 19-foot-tall (5.7 m) statue of a seated Lincoln was carved from 28 blocks of white Georgia marble. The walls of the memorial are inscribed with words from the Gettysburg Address and Lincoln's second Inaugural Address.

Just to the southeast is the **Korean War Veterans Memorial ❺.** Dedicated in 1995, it features 19 gray soldiers warily crossing a field of scrubby junipers. Next to this riveting stainless-steel group, a black-granite wall is etched with a mural of those who served, while another wall bears the simple message: "Freedom Is Not Free." Beside a "pool of remembrance" stands a stone carved with the war's toll—the numbers of killed, wounded, missing, and captured.

Walk east, in the direction of the **Tidal Basin,** and cross West Basin Drive at the second traffic light, in front of the nearly hidden **D.C. WWI Veterans Memorial,** honoring the District's veterans of that war.

A broad walk leads you through two towering hunks of granite, part of the new **Martin Luther King, Jr. National Memorial ❻.** Dedicated in 2011, the memorial's centerpiece is a 30-foot-high (9 m) relief of King carved out of rock and gazing across the Tidal Basin. The design represents a line from his 1963 "I Have a Dream" speech: "Out of a mountain of despair, a stone of hope."

Amid the trees of West Potomac Park on the basin's west side is the **Franklin Delano Roosevelt Memorial ❼,** honoring the 32nd President. Four unroofed, granite-walled alcoves—one for each of his four terms in office—spread along the water's edge, surrounded by landscaped plazas, statuary, and waterfalls.

On the south side of the Tidal Basin stands the **Jefferson Memorial ❽.** The view from here, across the Tidal Basin with its gulls and paddleboats and springtime cherry blossoms, is not to be missed. Dedicated to the author of the Declaration of Independence and third President of the United States, the structure was designed by John Russell Pope in the style of the ancient

Springtime Display: Cherry Blossoms as D.C. Icon

The first cherry tree near the Tidal Basin and Washington Monument was planted on March 27, 1912, by First Lady Helen Taft. But the idea had been put forward more than 25 years earlier. Washington resident Eliza Scidmore, who became a well-known travel writer, so admired groves of flowering cherries during a trip to Japan that she pitched a similar scheme to park officials in 1885. They showed no interest.

The idea gained support at the turn of the 20th century after a botanist at the U.S. Department of Agriculture, David Fairchild, tested flowering cherries at his estate and had several hundred planted in Chevy Chase, Maryland. Soon afterward, Mrs. Taft chose Japanese cherries to beautify a drab area along the Potomac. Things went awry when 2,000 of the trees, a gift from Japan, arrived full of pests and disease. They had to be burned. Japan graciously sent a new collection of carefully cultivated trees.

The Washington Monument appears to rise from a wreath of cherry blossoms.

Roman Pantheon and completed in 1943. Inside the airy colonnaded building a 19-foot (5.7 m) bronze of Jefferson stands beneath a towering dome. Among the quotes on the wall is one from a letter written in 1800: "I have sworn upon the altar of God eternal hostility against every form of tyranny over the mind of man."

Behind the monument on Ohio Drive is the **George Mason Memorial Garden.** In keeping with the quiet patriot's love of his gardens at Gunston Hall (see p. 228), across the river in Virginia and not far from Mount Vernon, the setting is a classical landscape designed as a peaceful, contemplative place.

The act of commemoration is a perennial work in progress. More projects are planned for the Mall, including the Smithsonian's National Museum of African-American History and Culture, opening just to the east of the Washington Monument. Meanwhile, Arlington, Virginia, has two landmarks worth visiting: the **Air Force Memorial** (see p. 209), with three elegant stainless-steel spires visible from downtown D.C., and the **Pentagon Memorial** (see p. 209), honoring the 184 people who died when American Airlines Flight 77 was hijacked and flown into the Pentagon on September 11, 2001.

U.S. Holocaust Memorial Museum

Opened in 1993, this museum serves as a memorial to the millions of people murdered during Nazi rule in Germany from 1933 to 1945. The architecture—windowless recesses, brickwork guard towers, and obscured windows—suggests some of the themes and images documented within. Inside, the skylit first-floor atrium is overshadowed by heavy steel trusses. A factory-like brick wall on one side is where visitors enter and ascend, via a cargo-style elevator, to see the permanent exhibition, starting on the fourth floor.

Despite the light, the Holocaust Museum's first floor sets a somber tone for a visit to the galleries.

U.S. Holocaust Memorial Museum

 Map pp. 70–71

✉ 100 Raoul Wallenberg Pl. (15th St.) S.W., just S of Independence Ave.

☎ 202/488-0400

🚇 Metro: Smithsonian; Bus: 13F–G, V7–9, Circulator

ushmm.org

Visiting

Pick up timed passes at the museum on the day of your visit or visit the website for advance passes ($). The exhibition is self-guided and takes two to three hours. You begin on the fourth floor. There are several films, audio programs, and a lot of text on the three-floor exhibit; you may want to make a selective tour of this section. Most of the exhibits are not recommended for children under 11; it's also a good idea to prepare older children for what they will experience.

On the **fourth floor,** which covers the spread of Nazism from 1933 to 1939, visitors are funneled through hallways from one exhibit area to the next. The dim, quiet halls reflect the museum's somber content. A theater, grim photographs, and monitors displaying silent footage bespeak the early years of the Third Reich and the start of its sanctioned violence toward Jews, Poles, Gypsies, homosexuals, political dissidents, the handicapped, and others.

The **third floor** is a walk-through tower lined with family photos from a shtetl, a Jewish village; you later learn that this entire village of 4,000 was destroyed in 1941, bringing 900 years of continuous history to an abrupt end. Perhaps most telling are the shelf loads of victims' belongings—rusty scissors, can openers, graters, razors, toothbrushes—and the huge piles of old shoes. There are bunks from Auschwitz and a scale model that shows how the gas chambers and crematoria worked.

Video monitors show unsettling images such as medical experiments, executions, and malnourished children. The monitors are shielded by walls so young children cannot see them; adults can elect not to watch.

The Big Picture

In addition to its powerful exhibits, the U.S. Holocaust Memorial Museum houses a study center and a vast archive of photos, film footage, eyewitness accounts, artifacts, and other materials that document Jewish history and events relating to the Holocaust. Many of the items here have been donated by families whose members were affected by the tragic events. The Steven Spielberg Film and Video Archive includes more than 1,000 hours of motion picture footage dating primarily from the 1920s to 1948 that can be viewed by appointment *(tel 202/488-6104, e-mail: filmvideo@ushmm.org).*

The museum's extensive online Holocaust Encyclopedia *(ushmm.org/learn/holocaust-encyclopedia),* accessible in a dozen languages, offers the history of Nazi tyranny through articles, podcasts, lesson plans, and mapping tools.

INSIDER TIP:

Amid all the horror is redemption in those who tried to save Jews. The museum does a fine job highlighting these people.

—SHEILA BUCKMASTER
National Geographic Traveler
magazine editor at large

Also on the third floor, the years from 1940 to 1945 are examined in detail through displays on ghettos, deportations, slave labor, and extermination camps. Among the powerful artifacts are cobblestones from a street in a Warsaw ghetto, clothing, and a cemetery gate from Karnow where Jews were routinely shot.

Efforts at resistance and the ultimate liberation of survivors are documented on the **second floor.** In the **Hall of Remembrance,** an eternal flame honors victims of the Holocaust; visitors may light candles in their memory.

On the **first floor,** the exhibit **Remember the Children: Daniel's Story** is targeted to families, including children eight years and older. It recounts the Holocaust from a child's perspective. The **lower level** has the **Children's Tile Wall,** with more than 3,000 tiles painted by American schoolchildren in memory of the estimated 1.5 million children who died. Outside the museum, it's a relief to look across the Tidal Basin to the Jefferson and FDR Memorials and remember those who stood against tyranny. ∎

More Places to Visit on the National Mall

Bureau of Engraving & Printing

The bureau is the place to see a lot of money—millions upon millions of dollars—being printed daily. To replace worn-out bills and follow the requests of the Federal Reserve Board, this facility and a similar one in Fort Worth, Texas, churn out billions of notes a year in denominations from $1 to $100. Each 50-foot-long (15 m) high-speed press can print 10,000 sheets per hour, turning out mainly $20 bills, which have a shelf life of 7.7 years. You can see 32-note currency sheets as they roll through production and 4,000-note "bricks" of bills being prepared for distribution to the 12 Federal Reserve Banks around the country. *moneyfactory.gov* Map pp. 70–71 ✉ 14th & C Sts., S.W. ☎ 202/874-2330 ⏱ Call for tour hours; get free tickets at booth on Raoul Wallenberg Pl. 🚇 Metro: Smithsonian

Discovery Theater in Smithsonian's S. Dillon Ripley Center

The Smithsonian's Discovery Theater relocated to this building in 2004 after its former home, the nearby Arts and Industries Building, closed for renovations. The theater presents a wide range of performances for children on a specially built stage. Visit the website for ticket and program information. *discoverytheater.org* 🅰 Map pp. 70–71 ✉ 1100 Jefferson Dr., S.W. ☎ 202/633-8700 🚇 Metro: Smithsonian, L'Enfant Plaza

Voice of America

This government-run news service has operated continuously since it went on the air in February 1942, soon after America entered World War II. Today, the service broadcasts news and educational and cultural programs in nearly four dozen languages to millions of people in other countries. It's transmitted by radio, satellite television, and the Internet. On 45-minute tours you can see exquisite 1940s murals by Ben Shahn and observe production of broadcasts. *voa.gov* 🅰 Map pp. 70–71 ✉ 330 Independence Ave., S.W. ☎ 202/203-4990 ⏱ Tours Mon.–Fri. noon & 2:30 p.m., except federal holidays 🚇 Metro: Federal Center

At the Bureau of Engraving & Printing, presses print money around the clock, five days a week.

Starring America's most famous home, 1600 Pennsylvania Avenue, with surrounding streets filled with places of cultural interest

White House & Around

The south portico of the White House remains a Washington icon.

White House & Around

The home of the Chief Executive is a living museum of the U.S. Presidency in downtown Washington, and the surrounding streets have additional attractions that make this a rich and charming neighborhood to explore.

In 1791 a surveyor and an engineer picked the site for a presidential "palace." The surveyor was George Washington, the engineer was Pierre-Charles L'Enfant, and the site was a cornfield above a tidal marsh where hunters shot ducks and geese. Just a mile (1.6 km) from the site of the future Capitol, the manse they envisioned would be about four times the size of the current White House.

Thomas Jefferson, Secretary of State at the time, persuaded Washington to hold a competition for the design. Unimpressed by the mundane entries, Washington urged Irish-born architect James Hoban to have a go. Hoban's entry, selected in 1792, was an adaptation of the Duke of Leinster's palace near Dublin. Regrettably, Washington—then on the verge of his second term as President—would not live to see the structure completed.

By the turn of the 20th century, after more than a century's worth of growing pains, it was clear that the White House—Theodore Roosevelt's designation for it—truly enshrined the American presidential legacy.

The presidential neighborhood grew in tandem with the White House. In the 1810s,

NOT TO BE MISSED:

St. John's Church, Decatur House, and other posh, federal-style residences were built around President's Park (renamed Lafayette Square in 1824). By 1900, the area was a thriving mix of government buildings, art galleries, hotels, and homes. Notable landmarks include the Treasury Building, Old Executive Office Building (now officially the Eisenhower Executive Office Building), Corcoran Gallery, Renwick building, Blair House, and the Octagon architecture museum.

From west of 20th Street to the Potomac River, the Foggy Bottom neighborhood is a mix of 19th-century row houses, apartment buildings, and major institutions, among them the State Department, World Bank, Kennedy Center, and George Washington University.

The White House area maintains and inspires a timeless polished decorum. At the same time, this segment of Washington underscores just how much times have changed. Until World War II, you could walk to the front door of the White House and leave your calling card. Today, security concerns have made visits understandably restrictive. ■

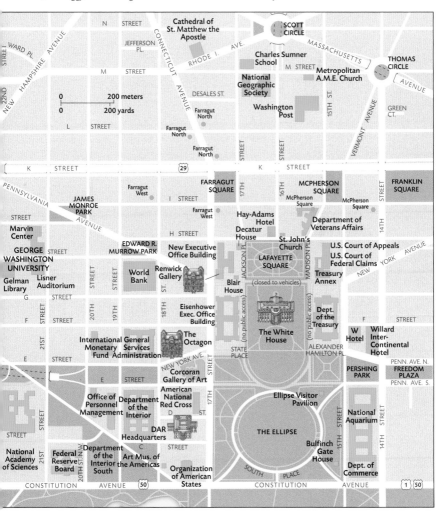

White House

The oldest public building in the District of Columbia, the White House has been the home of every U.S. President except George Washington. In this most famous of residences, the President signs bills into law, meets with national and international leaders, entertains guests, and does his best to lead a private family life. Despite more than 200 years of expansions and renovations, the White House has kept its essential appearance and design.

The dignified north portico of the White House basks in the glow of early evening.

White House

 Map pp. 108–109

✉ 1600 Pennsylvania Ave., N.W.

☎ 202/456-1414

🕐 Closed Sun.–Mon.

🚇 Metro: Federal Triangle, McPherson Square, Metro Center; Bus: 32–36, Circulator

whitehouse.gov

Washington's designers intended the executive mansion to be one of two focal points of the new Federal City (the Capitol would be the other). Nine blueprints were submitted to a competitive design panel; among those rejected was a plan put forward anonymously by Thomas Jefferson.

The winning design—the work of Irish-born architect James Hoban—honored the stately symmetries of Georgian manor houses in the British Isles. Not that the design lacked detractors: Benjamin Henry Latrobe, who worked on the White House in the early 1800s and is considered the country's first professional architect, assailed Hoban's concept as "a mutilated copy of a badly designed original near Dublin."

Nonetheless, the cornerstone

If you're near the White House and hear helicopters overhead, run to the South Lawn; you might just see the President boarding or deplaning *Marine One*.

—CAROLINE HICKEY
*National Geographic
Travel Books editor*

of the President's House (George Washington's preferred term for it) was laid in October 1792, a year before work began on the Capitol Building. The pale sandstone for the white-painted walls came from Aquia Creek, on the Virginia side of the Potomac. Eight years later, with President John Adams nearing the end of his term, the house was finally ready for occupation.

Jefferson, the third President, held the first Inaugural open house in 1805 and forged the tradition of throwing the house open to the public. The custom got out of hand in 1829, when some 20,000 well-wishers tromped through the White House, muddy boots and all; while President Jackson slipped away to a nearby hotel, his aides filled tubs with juice and whiskey and set them on the lawn to coax the crowds to remain outside. The Inaugural open houses continued until 1869, when Ulysses Grant replaced them with a parade, which he watched from the safety of a grandstand right in front of the White House.

During the War of 1812, the British retaliated for the American burning of public buildings in Canada by burning down the President's House and other city landmarks. When British soldiers arrived at the hastily vacated mansion on the night of August 24, 1814, they found Dolley Madison's dinner still on the table (a few of them sat down and polished it off). Shortly after midnight, soldiers threw flaming javelins into the mansion. By morning it was a smoldering shell. The house was rebuilt within its original walls over the next few years.

By the mid-20th century, the White House was suffering major structural problems: The walls and floors could no longer support the alterations and additions of previous decades. From 1948 to 1952, Harry and Bess Truman lived

Visiting the White House

The fact that you can step into the home of its President is one of the most endearingly democratic traditions of the United States. To go inside the White House you must schedule a tour. Requests must be submitted one to six months in advance through your member of Congress *(tel 202/224-3121)* or your country's embassy in Washington, D.C. The free self-guided tours *(7:30 a.m.–11:30 a.m. Tues.–Thurs. & 7:30 a.m.–1:30 p.m. Fri.–Sat.)* are assigned on a first-come, first-served basis. Before your arrival, call the 24-hour line *(tel 202/456-7041)*; tours are subject to cancellations. You can check security requirements and take a virtual tour online *(whitehouse.gov)*, or stop by the White House Visitor Center *(currently in the Ellipse Visitor Pavilion, open 7:30 a.m.–4 p.m. daily)* for exhibits and a background video.

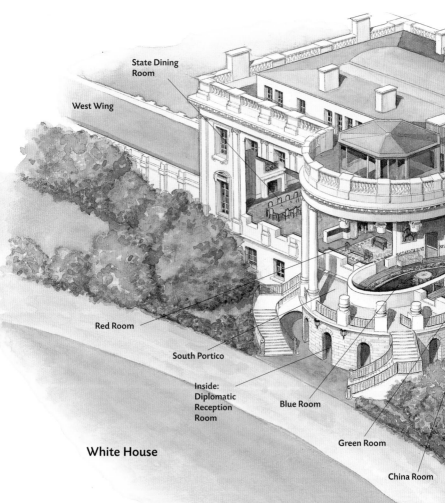

State Dining Room

West Wing

Red Room

South Portico

Inside: Diplomatic Reception Room

Blue Room

Green Room

China Room

White House

in Blair House across Pennsylvania Avenue, while the White House was gutted. Everything from furniture to paneling was taken out, a new basement dug, new foundations laid, and a steel framework installed. The basic house was still there, but it was now much safer. Since then, each First Family has added its own decorative touches. The Kennedys, for example, redesigned the Rose Garden, while the Reagans contributed a new 4,730-piece set of Lenox china.

A Look Inside

If you have arranged a group tour in advance, enter the grounds from a visitor entrance around the corner from Pennsylvania Avenue on 15th Street, next to the Treasury building. When you arrive, take a minute to look through the gate to see a portion of the mansion's beautifully planted 18-acre (7.2 ha) grounds.

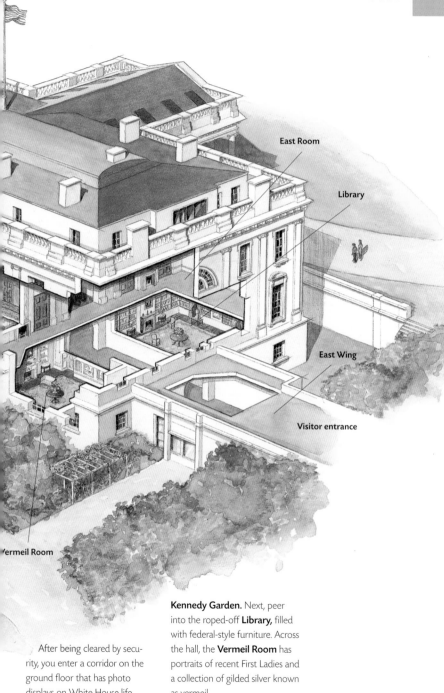

East Room

Library

East Wing

Visitor entrance

Vermeil Room

Kennedy Garden. Next, peer into the roped-off **Library**, filled with federal-style furniture. Across the hall, the **Vermeil Room** has portraits of recent First Ladies and a collection of gilded silver known as vermeil.

The rooms you can actually walk through are up on the State

After being cleared by security, you enter a corridor on the ground floor that has photo displays on White House life and glass-walled views of the carefully manicured **Jacqueline**

Floor. The first one you enter—the expansive **East Room—**is also the largest in the house: It hosts press conferences, award ceremonies, and concerts. Among the weddings held here were those of Nellie Grant, Alice Roosevelt, and Lynda Bird Johnson. The energetic children of Theodore Roosevelt are said to have roller-skated across the floor here.

Continue around to the **Green Room,** used by Jefferson as a dining room but now functioning as a reception parlor. The window affords a great view beyond the Ellipse (an open greensward just north of Constitution Avenue) to the Jefferson Memorial. Much of the Green Room's furniture came from the New York City workshop of Duncan Phyfe in the early 1800s. The green watered silk wall coverings were chosen by Jacqueline Kennedy.

The oval **Blue Room** contains several pieces of furniture bought by James Monroe, who refurbished the elegant room after the 1814 fire. Presidents still receive guests here in part because of the lovely view of the South Lawn. The Blue Room is the traditional location of the primary White House Christmas tree.

First Ladies frequently entertain in the adjacent **Red Room,** furnished as an American Empire parlor of 1810 to 1830. It was the favorite sitting room of Mary Todd Lincoln.

Some 140 guests can be seated in the **State Dining Room,** which boasts painted oak paneling from a 1902 renovation. In the **Cross Hall** and **Entrance Hall** the floors are made out of Tennessee marble. The decorated concert grand piano was a 1938 gift from the Steinway company.

A carpeted marble staircase leads to the second and third floors, open only to the First Family and their guests. Notable rooms there include the Queen's Bedroom, named for its many

The Red Room: A Favorite of First Ladies

Painted various shades of red since the 1840s, the small Red Room parlor had walls of yellow when legendary Washington hostess Dolley Madison used the room for bipartisan entertaining during a period of fierce political rivalry.

Eleanor Roosevelt launched her famous women-only press sessions here in response to the banning of women from presidential news conferences. Through the years, the room also has functioned as a living room, a music room, a venue for official photographs, and an intimate setting for small dinner parties.

But the space has seen sad moments, too. Mrs. Kennedy received foreign heads of state in the Red Room following President John F. Kennedy's state funeral.

President James Monroe chose Empire-style furnishings for the room when the White House was rebuilt after the British burned it in the War of 1812. The style changed many times, until the present American Empire decor was adopted during the Kennedy White House renovation. In 2000, the walls and upholstery were made deep carmine as more authentically reflective of the 19th century.

Fabrics in the Red Room were woven in the United States, using French Empire designs.

royal guests (including the queens of Great Britain, Norway, Greece, and the Netherlands), and the now famous Lincoln Bedroom.

In fact, the Lincoln Bedroom wasn't the 16th President's sleeping quarters but his office and Cabinet room. Under Mr. and Mrs. Theodore Roosevelt the space was converted to a guest suite known as the Blue Bedroom. It was President Harry Truman who decided to fill the room with Lincoln memorabilia. Scandal surrounded the historic chamber in the Clinton Administration when it was revealed that campaign donors were offered overnight stays here. Among the high-profile guests who spent the night were Steven Spielberg, Barbra Streisand, and Lee Iacocca.

The West Wing (you can take a virtual tour of the wing at whitehouse.gov) holds the Cabinet Room, numerous staff and reception rooms, and the President's Oval Office (built in 1909) and its adjoining Rose Garden. The White House also contains a jogging track, swimming pool, movie theater, and bowling lane. The total number of rooms in the White House: 132.

Your tour will exit the front door beneath a columned portico, then follow the walkway to the front gate. As photographing is forbidden inside, many people pause here to take pictures of the White House before leaving. ■

A White House Area Walk

Strolling the streets around the White House will give you a concentrated taste of the capital's core. The tourists, security officers, and limousines that buzz around the executive mansion like drones around a queen bee are part of the picture, but so are restaurants, museums, art galleries, benches for idling, and, because local laws bar skyscrapers, long, green views across the Ellipse and the Mall.

Once you've viewed or visited the White House, you tend to forget it's there, as do the locals who go about their business in the area. The section of Pennsylvania Avenue in front of the **White House ❶** (see pp. 110–115) is closed to traffic, so it offers good photo opportunities if you aren't

NOT TO BE MISSED:

White House • Lafayette Square • Octagon • Corcoran Gallery of Art

A short walk from the White House, Blair-Lee House is where foreign dignitaries often stay.

hampered at the time of your visit by security constraints and construction fences.

The park just north of the White House, **Lafayette Square ❷**, is a perfect place to sit with a sandwich and people-watch. As a public park in full view of the White House, the square is strategically ideal for demonstrating for or against something. Activists for nuclear disarmament and other causes have mounted peaceful vigils here. In the middle of the square is Clark Mills's statue of Andrew Jackson on a rearing horse. The self-taught Mills made this piece in the 1850s. Statues of foreign-born Revolutionary War heroes occupy the four corners: Marquis de Lafayette, Baron Friedrich von Steuben, Thaddeus Kosciusko, and Comte de Rochambeau. Many of the federal-style row houses along the square are White House offices, saved from the wrecking ball by Jackie Kennedy's determination to preserve the historical character of the square.

Across H Street from the square stands the gold-domed **St. John's Church ❸** (see p. 130), known as the "Church of the Presidents." Services are in English and Spanish. Diagonally across the corner from here, at Jackson Place and H Street, is **Decatur House ❹** (see p. 128), built in 1818 for naval hero Stephen Decatur.

Next, head south and turn right on Pennsylvania Avenue to see the 1810 white brick

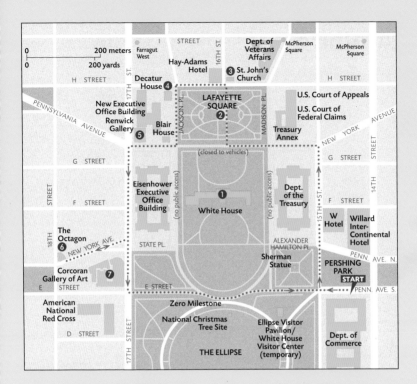

Blair House, the small building where foreign dignitaries often stay; Robert E. Lee was offered command of the Federal Army here in 1861. On November 1, 1950—about midway through the Trumans' four-year stay at Blair House while the White House was under renovation—a policeman was killed on the street defending the President from an assassination attempt.

In the same block, the **Renwick Gallery** ⑤ (see p. 130), a Smithsonian museum, shows off its mansard roof and redbrick-and-sandstone exterior opposite the even more flamboyant **Eisenhower Executive Office Building.** A massive piece of architecture originally named the Old Executive Office Building, the OEOB is one of the country's finest Second Empire–style structures. Built from 1871 to 1888 (just after the Renwick), the granite pile shocked locals who had expected a neoclassical temple to house the State, War, and Navy Departments. It now holds offices of White House

> ⓜ See also area map pp. 108–109
> ► White House Visitor Center
> ⊕ 3 hours
> ↔ 1.5 miles (2.4 km)
> ► Corcoran Gallery of Art

staff members, the Office of Management and Budget, and the Office of the Vice President.

Head south on 17th Street and turn right on New York Avenue. The historic **Octagon** ⑥ (see p. 130) stands on the corner of 18th Street. The brilliant design of the three-story brick house exemplifies federal architecture. Go back to 17th and turn right; on your right is the **Corcoran Gallery of Art** ⑦ (see p. 121), housed in an attractive beaux arts building. From here, walk east on E Street, between the South Lawn of the White House and the Ellipse. *Marine One,* the President's helicopter, lands on the South Lawn, site of the annual Easter

The Willard Hotel

While you're in the vicinity of the White House, drop into the Willard Hotel (*1401 Pennsylvania Ave., N.W., tel 202/628-9100; see Travelwise p. 246*), a Washington landmark since the 1850s. Nathaniel Hawthorne called it the "center of Washington" for its role as the heart of political lobbying in the 19th century. The hotel has hosted Presidents, heads of state, and a gaggle of household names, from Mark Twain to Mae West. Martin Luther King, Jr., penned part of his "I Have a Dream" speech here in August 1963.

In 1901, the venerable hostelry was rebuilt as a 12-story beaux arts hotel under the guidance of Henry Hardenbergh, architect of New York's famous Plaza Hotel. Closed in 1968 when much of Pennsylvania Avenue hit the skids, the Willard reopened in grand style in 1986.

The restored Willard boasts marble columns, polished wood paneling, glittering chandeliers, and other trappings of opulence. Shops, a bar, a café, and an elegant restaurant provide multiple opportunities to splurge.

Egg Roll. The National Christmas Tree, planted during the Carter Administration, stands on the Ellipse near the Zero Milestone, the spot from which city distances are measured.

On the corner of E and 15th Streets, a bronze William Tecumseh Sherman sits astride a horse, its tail raised toward the South, on the spot where he reviewed victorious Union troops. He faces the Greek Revival **Department of the Treasury** and its statue of Alexander Hamilton; sadly, the building blocks the view from the White House to the Capitol.

Cap the day with a drink at the trendy P.O.V. Roof Terrace bar of the **W Hotel** (see Travelwise p. 246), formerly the Hotel Washington. On clear days, this local favorite meeting place offers a great panoramic view of the White House, Mall, and abundant treetops of the city and neighboring Virginia.

The Willard Hotel is worth a peek for its grand historic style.

National Geographic Society

Robert Peary, Jacques Cousteau, and Jane Goodall are among the explorers and scientists who have been supported by the National Geographic Society, founded in Washington, D.C., in 1888. At the headquarters of the Society—one of the world's largest nonprofit scientific and educational institutions—visitors find exhibits at the National Geographic Museum and a wealth of cultural programs.

Home base: National Geographic's explorers, writers, and photographers have traveled the Earth, sharing its amazing stories with each new generation. A rich sampling of discoveries awaits visitors.

The National Geographic Society's magazines, books and guidebooks (including this one), maps, websites, TV programs, and classroom materials—all aimed at "the increase and diffusion of geographic knowledge" and to "inspire people to care about the planet"—are produced here at the headquarters.

Explorers Hall often displays the work of National Geographic photographers, researchers, and explorers, including conservationist Mike Fay, whose grueling two-year, 2,000-mile (3,220 km) trek across the heart of Africa inspired the country of Gabon to set aside 10 percent of its land as national park, and paleontologist Paul Sereno with his newest dinosaur discoveries. Likewise special exhibits frequently appear, such as the recent exhibit on ancient Peruvian gold.

Explorers Hall also houses the National Geographic Store, which offers a wide array of maps, books, magazines, toys, games, international music CDs, as well as a variety of other educational, entertainment, and decorative items from around the world. ■

National Geographic Society

🅰 Map pp. 108–109

✉ 17th & M Sts., N.W.

☎ 202/857-7588 (museum); 202/857-7700 (ticket office)

🚇 Metro: Farragut North, Farragut West

nationalgeographic.com

DAR Headquarters

This robust beaux arts building was built between 1905 and 1929 to serve as the headquarters of the Daughters of the American Revolution (female descendants of American Revolution patriots). Encompassing an entire city block, it is one of the largest buildings in the world exclusively owned and maintained by women.

The DAR building hosts many private parties and events.

DAR Headquarters

🅰 Map pp. 108–109

✉ 1776 D St., N.W.

☎ 202/628-1776 or 202/628-4780 (Constitution Hall event info)

Ⓜ Metro: Farragut West

dar.org

The oldest part of the DAR Headquarters, **Memorial Continental Hall,** was designed by architect Edward Pearce Casey (1864-1940), who also designed the interior of the Library of Congress. Inside, visitors can tour more than 30 period rooms, each outfitted by a different state organization of the DAR. The California room recreates an 1860s parlor of the oldest adobe house in Monterey; the Michigan room presents a 1920s library with red bookshelves and blue-glazed earthenware; and the New Hampshire room is a

playful children's attic with toys and dolls from the late 18th to the early 20th centuries. A museum displays exhibits drawn from the DAR's collection of textiles, silver, glass, and furniture.

Built in the 1920s on the building's west side, **Constitution Hall** is a 3,702-seat auditorium designed by John Russell Pope (the architect behind the National Gallery of Art's West Building and

INSIDER TIP:

Before your visit, take the online virtual 360° tour of DAR Headquarters—especially useful for choosing seats for a show in Constitution Hall.

—JUSTIN KAVANAGH
National Geographic Travel Books editor

the Jefferson Memorial). All kinds of concerts and lectures are held here, but Constitution Hall is best (or most notoriously) known for the one that never took place: After the DAR's 1939 refusal to let black contralto Marian Anderson perform, Eleanor Roosevelt stepped in, and Anderson sang at the Lincoln Memorial. ∎

Corcoran Gallery of Art

Washington's oldest art museum (and the third oldest in the United States), the Corcoran Gallery holds American and European artworks. It is the largest nonfederal art museum in Washington, D.C. Long an independent institution, the museum is now entering a new chapter in partnership with the National Gallery of Art and George Washington University.

William Corcoran founded his art gallery "for the purpose of encouraging American genius."

The Corcoran started out three blocks north, in the building that now houses the Smithsonian's Renwick Gallery (see p. 130). The stately redbrick mansion was built to hold the collection of banker-philanthropist William Wilson Corcoran (1798–1888).

An enthusiastic patron of contemporary American art at a time when most collectors favored European works, Corcoran was a personal friend to several of the artists whose work has hung in the gallery, including Albert Bierstadt, Frederic Church, Thomas Doughty, and George Inness.

Corcoran's holdings came to include American and European landscapes and genre paintings, as well as sculpture.

When Corcoran's collection outgrew its available space, an architectural competition was held, which resulted in the hiring of New York architect Ernest Flagg. His stately beaux arts–style building, the first of its kind in the city, was completed in 1897. Bronze lions flank the entrance to the symmetrical white marble building; the green copper roof caps an architrave inscribed with

(Continued on p. 124)

Corcoran Gallery of Art

- Map pp. 108–109
- 500 17th St., N.W.
- 202/639-1700
- Closed Mon.–Tues.
- Metro: Farragut West; Bus: 32–36, Circulator

corcoran.org

It's a Spooky Little Town

Intrigue. Mystery. Romance. Spies have captured the imagination of moviegoers for decades, but in Washington—home of the CIA, the FBI, and the Pentagon—such cinematic fare is real, with city streets alive with secret agents seeking or supplying classified information. Every now and then an agent is nabbed, exposing a world in which backyard barbecuers such as Aldrich Ames or Robert Hanssen turn out to have led lives of deceit.

Spying caught on in Washington during the Civil War, when amateur agents on both sides of the Mason-Dixon Line scoured the capital city for war-related information. Thomas Nelson Conrad, a former Georgetown College headmaster, sat in Lafayette Park across from the White House for hours, meticulously noting President Lincoln's comings and goings. Conrad hoped to kidnap the President, then exchange him for prisoners of war. The Confederacy rejected his plan as infeasible.

The most romantic figure in Washington's espionage history may be the Rebel Rose. Intelligent, beautiful, and duplicitous, Rose O'Neal Greenhow (1815–1864) haunted Washington's loftiest social circles before the Civil War, befriending Presidents, senators, and tycoons. When war broke out and men left for battle, spying became women's work. None was more deft than Greenhow. Inside her modest Northwest house at 398 16th Street (it's no longer standing), she plied unsuspecting targets with oysters, wild turkey, and champagne, pumping them for information all the while.

At one dinner party, Greenhow learned that the Federals were planning to move into Virginia. By quickly passing a coded message to Confederate Gen. Pierre G. T. Beauregard inside a woman's hair bun, she enabled him to reposition some of his troops—and, ultimately, to win the First Battle of Bull Run.

Soviet KGB colonel Vitaly Yurchenko made world headlines when he strolled into the U.S. Embassy in Rome in August 1985 and stated he wished to defect. Among the tidbits he had to share: NSA analyst Ronald Pelton had served as a double agent since 1980 and CIA officer Edward Lee Howard since 1984.

But Yurchenko was not a happy decamper. His ex-girlfriend, who married a Russian diplomat stationed in Montreal, had no plans to leave her husband. Worse, the good colonel was relegated to a prisonlike existence in the United States, where his CIA case officers insisted on escorting him everywhere.

EXPERIENCE: Tracing the Routes of Espionage

Why is there a tunnel under the Russian Embassy? What does the National Cathedral have to do with spying? Learn the answers to questions like these in **spy walking tours** led by Carol Bessette, a retired Air Force officer and military intelligence expert (tel 703/ 569-1875, spiesofwashingtontour.com, $$). Various tours focus on tales of intrigue that unfolded inside chic homes of Georgetown, around the White House during the Civil War, in embassies, apartments, and restaurants of upper Northwest D.C.

To try your hand at intelligence activities, check out **Operation Spy** ($$) at the International Spy Museum (see p. 137). You'll decrypt secret conversations and arrange video surveillance of clandestine meetings.

At this K Street spot, traitorous Aldrich Ames spilled critically important beans to Russian agents.

On November 2, 1985, Yurchenko and his CIA handler repaired to a popular neighborhood restaurant in Georgetown that is now defunct. At some point Yurchenko stepped out for a breath of fresh air—and grabbed a cab to the Soviet Embassy, where he rescinded his defection. Four days later he was on a plane to the Soviet Union, leaving the intelligence community to debate whether he had been a legitimate defector or a KGB plant.

Following in the forked footsteps of Greenhow and Yurchenko came career CIA officer Aldrich Ames, who in 1994 was accused of exposing U.S. intelligence assets inside the former Soviet Union. The info swap occurred at Chadwicks, at 3205 K Street in Georgetown; Ames chalk-marked a blue mailbox on R Street at 37th Street as a dead-drop signal. For his tip-offs, Ames received more than $2.7 million from the Soviets—and from the Americans, a lifelong prison sentence.

Bird's-eye Views

The **Washington Monument** (see sidebar p. 101) isn't the only place with a panoramic perspective. Though few people know it, the **Old Post Office Tower** (see p. 146; currently closed for renovations) offers one of the best views of the Mall. And from the sixth-floor terrace of the **Newseum** (see p. 139), the U.S. Capitol looks truly monumental. For decades the open-air roof deck of the old Hotel Washington was a favorite hideaway for its treetop views of the White House; today it's part of the **W Hotel** (see p. 118) and still a great place for cocktails. The **National Cathedral** (see pp. 189–191) sits on one of the highest points in the city. From the observation gallery you can see for miles across the Potomac and into Virginia.

the names of Rembrandt and other great artists.

Inside is the gold-and-white **Salon Doré,** an 18th-century room from Paris's St.-Germain quarter. Part of an extensive donation of European art works and objects from industrialist and U.S. Senator William A. Clark (1839–1925) of Montana, the grand gilded room glitters with Corinthian pilasters, huge framed mirrors, and a ceiling mural.

The historic American collection encompasses works from colonial times through 1980, including colonial and federalist portraiture, neoclassical sculpture, Hudson River School painting, art of the American West, American impressionism, and 20th-century realism. The Corcoran also has sizable collections of contemporary art, photography, and decorative arts.

Special exhibitions at the Corcoran have run for several months at a time and have featured well-known artists and photographers such as Annie Leibovitz and Ansel Adams. A 2010 exhibition of more than a hundred of Chuck Close's prints and objects offered the first survey of this important artist's innovative work in printmaking.

Financial difficulties have long plagued the gallery, however, and in February 2014, the Corcoran's board of trustees announced that it would cease to operate as an independent institution and enter into partnership with the National Gallery of Art and George Washington University.

Under the provisional agreement, the Corcoran's historic 17th Street building will remain open as a museum and exhibition space, with free general admission. The National Gallery will curate a Corcoran Legacy Gallery within the building that will display a selection of iconic works from the core collection, as well as organize exhibitions of modern and contemporary art under the name Corcoran Contemporary, National Gallery of Art.

The Corcoran School of Art and Design, formerly Washington's only four-year accredited fine-arts institution, will retain its identity but become part of George Washington University. The terms of the collaboration may shift going forward, but all involved in the partnership are dedicated to safeguarding the Corcoran's historic legacy. ∎

Organization of American States & Art Museum

Blending classical and Spanish colonial elements, this striking white building is the headquarters of the Organization of American States, a regional alliance of 35 nations promoting peace and economic cooperation among its member countries from the Americas and the Caribbean.

Removed from typical city energy, the OAS courtyard offers a relaxing sense of the tropics.

Dedicated in 1910, the grand building with its marble facade and monumental bronze gates was the work of architects Paul Cret, designer of the Folger Shakespeare Library (see p. 64), and Albert Kelsey. Just inside the elaborate triple-arched entry, a lush villa-like courtyard boasts an octagonal Aztec-style fountain and overflows with tropical plants. Upstairs, the large **Hall of the Americas** auditorium is graced by Tiffany stained-glass windows, massive Corinthian columns, and a vaulted ceiling.

In the back, a walkway through an Aztec garden leads to the **Art Museum of the Americas,** roofed in red tile (the museum must be entered from 201 18th St.). Several attractive galleries host exhibits from the museum's permanent collection, plus traveling shows of Latin American and Caribbean art and photography.

After your visit, head for the triangular park across 18th Street to view the raised-sword equestrian statue of Simón Bolívar the Liberator, a gift to the United States in 1958 from Venezuela. ∎

Organization of American States & Art Museum

- 🅜 Map pp. 108–109
- ✉ 17th St. & Constitution Ave., N.W.
- ☎ 202/370-0147
- 🕐 Museum closed Mon.
- 🚇 Metro: Farragut West; Bus: 80, H1, L1, S1

oas.org
museum.oas.org

John F. Kennedy Center for the Performing Arts

Once maligned as an unsightly pillbox along the Potomac, the Kennedy Center has since earned the affection of Washingtonians. Its 1971 opening elevated the city from a cultural backwater to a leader in the live arts. The world's foremost singers, pianists, jazz musicians, classical artists, dancers, and actors have performed on Kennedy Center stages. Based here, the National Symphony Orchestra and Washington National Opera have achieved international respect.

The Kennedy Center, Washington's premier bastion of culture, stretches along the Potomac River.

John F. Kennedy Center for the Performing Arts

⬛ Map pp. 108–109

✉ 2700 F St., N.W.

☎ 202/467-4600

🚇 Metro: Foggy Bottom–GWU; Bus: Shuttle from Metro

kennedy-center.org

The Kennedy Center is the "national living memorial" to a fallen President, John F. Kennedy. A presidentially appointed board of trustees oversees the operation of the center, which is supported both by ticket sales and by private donations.

Visiting

Free guided tours are offered daily; call for times. You may also wander about on your own, but some theaters are closed to the public during rehearsals. Tickets (purchase at box office or call 202/467-4600

or 800/444-1324) are necessary for most performances. The Millennium Stage program, however, offers free daily performances at 6 p.m. in the Grand Foyer.

The Kennedy Center is at its best at night, when floodlights envelop its white Carrara marble in a vibrant glow. The north entrance opens into the **Hall of States**, its soaring ceiling lined with state flags; at the south entrance the **Hall of Nations** contains the flags of countries with diplomatic ties to the United States. Both halls lead to the

Grand Foyer—at 630 feet (192 m) one of the longest rooms in the world. This royal, red-carpeted space is outfitted with floor-to-ceiling mirrors and 16 crystal chandeliers donated by Sweden. Halfway down the hall you'll find Robert Berks's big, emotive bronze bust of John F. Kennedy.

Attending a performance is the reason to come here—and the best way to take in the auditoriums. The 2,465-seat **Concert Hall,** renovated in 1997, is home to the National Symphony; the 1,164-seat **Eisenhower Theater** is named for the President who signed legislation for a National Cultural Center; and the spectacular 2,362-seat **Opera House** completes the trio of fine performance spaces. Just inside the north entrance, off the Hall of States, the 324-seat **Family Theater** presents performances for young audiences.

On the Roof Terrace level,

the 513-seat **Terrace Theater** is a delightful venue for jazz, solo recitals, chamber music, and drama. You can also take in an experimental or family show at the 399-seat **Theater Lab**. The 200-seat **Jazz Club** swings on this level, too. On the Roof Terrace, walk onto the patio for views of the memorials, the Potomac, Arlington high-rises across the river, and the distant hilltop Washington National Cathedral as you stroll around the building. ■

EXPERIENCE: Tuning in to Free Concerts in D.C.

Numerous groups offer no-charge music performances, but the most ambitious lineup is the Kennedy Center's **Millennium Stage** concerts at 6 p.m. every day in the Grand Foyer. Marimba, show tunes, classical works, jazz—programs run the gamut. No tickets needed. The Harman Center for the Arts (see p. 138), in Penn Quarter, offers free hour-long performances Wednesdays at noon from September through May as part of its **Happenings Lunchtime** program; you can even bring your own lunch. Performers include many local arts groups. Post-work **Happenings Happy Hours** are staged at 5:30 p.m. in select months;

visit the website (*shakespearetheatre.org*) for the schedule.

The Church of the Epiphany (*epiphanydc.org*) downtown also hosts free midday concerts every Tuesday with its **Tuesday Concert Series.** Less well known is the excellent concert series sponsored by the Library of Congress (see pp. 62–63). View the program schedule and reserve free tickets online (*loc.gov/rr/perform/concert*). The **Friday Morning Music Club** (*fmmc .org*) has arranged free concerts in the Washington area for 120 years as a public service under its mission of promoting classical music. Performances are now held throughout the week.

More Places to Visit Around the White House

B'nai B'rith Klutznick National Jewish Museum

This museum of Jewish art, history, and culture documents the life and festival cycles of Judaism. Named for the B'nai B'rith service organization and Chicago attorney Philip Klutznick, highlights of the collection on view include ceremonial and folk art, coins, maps, and paintings and sculpture by artists ranging from Marc Chagall to Ben Zion. ✉ 2020 K St., N.W., 7th floor ☎ 202/857-6647 🕐 Call for appt. 🚇 Metro: Farragut West, Farragut North, Foggy Bottom–GWU

Cathedral of St. Matthew the Apostle

This redbrick 1890s cathedral, with its ribbed copper dome, is where the funeral Mass of President John F. Kennedy was held in 1963. The cavernous interior, embellished with mosaics, a skylit dome, flickering votive candles, and paintings and statues, is a haven for prayer. *stmatthewscathedral.org* 🗺 Map pp. 108–109 ✉ 1725 Rhode Island Ave., N.W. ☎ 202/347-3215 🚇 Metro: Dupont Circle, Farragut North

Charles Sumner School

This building was opened in 1872 as a school for African-American children and named for the abolitionist senator from Massachusetts. It is now an archive and a D.C. public schools conference center and museum. The Sumner School also hosts concerts, lectures, films, and art exhibitions. 🗺 Map pp. 108–109 ✉ 1201 17th St., N.W. ☎ 202/730-0478 🕐 Closed Sat.–Sun. 🚇 Metro: Farragut North, Dupont Circle

Decatur House

For his triumphs in the War of 1812, Commodore Stephen Decatur earned enough to build this federal-style town house on Lafayette Square. Benjamin Henry Latrobe designed the house, completed in 1818, but Decatur never really got to enjoy it: He was killed in a duel with a fellow officer 14 months after moving in. His wife rented the house to the likes of Henry Clay. In 1829, Charlotte Dupuy, a woman enslaved by Clay, then the Secretary of State, sued him for her freedom while living at Decatur House. In January 2010, the National Center for White House History was established here for research and events. *decaturhouse.org* 🗺 Map pp. 108–109 ✉ 1610 H St., N.W. 🚇 Metro: Farragut West

Department of the Interior Museum

Recently reopened after a four-and-a-half-year hiatus, this small, quiet museum

A bronze Albert Einstein sits in thought at the National Academy of Sciences (see opposite).

chronicles the Interior Department's 1930s origins, when it comprised the National Park Service, U.S. Fish and Wildlife Service, U.S. Geological Survey, and the Bureaus of Mines, Indian Affairs, Reclamation, and Land Management. Drawings, handmade maps, tools, and videos tell the story of the country's settlement. Adults must present photo ID to enter. *doi.gov/interiormuseum* 🅰 Map pp. 108–109 ✉ 1849 C St., N.W. ☎ 202/208-4743 🕐 Closed Sat.–Sun. & federal holidays 🚇 Metro: Farragut West, Foggy Bottom–GWU

INSIDER TIP:

Schedule an hour-long tour of the 1941–1942 murals by photographer Ansel Adams at the Department of the Interior. For details, contact the DOI [tel 202/638-6600].

—CAROLINE HICKEY
*National Geographic
Travel Books editor*

Department of State

On the eighth floor of the imposing State Department building you will find the elegant suite of **Diplomatic Reception Rooms** decorated with one of the country's finest collections of early American furnishings. Take the 45-minute tour and you will discover such surprises as George Washington's Chinese porcelain *(reservations required, often months ahead)*. The rooms on the south side—among them the State Dining Room— offer views of the Mall and its monuments. *state.gov/m/drr* 🅰 Map pp. 108–109 ✉ 23rd & C Sts., N.W. ☎ 202/647-3241 🕐 Closed Sat.–Sun. & federal holidays 🚇 Metro: Foggy Bottom–GWU

Tea Time

Whether you take it with honey and milk or prefer to sip green-leaf varieties, there are plenty of spots in Washington to enjoy afternoon tea. Two of the poshest locales are elegant **Peacock Alley** (take a peek at the mosaic floor) at the historic Willard Hotel (see sidebar p. 118) and the radiantly skylit **Greenhouse** atrium in the renovated Jefferson Hotel *(1200 16th St., N.W., tel 202/ 448-2300, jeffersondc.com).* For an authentic Asian atmosphere, try **Teaism** *(teaism.com),* with several locations around town. For garden-style settings, options include **Hillwood Estate** (see pp. 187–188) and the **National Cathedral** (see pp. 189–191).

Hay-Adams Hotel

The elegant Italian Renaissance–style Hay-Adams, one of Washington's finest small hotels, fronts Lafayette Park, with a good view of the White House. Built in the 1920s, it occupies the site of residences owned by statesman John Hay and historian Henry Adams. Stop in for fine dining at the hotel's Lafayette Restaurant or sip cocktails at its cozy bar Off the Record. *hayadams.com* 🅰 Map pp. 108–109 ✉ 16th & H Sts., N.W. ☎ 202/638-6600 🚇 Metro: Farragut West, Farragut North, McPherson Square

National Academy of Sciences

Housed here are committees representing foremost U.S. experts in science, medicine, and engineering. Outside is a bronze of Albert Einstein (see opposite) by Robert Berks, who sculpted the Kennedy Center's JFK bust. *nasonline.org* 🅰 Map pp. 108–109 ✉ 2101 Constitution Ave., N.W. ☎ 202/ 334-2000 🚇 Metro: Foggy Bottom–GWU

Octagon Museum

A gem of early Washington history, the redbrick Octagon was the neighborhood's first private residence, built about the same time as the White House. Its longevity owes much to its designer, William Thornton, who was also the first architect of the Capitol. The house was completed in 1801 for entrepreneur John Tayloe III. When the British burned the President's House in 1814, the Madisons took shelter here, just a five-minute walk from the executive mansion. President Madison signed the war-ending Treaty of Ghent in an upstairs parlor.

INSIDER TIP:

Breakfast at the Hay-Adams Hotel might be a splurge, but it sometimes comes with paparazzi-worthy sightings of household-name folks in the worlds of politics and entertainment. You never know.

—AMY ALIPIO
National Geographic Traveler
magazine associate editor

The Tayloes moved back in and raised 15 children here. After Mrs. Tayloe's death in 1855, the Octagon was rented out for various purposes. The American Institute of Architects bought it in 1902. It now houses a museum operated by the American Architectural Foundation. Despite its name, the Octagon house only has six sides. *theoctagon.org* ⓜ Map pp. 108–109 ✉ 1799 New York Ave., N.W. ☎ 202/626-7439 ⓛ Open Thurs.–Fri. 1–4 p.m.; call for guided tours Ⓜ Metro: Farragut West, Farragut North

Renwick Gallery

The architecturally distinctive Renwick Gallery has housed the Smithsonian American Art Museum's contemporary craft program since 1972. Designed in 1858 by James Renwick, Jr., architect of the Smithsonian's Castle, the striking Second Empire–style building features sandstone pilasters and garlands gracing the redbrick and decorative ironwork crowning the tripartite mansard roof.

During the Civil War it housed military records and uniforms, and the U.S. Court of Claims occupied the building from 1899 to 1964. Jacqueline Kennedy led efforts to save the building from demolition, and it came under the aegis of the Smithsonian Institution in 1965. Works by artists such as Larry Fuente, Anni Albers, Dale Chihuly, Albert Paley, Wendell Castle, James Cederquist, Lia Cook, and Claire Zeisler have been featured. The Renwick is closed for renovations until 2016. *americanart .si.edu/renwick* ⓜ Map pp. 108–109 ✉ 17th St. & Pennsylvania Ave., N.W. ☎ 202/633-7970 Ⓜ Metro: Farragut West; Bus: 32, 36, Circulator

St. John's Church

Presidents since James Madison have worshipped at this Episcopal church on occasion. A brass plate marks the President's pew, No. 54, and the kneelers are covered in needlepoint. A national historic landmark, the gold-domed yellow stucco church, completed in 1815, has daily services, as well as concerts and community events. *stjohns-dc.org* ⓜ Map pp. 108–109 ✉ 1525 H St., N.W. ☎ 202/347-8766 Ⓜ Metro: Farragut West, McPherson Square

St. Mary's Episcopal Church

Called St. Mary's Church for Colored People when it opened in 1887, this was Washington's first house of worship for African-American Episcopalians. The altar triptych depicts two saints of African descent; the center window is Tiffany stained glass. ⓜ Map pp. 108–109 ✉ 728 23rd St., N.W. ☎ 202/333-3985 ⓛ Closed Fri.–Sat. Ⓜ Metro: Foggy Bottom–GWU

A metropolitan mélange of historic structures, entertainment spots, museums, office buildings, shops, hotels, and a slew of restaurants

Downtown

An imposing figure adorns the National Building Museum.

Downtown

Just north of the Mall since the city's founding in 1791, downtown D.C. sprung from the intersection of Pennsylvania Avenue (the city's main street) and 7th Street (the main northern thoroughfare). The area now sprawls to 14th Street and Louisiana and Massachusetts Avenues. Booming with new vitality, downtown buzzes with restaurants, shops, theaters, and galleries, as well as several long-established museums.

Throughout the 1800s, boutiques, hotels, and theaters thrived downtown, catering to the area's residents. The turn of the 20th century, however, brought the exodus of affluent merchants and residents to the suburbs, thereby opening up the downtown area to successive groups of lower income citizens. Then came the assassination of Martin Luther King, Jr., in 1968, instigating riots and the large-scale abandonment of commercial ventures. As buildings fell into miserable disrepair and the crime rate exploded, the area became one to avoid.

That outlook soon changed. In 1972, Congress created the Pennsylvania Avenue

R.I. AVE.

14TH STREET
VERMONT AVE.

Mary McLeod Bethune
Council House N.H.S.

N STREET

14TH STREET

N STREET

STREET

National City
Christian Church

M ST.

12TH STREET

11TH STREET

STREET

THOMAS
CIRCLE

To Metropolitan
A.M.E. Church
GREEN
CT.

ST.

MASSACHUSETTS

L STREET

13TH

L STREET

Washington
Convention
Center

STREET

AVENUE

29

10TH STREET

MT. VERNON
SQUARE

13TH

STREET

Carnegie
Library

STREET

STREET

STREET

14TH

29

K STREET

AVENUE

I ST.

I ST.

MASSACHUSETTS

FRANKLIN
SQUARE

STREET

8TH

7TH

Friendship
Arch

6TH STREET

AVENUE

McPherson
Square

YORK

AVENUE

Gallery Place-
Chinatown

National Mus. of
Women in the Arts

NEW

H STREET

G PL.

CHINATOWN

H STREET

National
Building
Museum

G ST.

New York Avenue
Presbyterian
Church

STREET

9TH STREET

Smithsonian
American
Art Museum

Verizon
Center

G

13TH ST.

12TH STREET

Metro
Center

Gallery Place-
Chinatown

Harman
Center
for the
Arts

Metro Center

F

11TH ST.

Metro
Center

Nat. Portrait
Gallery

Gallery Place-
Chinatown

National Museum of
Crime & Punishment

Judiciary
Square

STREET

395

F

Metro Center

Madame
Tussaud's

National
Theatre

13TH ST.

12TH STREET

Petersen
House

Warner
Theatre

Ford's
Theatre
N.H.S.

International
Spy Museum

Marian Koshland
Science Museum

STREET

3RD STREET

2ND STREET

1ST STREET

E STREET

PENN. AVE. N.

FREEDOM PLAZA

PENN. AVE. S.

District
Building

14TH STREET

PENNSYLVANIA

STREET

10TH STREET

J. Edgar
Hoover
FBI
Building

1
50

Shakespeare
Theatre

7TH ST.

PENNSYLVANIA
QUARTER

1
50

JUDICIARY
SQUARE

5TH

D ST.

4TH STREET

Judiciary
Square

Ronald Reagan
Building &
International
Trade Center

Federal
Triangle

Old
Post
Office

Market Square

INDIANA
AVE.

Environmental
Protection Agency

Internal
Revenue
Service

10TH ST.

U.S. Navy Mem. &
Naval Heritage Ctr.

Dept. of
Justice

Archives-
Navy Memorial

Newseum

To Surratt
Boardinghouse

JOHN
MARSHALL
PARK

CONSTITUTION

1
50

AVENUE

National
Archives

AVENUE

Federal Trade
Commission

C STREET

Washington, D.C.

NW

NE

Subject
area

Potomac

SW

SE

Anacostia

Virginia

Md.

Md.

Snack vendors and stylish couples are routinely spotted on downtown sidewalks.

Development Corporation (PADC) to plan the revitalization of Pennsylvania Avenue—the neglected streetscape was unbefitting what many consider to be America's Main Street.

Initially, the PADC focused on renovating Pennsylvania Avenue's historic buildings: the Old Post Office, the Willard Hotel, and the National and Warner Theatres. Each successful venture encouraged the next, as city planners and developers saw the exciting possibility of reviving downtown.

Coupled with renovation, new construction brought Market Square (1989; *N of the Archives*), with offices and apartments; the Lansburgh (1992; *8th & E Sts.*), a residential/retail/cultural arts complex; and in 2003 the new convention center *(N of Mt. Vernon Sq.)*. In the last few years, billions of dollars have been invested in the area's development, including many new restaurants. A popular attraction is the Harman Center for the Arts.

The arrival of the MCI Center in 1997 (now the Verizon Center) has been important to development, drawing large numbers of visitors to basketball and hockey games, concerts and other special events.

All this new life complements several museums often overshadowed by those on the nearby Mall. Highlights include the Smithsonian American Art Museum, National Portrait Gallery, National Museum of Women in the Arts, and National Building Museum. The Newseum is the newest addition to the lineup.

Amid the modernization, tiny Chinatown clings to its heritage. Clustered on the north side of Pennsylvania Avenue in the 1880s, the enclave established its distinctive appearance after moving to the H Street area in the 1930s, where it remains today, with Cantonese, Szechuan, and Hunan restaurants, as well as traditional Chinese pharmacies. ■

NOT TO BE MISSED:

Role-playing and cool gadgets at the International Spy Museum 137

Creative stagings of Shakespeare at the Lansburgh or Harman 138–139

Experiencing the special effects of the Newseum's 4-D film 139

Seeing the theater box where President Lincoln was shot 140

The Charters of Freedom at the National Archives 142–143

The Great Hall of the National Building Museum 144

Pennsylvania Quarter

The shining star of downtown's revitalization, the Pennsylvania Quarter neighborhood—also called the 7th Street corridor—has become a hip hangout. With an explosion of luxury apartment complexes, trendy restaurants, theaters, and galleries joining a panoply of established and new museums, the once neglected area now teems with life both day and night.

Chinese influences along lively 7th Street endure amid new shops and businesses.

Pennsylvania Quarter

- Map pp. 132–133
- 5th to 9th & E to I Sts., N.W.
- Metro: Gallery Place–Chinatown; Bus: 70, 79, Circulator

The real success story of the Pennsylvania Quarter begins with the abandoned Lansburgh department store. In 1992 this imposing building was rehabilitated into a mixed-use complex housing several hundred residential units, retail space, and a cultural arts venue. The Lansburgh's reigning tenant, the nationally renowned **Shakespeare Theatre** (see pp. 138–139) moved to 7th Street from Capitol Hill in 1992. Devoted to presenting the Bard's works—as well as those of his contemporaries and of the playwrights he influenced—the theater is considered one of the nation's most prestigious. It expanded dramatically in October 2007, when the new **Harman Center for the Arts** opened. The center's **Sidney Harman Hall** added 774 seats and a second venue to the theater's performance capacity. The well-established repertory **Woolly Mammoth Theatre** (641 D St., N.W., tel 202/393-3939, woolly mammoth.net) is located nearby.

Another major contributor to revitalization was the colossal **Verizon Center** (601 F St., N.W., tel 202/628-3200, verizoncenter .monumentalnetwork.com), which draws thousands of visitors on any given day. Opened in 1997, the

INSIDER TIP:

There's a vibrant theater scene on 14th Street, N.W., a quick cab ride or long walk from Penn Quarter. Before you head in to see the show, have Thai food at Rice [1608 14th Street, N.W.]

—M. J. JACOBSEN
National Geographic
vice president of communications

20,000-seat arena hosts circuses, ice skating performances, concerts, and other special events. It's also home to the Washington Wizards and Mystics professional basketball teams (men and women, respectively), the Georgetown Hoyas college basketball team, and the Washington Capitals hockey team.

An even bigger addition to downtown is the **Washington Convention Center** *(801 Mount Vernon Pl., dcconvention.com)*, which opened in 2003. With 2.3 million square feet (more than 2 million sq m) of space—covering six city blocks on 17 acres (6.8 ha)—the behemoth is more than double the size of the old convention center that was just blocks away.

Keeping in step with the quarter's new face, many of its museums—including the **National Portrait Gallery** (see pp. 136–137) and the **Smithsonian American Art Museum** (see this page)— have been renovated.

Increasing the area's appeal are several museums added in recent years. The most dynamic is the imposing block-long **Newseum** (see p. 139), dedicated to all aspects of journalism. The highly popular **International Spy Museum** (see p. 137), opened in 2002, now has serious competition from the nearby **National Museum of Crime & Punishment** (see pp. 137–138). Also nearby is an outpost of **Madame Tussauds wax museum** *(1001 F St., N.W., madametussauds.com /washington)*. Several blocks away, the **Washington Historical Society** *(8th & K Sts., N.W.)* has moved into a beaux arts building, the former Carnegie Library.

Sandwiched amid all this growth is Washington's small but distinctive **Chinatown** *(6th to 8th Sts. & G to H Sts., N.W.)*, which has thrived since it was established here in the 1930s.

Smithsonian American Art Museum

Housed in a historic landmark that Walt Whitman called the "noblest of Washington buildings" is the nation's first collection of American art. Here and at its Renwick Gallery (see p. 130) are works in every medium—all by American artists and spanning more than three centuries. The National Portrait Gallery shares the impressive building, which reopened after a major overhaul.

One of the finest examples of Greek Revival public architecture in the United States, this stunning building has porticos modeled on the Parthenon in Athens, a curving double staircase, colonnades,

Smithsonian American Art Museum

- Map pp. 132–133
- 8th & F Sts., N.W.
- 202/633-7970
- Metro: Gallery Place– Chinatown; Bus: 42, 70, 79, D3–D6, Circulator

americanart.si.edu

National Portrait Gallery

🅐 Map pp. 132–133

✉ 8th & F Sts., N.W.

☎ 202/633-8300

🚇 Metro: Gallery Place–Chinatown; Bus: 42, 70, 79, D3–D6, Circulator

npg.si.edu

and vaulted galleries. Construction began in 1836 under the direction of Robert Mills, then architect of public buildings.

Pierre-Charles L'Enfant's original plan for the capital called for putting a national nondenominational church or a pantheon for the nation's heroes on this site. Instead, Congress claimed it for a patent office, which moved into the south wing in 1840 while construction continued. The

sculpture, photography, prints and drawings, African-American art, Latino art, and folk art.

Among the several public spaces are a courtyard with café and free Wi-Fi, as well as a conservation center where visitors can observe restoration and repair of important works of art.

National Portrait Gallery

Recognizing the nation's heroes, intellects, and rogues, the National Portrait Gallery reveals America's history through portraiture and sculpture. The idea of a national portrait gallery dates back to 1857, when Congress commissioned George P. A. Healy to paint official portraits of all the Presidents for the White House. After World War I, a national portrait gallery was proposed, yet this gallery didn't open until 1968.

The collection consists of more than 20,000 objects in a wide range of media, including marble, oil on canvas, drawing, and photography. Among the formal portraits of all the Presidents is Gilbert Stuart's famous "Lansdowne" portrait of George Washington.

Opening onto the magnificent third-floor Great Hall are four galleries that feature 20th-century Americans who were significant in politics, culture, and science. **"Champions"** salutes figures whose impact has extended beyond their achievement in American sports. **"Bravo!"** showcases composers and performers from the beginning of the 20th century to the present, with video clips of performances by such legends as P. T. Barnum, John Wayne,

The National Portrait Gallery contains the only complete collection of presidential portraits outside the White House.

building was used as a hospital and barracks during the Civil War, and President Abraham Lincoln held his second Inaugural Ball here in 1865.

More than 7,000 artists are represented in the Smithsonian American Art Museum's collection, which features colonial portraits, 19th-century landscapes, American Impressionism, 20th-century realism and abstraction,

Katharine Hepburn, Leonard Bernstein, and Aaron Copland.

Other notable personalities appear in the exhibit **"American Origins,"** from the first meeting of Native Americans and European explorers through the onset of the gilded age. The Civil War galleries have selections from the museum's outstanding daguerreotypes. Caricatures by Al Hirschfeld, *Time* magazine portrait covers, and sculptor Jo Davidson's bronze and terra-cotta portraits of famous Americans such as Franklin D. Roosevelt, Gertrude Stein, and Gertrude Vanderbilt Whitney all round out the museum experience.

International Spy Museum

Fans of espionage will love this spot, which offers inside looks at how professionals track and nail their targets. It has a wide range of interactive exhibits highlighting tools and techniques of the trade, historically significant people and events, and an array of fascinating artifacts.

Highly popular since it opened more than a decade ago, the International Spy Museum occupies the shell of five historic buildings dating from 1875 to 1892; the American Communist Party had offices here during World War II. In the refurbished space, the exhibits were developed with the guidance of real agents and spy-catchers such as CIA masters of disguise. The displays incorporate hundreds of objects ranging from popular 1930s and 1940s G-Man toys (G for "government")

to spying devices such as a KGB pistol encased in a lipstick tube.

You begin the self-guided tour by adopting an alias. The role-playing continues through exhibits that test your skill at analyzing situations and maintaining your cover, as real agents must do. Find out in School for Spies if you have what it takes for this risky business. Other exhibits convey stories of notable spy rings and intelligence gathering through time, such as the brilliant work of Navajo code talkers and the methods of convicted spies such as Robert Hanssen.

During weekends, holidays, and the peak tourist season, the lines are often long for same-day admission, so it's a good idea to reserve in advance. Check the website for details.

National Museum of Crime & Punishment

Piggybacking on the success of its spy museum neighbor, the

International Spy Museum

- Map pp. 132–133
- 800 F St., N.W.
- 202/393-7798
- $$$$
- Metro: Gallery Place–Chinatown; Bus: 42, 70, 79, D3–D6, Circulator

spymuseum.org

National Museum of Crime & Punishment

- Map pp. 132–133
- 575 7th St., N.W.
- 202/393-1099
- $$$$
- Metro: Gallery Place–Chinatown; Bus: 42, 70, 74, 79, D3–D6, Circulator

crimemuseum.org

Sightseeing With a Twist

If walking from one big monument to another feels ho-hum, add something different to your day. Follow a guide as you glide past the sites on a motorized Segway (*citysegwaytours.com*), or explore with amphibious **DC Ducks** (*dcducks.com*). The **Poetry Foundation** (*poetryfoundation .org*) tour reveals the city through the eyes of its poets; visit the website to load your MP3 player with the narration and print a corresponding map. **Monuments by Moonlight** (*historictours.com*) offers trolley tours that feature major sites after dark. **Bike the Sites** (*bikethesites.com*) will deck you in reflective gear for its own version of an evening tour.

National Museum of Crime & Punishment provides an experience that mimics the drama of TV's *CSI* and *America's Most Wanted*. On three floors that total some 25,000 square feet (2,320 sq m) of space, you can immerse yourself in a crime scene with fresh evidence, then aid the investigation using such

The International Spy Museum entrance is no secret.

Shakespeare Theatre & Harman Center for the Arts

- Map pp. 132–133
- Lansburgh Theatre: 450 7th St., N.W. Sidney Harman Hall: 610 F St., N.W.
- 202/547-1122
- Metro: Archives– Navy Memorial, Gallery Place– Chinatown, Judiciary Square; Bus: 70, 74, D3– D6, Circulator

shakespearetheatre .org

forensic science techniques as fingerprinting, ballistics, and DNA testing to solve the case.

Other interactive activities allow you to engage in FBI-style firearms training, simulate a high-speed police chase, and try to crack a safe. The museum houses the actual television set of *America's Most Wanted*. During its time on the air, the show helped lead to the capture of more than 1,200 fugitives.

Shakespeare Theatre & Harman Center for the Arts

Since its founding in 1985, Washington's Shakespeare Theatre has become one of the city's most beloved cultural institutions. Under artistic director Michael Kahn, the company has won wide acclaim for its highly imaginative modern interpretations of classical plays that in some cases make them more comprehensible and relevant to 21st-century audiences.

In 1992 the Shakespeare Theatre helped spearhead a renaissance of the downtown area near Pennsylvania Avenue by moving from its Capitol Hill quarters to the converted Lansburgh department store on 7th Street. Steady audience growth led the company to expand in 2007 to additional space around the corner in a handsome new $89 million glass-fronted building.

Today, the existing 451-seat **Lansburgh Theatre** and the 774-seat **Sidney Harman Hall**– together known as the Harman Center for the Arts–provide multiple spaces for staging a broad range of works.

Besides presenting familiar plays like *Hamlet, Romeo and Juliet, The Tempest,* and *A Midsummer Night's Dream,* the Shakespeare Theatre has undertaken ambitious productions of rarely produced works such as *Coriolanus, King John, Troilus and Cressida,* and *Pericles.* Modern masterpieces by George Bernard Shaw, Oscar Wilde, Eugene O'Neill, Henrik Ibsen, and others also are represented.

In its nearly three decades, the Shakespeare repertory company has received numerous Helen Hayes awards for excellence in its theatrical presentations. They often include renowned guest artists, such as Stacy Keach playing King Lear.

In 2010, a Harman performance of *Phèdre,* produced by the National Theatre of Great Britain and starring Helen Mirren, sold out within five hours after tickets went on sale.

As part of its commitment to make classical theater more widely accessible, the Shakespeare Theatre offers a Free for All performance every summer. It also organizes educational programs for students, and partners with many groups to provide concerts, ballet, and other arts performances.

Newseum

The Newseum, an array of fast-paced exhibits that convey the nature of modern journalism, has brought a new vitality to Pennsylvania Avenue in the shape of an elaborate building that lies near the U.S. Capitol, amid the imposing structures of "official" Washington, D.C.

A project of the Freedom Forum, the Newseum, which opened at this location in early 2008, shares the block-long building with apartments, a conference center, and the Source, a restaurant featuring the cuisine of noted chef Wolfgang Puck. The **terrace** offers panoramic views of the Capitol and the National Mall.

Emblazoned on the exterior is a 74-foot-high (22.5 m) marble engraving of the First Amendment, which guarantees press freedom. Inside, in the 90-foot-high (27 m) **Great Hall of News,** images of historical and current news events are projected on a wall-size screen.

The museum has six floors of exhibits on all aspects of the press and news reporting. Especially moving are galleries devoted to the fall of the Berlin Wall and the 2001 terrorist attacks on the United States; 127 newspaper front pages from around the world tell the story of the latter. Another gallery displays a collection of iconic Pulitzer Prize–winning photographs, such as Marines raising the flag at Iwo Jima.

The interactive displays and programs allow visitors to cast themselves in various news roles or serve as audience members for news programs hosted in the Newseum's **TV studio and theaters** (see sidebar above).

After you enter the building on level one, take the escalator down to the concourse level. Begin with the orientation films and other introductory exhibits. Then take the glass elevator to the sixth level and work your way down. ∎

EXPERIENCE:
Put Yourself in the News

Always harbored a secret desire to be a TV personality? See if you have what it takes in the **Newseum's interactive newsroom.** Stations equipped with cameras, teleprompters, and scripts let you try reporting and delivering the news. TV screens project your performance, and you can download the video ($). Newsmania, an interactive game, tests your knowledge of First Amendment rights. Don't miss the riveting 13-minute 4-D film that offers a "take you there" experience of news reporting through the ages. Don the special glasses and you'll find yourself alongside Nellie Bly as she goes undercover in 1887 to expose conditions at a women's insane asylum. Some of the special effects seem frightfully real.

Newseum

⬛ Map pp. 132–133

✉ 555 Pennsylvania Ave., N.W.

☎ 888/639-7386

💲 $$$$

Ⓜ Metro: Archives–Navy Memorial; Bus: 32–36, 54, 70, P6

newseum.org

Ford's Theatre National Historic Site

A working theater and a museum dedicated to one of the nation's most tragic dramas, Ford's Theatre has a morbidly compelling quality. John Wilkes Booth shot President Abraham Lincoln here on April 14, 1865, five days after Lee's surrender at Appomattox. Lincoln's untimely death pushed to legendary heights the historical greatness he had achieved by keeping the Union from falling apart. The theater closed shortly thereafter.

Ford's Theatre National Historic Site

- Map pp. 132–133
- 511 10th St., N.W.
- 202/347-4833
- $
- Metro: Metro Center; Bus: 42, 79, D3–D6

fordstheatre.org

Serving as a government office building and then a storage facility, the small 10th Street edifice was acquired by the National Park Service in 1933, restored to its original 1865 splendor in the 1960s, and renovated again in 2008. The theater now hosts a full program of contemporary American plays, musicals, and other entertainment.

The ornate interior boasts the authentically re-created Presidential Box with American flags, lace curtains, red velvet wallpaper, plush seats, and the original settee. The museum downstairs contains various historic artifacts.

When the theater is not in use, Park Service officials offer short informative talks on the night's events. Booth, a disgruntled actor and Confederate sympathizer, shot Lincoln in the head and then jumped down to the stage, breaking a bone in his leg. He hobbled off and fled on horseback through the southern Maryland countryside, only to be caught 12 days later and shot dead.

Continue following the night's events across the street at the **Petersen House** *(516 10th St., N.W.)*, where Lincoln was taken after the shooting. Never regaining consciousness, the President died the next day. Peek into the parlor where Mary Todd Lincoln waited through the night, the back parlor where Lincoln's secretary of war began investigating the murder, and the period-furnished bedroom in which Lincoln died. Pick up tickets *($)* to enter the museum and house at the box office, or visit the website. Occasional walking tours *($$$)* are led by costumed actors. ■

The Presidential Box is on permanent display at Ford's.

National Museum of Women in the Arts

This well-designed museum focuses solely on the work of women artists. Founder and art collector Wilhelmina Cole Holladay maintained that women were often completely overlooked in standard art history texts. Determined to correct the imbalance, her resulting museum, which opened in 1987, showcases and promotes the talent of women artists around the world from the Renaissance to the present.

Notable in itself, the handsome Renaissance revival building began as a Masonic temple in 1907, served as a movie theater in the 1960s, and, after being threatened with demolition in the early 1980s, was purchased by Holladay in 1983. Restored to its former glory, the dazzling grand hall shines with polished marble floors and highly decorative plasterwork.

Select works in the permanent collection (which numbers about 4,500 pieces) are on view in the **Great Hall, Mezzanine,** and **third floor.** These works chronicle women's artistic achievements from the 16th century through to modern times. Look for Lavinia Fontana's 1580 "Portrait of a Noblewoman"; Fontana was the first widely known woman to sustain a career as an artist.

Other treasures include "Highland Raid" (1860) and other works by Rosa Bonheur (1822–1899), who was famous for her straightforward depictions of animals, as well as "The Bath" (1891) and other canvases by American Impressionist Mary Cassatt (1844–1926). Georgia O'Keeffe, Helen Frankenthaler, Lee Krasner, Judy Chicago, Alma Woodsey Thomas, Chakaia Booker, Jaune Quick-to-See Smith, and Hung Liu are among the artists represented. This museum is the only place in Washington where you can see work by Mexican painter Frida Kahlo. Her "Self-Portrait–Dedicated to Leon Trotsky" (1937),

INSIDER TIP:

The elegant National Museum of Women in the Arts occupies a gorgeously impressive building. Try the café on the mezzanine level for a snack or lunch.

—SUSAN STRAIGHT
National Geographic Travel Books editor

also known as "Between the Curtains," is part of the permanent collection. It was donated to the museum by journalist, playwright, and ambassador Clare Boothe Luce in 1988, shortly before her death.

Special exhibits are found on the second floor, while the fourth floor has an 18,500-volume library and research center. ■

National Museum of Women in the Arts

- ⬛ Map pp. 132–133
- ✉ 1250 New York Ave., N.W.
- ☎ 202/783-5000
- $ $$
- Ⓜ Metro: Metro Center; Bus: 80, D1–D6, S2–S4, X2

nmwa.org

National Archives

Serving as the nation's memory bank, the National Archives contains 12 billion pages of documents, including the original parchment copies of the Declaration of Independence, the U.S. Constitution, and the Bill of Rights. John Russell Pope, architect of the Jefferson Memorial, designed the 1935 building expressly to house these manifestos. In fact it was Jefferson, author of the Declaration, who first voiced concern about the deterioration of the national records.

The semicircular Rotunda is where America's Charters of Freedom are displayed for all to see.

National Archives

🅰 Map pp. 132–133

✉ Constitution Ave. bet. 7th & 9th Sts., N.W.

☎ 202/357-5000

🚇 Metro: Archives–Navy Memorial; Bus: 30–36, A42–A48, P1–P4

archives.gov

Ringed with 72 massive Corinthian columns, Pope's grand neoclassical edifice takes up a whole city block. Bas-reliefs decorate the pediments atop the north and south porticos. The 39 limestone steps that front the south portico on Constitution Avenue represent the 39 signers of the Constitution. The foot-thick (0.3 m) bronze doors at the top of the stairs soar 40 feet (12 m) high.

Inside, the echoing **Rotunda** rises to a 75-foot-high (23 m) dome. New York artist Barry Faulkner painted the two 1930s murals. "The Constitution" depicts James Madison presenting the document to George Washington. "The Declaration of Independence" shows Thomas Jefferson submitting the proclamation to John Hancock, presiding officer of the Continental Congress.

The low-lit Rotunda is where you can view the United States' most important documents: the **Charters of Freedom.** The Declaration of Independence, the U.S. Constitution, and the Bill of Rights lie in state-of-the-art cases that fiercely protects the them from air and moisture. The cases allow all four pages of the Constitution to be shown at the same time. In cases flanking the Charters of Freedom are documents related to the exhibit "The Charters of Freedom: Our Nation's Founding Documents."

The interactive exhibit **"Public Vaults"** presents stories of how records in the National Archives "stacks"—documents, maps, photos, and films—are used by the federal government, organizations, and individual citizens to clarify historical events, investigate mysteries, make documentaries, and pursue family history.

Every few months, the Archives presents fresh exhibits in the **Lawrence F. O'Brien Gallery.** The focus ranges from photographic displays to selected holdings from the presidential libraries and other museums. The **McGowan Theater** shows a short film about the Archives between 11 a.m. and 12 p.m. and 1 p.m. and 2 p.m., and screens documentary films at night. The **Boeing Learning Center** (closed Sat.–Sun. & federal holidays) offers a variety of programs for children and adults that detail the methods of document-based research.

A Rich Repository

The Archives preserves more than 12 million maps, charts, and architectural drawings; 25 million photos; hundreds of thousands of films, videos, and sound recordings; and more. The National Archives and Records Administration, established in 1934 to oversee what to save, deems about 3 percent of federal records generated annually to be worthy of permanent storage.

Representing more than 200 years of history, the repository is creating a rich paper trail. Among the original treasures are the Louisiana Purchase Treaty, the Emancipation Proclamation, Mathew Brady's Civil War photographs, Robert Peary's polar expedition journals, Dust Bowl photographs, Indian treaties, recordings of FDR's fireside chats, captured German records and

Family Traces

People seeking genealogical history are heavy users of the National Archives. Every one of its twelve billion documents helps tell the story of some person or event. But putting it all together isn't straightforward. There's no master index, so you have to search individual collections; raw records are stored in boxes arranged by agency and program. A few records collections are available online, such as those on census data, military service, naturalization, and land claims. For more complex searches, you might need to visit other Archives branches around the country. The National Archives website (archives .gov) offers tips on getting started.

Japanese surrender documents from World War II, and Richard Nixon's letter of resignation.

The Archives is popular among scholars, historians, and researchers, who use the research facilities here and in College Park, Maryland. Alex Haley used slave ship manifests in researching his novel *Roots.* Opened in 1994, the Maryland branch is the largest archival facility in the world. ■

National Building Museum

The huge redbrick Pension Building designed by Gen. Montgomery C. Meigs is one of Washington's architectural treasures. The 1887 structure, however, modeled on the 18th-century Palazzo Farnese in Rome, was called Meig's Old Barn by critics. Though it had deteriorated by the 1960s, a study highlighted its potential as a museum. And so it was spared the wrecking ball.

Arcaded galleries and marbleized columns define the Great Hall.

National Building Museum

- Map pp. 132–133
- 401 F St., N.W.
- 202/272-2448
- $$
- Metro: Judiciary Square; Bus: D3–D6, Circulator

nbm.org

Congress called for the building's restoration in 1980 for an architecture, urban planning, and design museum. Girding the entire building, the most striking exterior feature is the 3-foot-high (0.9 m) terra-cotta frieze designed by sculptor Caspar Buberl (1834–1899). Depicting a procession of Civil War infantry, artillery, cavalry, and other units, it is emblematic of the building's original purpose: serving the needs of Union veterans.

Inside, the **Great Hall** will take your breath away. Standing in the middle of this immense, light-filled space bordered on all sides with four tiers of arcades and high clerestory windows, you feel as if you've stepped into an Italian gallery. Eight Corinthian columns, made of brick but plastered and painted to resemble marble, rise

75 feet high (23 m) on either side of a central fountain. Meigs modeled aspects of this room after several classical and Renaissance palaces and churches.

The museum galleries, featuring changing exhibits on the building arts, are on the Great Hall's first two levels. The long-term exhibit **"House and Home"** artfully arranges photographs, objects, models, and films to explore how ideas about American domestic life have changed due to the evolution of technology and consumer culture. The seven galleries feature touchable walls of materials used in residential construction and commissioned scale models of 14 iconic American homes.

The museum offers lectures, films, area building tours, a café, and an excellent gift shop. ■

More Places to Visit Downtown

Carnegie Library

In 1899, Andrew Carnegie donated $682,000 to build this main library and three additional branches in Washington. This classic white marble beaux arts–style structure was completed in 1903 and served as the city's central library until 1972. Today, the Historical Society of Washington, D.C., operates a research library here and sponsors activities that include workshops, author readings and lectures, and the Urban Photography series that documents D.C.'s neighborhoods. *historydc.org* 🄰 Map pp. 132–133 ✉ 801 K St., N.W. at Mount Vernon Square ☎ 202/249-3955 🄼 Metro: Mt. Vernon Square–7th Street, Gallery Place–Chinatown

Freedom Plaza

This granite plaza is anchored by an equestrian statue of Casimir Pulaski, the Polish nobleman who fought for America in the Revolutionary War and was mortally wounded at the siege of Savannah. The plaza, which was named in 1988 in honor of Dr. Martin Luther King, Jr., offers a sweeping view down Pennsylvania Avenue to the U.S. Capitol. Inlaid in bronze on the ground are depictions of L'Enfant's 1791 city plan, along with outlines for the Congress House and President's Palace. 🄰 Map pp. 132–133 ✉ Pennsylvania Ave. bet. 13th & 14th Sts., N.W. 🄼 Metro: Metro Center, Federal Triangle

Marian Koshland Science Museum of the National Academy of Sciences

This 5,700-square-foot (530 sq m) museum that opened in 2004 provides insight into scientific issues at the core of many of the nation's public policy decisions. Interactive exhibits explore climate change, satellite images of Earth, and the emerging health threats from infectious diseases. *koshland-science-museum.org* 🄰 Map pp. 132–133 ✉ 6th & E Sts., N.W. ☎ 202/334-1201 🕐 Closed Tues. 💲 $ 🄼 Metro: Gallery Place–Chinatown, Judiciary Square

Mary McLeod Bethune Council House

A national historic site, the former home of educator Bethune (1875–1955), who founded Bethune-Cookman College in Daytona Beach, Florida, and the National Council of Negro Women, stores and displays artifacts pertaining to African-American women's history. The house museum is decorated with Bethune's original furnishings and photographs. *nps.gov/mamc* 🄰 Map pp. 132–133 ✉ 1318 Vermont Ave., N.W. ☎ 202/673-2402 🄼 Metro: McPherson Square

INSIDER TIP:

L'Enfant's plan of the city, inlaid on the ground in Freedom Plaza, is the ultimate interactive map. In seconds you can get a feel for the city's layout without having to rely on a map, aerial photograph, or satellite image.

—JUAN JOSÉ VALDÉS
National Geographic Maps editorial & research

National Theatre

The sixth theater erected on this site since 1835, the National Theatre can claim to be Washington's oldest continuously operating theater. The sumptuous decor

Around the world in 80-plus steps: The 100-foot-diameter (30.5 m) map at the Navy Memorial plaza

includes dazzling chandeliers. Unlike most modern theaters, the mezzanine and balcony are close to the stage, lending an intimate feel for theatergoers. Lavish Broadway and pre-Broadway shows and other presentations are staged here, many with well-known performers from stage, screen, and concert hall. *thenationaldc.org*  Map pp. 132–133 ✉ 1321 Pennsylvania Ave., N.W. ☎ 202/628-6161 Metro: Federal Triangle, Metro Center

Old Post Office

This castlelike edifice along Pennsylvania Avenue was built in the 1890s as headquarters for the U.S. Post Office. For great views, take the elevator to the 270-foot-high (82 m) observation deck. The Bells of Congress, in the 315-foot (96 m) tower, were donated by England during the U.S. Bicentennial. The building is being transformed into a luxury hotel and is temporarily closed. *nps.gov/opot* Map pp. 132–133 ✉ Pennsylvania Ave. & 12th St., N.W. ☎ 202/606-8691 Metro: Federal Triangle

U.S. Navy Memorial & Naval Heritage Center

Situated directly behind the National Archives (see pp. 142–143), this heritage center contains artifacts and changing exhibits that highlight U.S. naval history.

A small theater screens films on historic maritime figures and events, and offers free noontime lectures. Outside on the plaza, the circular memorial features a 7-foot-tall (2.1 m) bronze statue of "The Lone Sailor" and a correctly oriented granite map of the world. Bronze relief sculptures depicting events in naval history ring the memorial's perimeter. *navymemorial.org* Map pp. 132–133 ✉ 701 Pennsylvania Ave., N.W. ☎ 202/380-0710 Metro: Archives–Navy Memorial

Warner Theatre

A block east of the National Theatre, the Warner Theatre started life in 1924 as a silent-movie palace and vaudeville stage. From the mid-1940s to the late 1960s, it only presented movies. Thereafter it functioned mainly as a rock concert venue until being shut down completely. The Warner Theatre reopened in 1992, after being refurbished with dazzling crystal, red velvet, and gold leaf. The Warner now hosts theater and dance performances as well as entertainers from Eddie Izzard to the Ramsey Lewis trio. In December there are performances of *The Nutcracker* presented by the Washington Ballet. *warnertheatredc .com* Map pp. 132–133 ✉ 13th & E Sts., N.W. ☎ 202/783-4000 Metro: Federal Triangle, Metro Center

Hip and historic: old row houses, shops brimming with hot fashions and furnishings, mule-drawn canal boats, a trendy after-dark scene

Georgetown

If only these worn-smooth Georgetown cobblestones could talk ...

Georgetown

Washington's poshest square mile is a high-octane cocktail of cultural refinement and giddy nightlife. While side streets exhibit elegant federal and Victorian architecture, Wisconsin Avenue and M Street inject excitement with boutiques, bars, and restaurants.

Casually elegant: Relax on a shady sidewalk.

Georgetown began life as a tobacco inspection and shipment port at the confluence of Rock Creek and the Potomac, the highest navigable point on the river, on a 795-acre (322 ha) tract acquired by Scottish immigrant Ninian Beall in 1703. The Maryland Assembly established a town there in the 1750s and named it for

George II. After independence, when the country was planning its federal city, Georgetown had become a thriving trade center, with lordly merchants' houses rising on the hill and artisans' houses and warehouses dotting the riverside. The new city proved a boon to Georgetown's silversmiths, cabinetmakers, and other craftspeople, who did a brisk business fitting the White House and other federal buildings. During the Civil War, Georgetown's significant black community made it an important Underground Railroad stop.

In 1871 the city of Washington annexed Georgetown. By then the little town needed the capital more than the reverse. The advent of the railroad and steam power had greatly diminished the importance of the C & O Canal

NOT TO BE MISSED:

DENT

Q

GEORGETOWN UNIVERSITY

P

O STREET

Healy Bldg.

37TH STREET

36TH STREET

35TH STREET

34TH

N

← To Kreeger Museum

CANAL ROAD

PROSPECT

C & O Canal Towpath

M

CHESAPEAKE AND OHIO CANAL NATIONAL HISTORICAL PARK

Francis Scott Key Memorial

| 0 | 200 meters |
| 0 | 200 yards |

Francis Scott Key Memorial Bridge

29

D.C. VA.

GEORGE WASHINGTON MEMORIAL PKWY.

and thus Georgetown at its eastern end. In the first half of the 20th century, Georgetown lost its cachet and functioned primarily as industrial muscle for Washington, its foundry and mills supplying iron, paper, and coal. During Roosevelt's administration, white-collar workers began moving back; then, in 1950, Congress declared it a national historic district, speeding its restoration and return to fashion.

Rock Creek and the Potomac River form Georgetown's eastern and southern borders; to the west lies Georgetown University and north the hill on which Dumbarton Oaks sits. In these blocks have lived members of such clans as the Washingtons, Lees, and Kennedys. Today diplomats, politicians, journalists, and socialites walk shady brick sidewalks and party in book- and art-filled houses. ∎

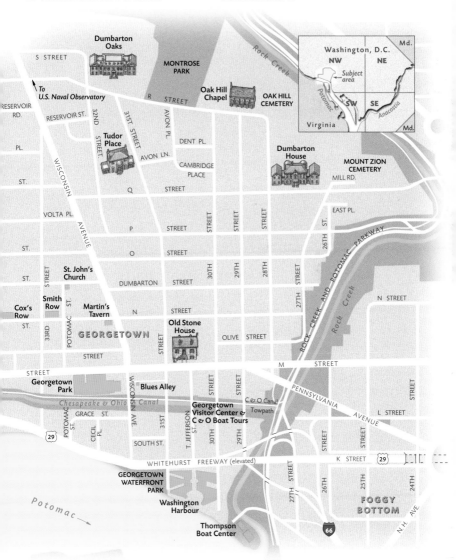

A Brick Sidewalk Tour

With its venerable tree-lined streets and historic architecture, Georgetown was made for the leisurely stroller. You can try seeing the city's oldest neighborhood by car, but traffic moves slowly on the narrow streets, some of which are still cobbled and veined with trolley tracks. Better to leave the car behind and lace up your walking shoes.

The C & O Canal, not your traditional city locale, is a sweet slice of Georgetown.

If you choose to drive, you can find street parking, but it may take a while, especially on the weekends. The network of streets north of M Street is your best bet for parking, though you should pay attention to the signs—most streets are zoned for two-hour parking from 7 a.m. to 9 p.m. (except Sunday). There are parking lots along M Street and below the canal. Metro buses service M Street and Wisconsin Avenue. You can also walk from the Foggy Bottom–GWU Metro station, just over a half mile (0.8 km) to the eastern edge of Georgetown.

If you do start from the Metro, you'll head west on Pennsylvania Avenue. Across the bridge, Pennsylvania feeds into M Street, Georgetown's main avenue for shopping, dining, and partying. Spring and summer evenings,

NOT TO BE MISSED:

Old Stone House • Washington Harbour • Cox's Row

the ten-block stretch from here to the Francis Scott Key Bridge is a steady parade of the chic, the casual, and the grungy. While the shops tend to be upscale, the bars, dance floors, and some restaurants cater to a young crowd, liberally supplied by Georgetown and George Washington Universities. A long-standing favorite restaurant for Sunday brunch, **Seasons ❶** (*2800 Pennsylvania Ave., N.W.,* see Travelwise p. 249), at the Four Seasons Hotel, features traditional and innovative cuisine, including organic dishes.

Continue west on M to the **Old Stone House** ❷ *(3051 M St., N.W., tel 202/895-6070, closed Mon.–Tues.)*, one of the oldest structures in the city. A craftsman named Christopher Layman built the first floor of the three-story house of local fieldstones in 1765, probably as both home and shop. A legend, later disproved, that George Washington had a headquarters here helped preserve the house. In 1953, the National Park Service acquired the property, restored it, and opened it to the public in 1960. The ground floor has a shop with replicas of 18th-century tools and a kitchen with cast-iron stove. On the second floor, built by the next owner, you'll find an oak-paneled dining room, a parlor, and bedrooms.

Cross M Street and head downhill on Thomas Jefferson Street to the eastern terminus of the **C & O Canal** ❸, a muddy-bottomed, shallow waterway, bordered by a towpath, that served as a key shipping link in the 19th century. Originally slated to stretch some 460 miles (740 km) to Pittsburgh and connect with the Ohio River, the Chesapeake and Ohio Canal, begun in 1828, made it only

Along the C & O Canal

A 184.5-mile (297 km) towpath parallels the C & O Canal, and the stretch of the path that runs through Georgetown invites hiking, strolling, or jogging. The **Georgetown Visitor Center** *(1057 Thomas Jefferson St., N.W., tel 202/653-5190)* has a good map. The towpath can be entered below M Street, at Thomas Jefferson Street. Some strollers pack picnic lunches to enjoy along the way. April through October, there are scenic rides on a replica 19th-century canal boat *(nps .gov/choh)*. You can also explore parts of the canal by canoe. Rent equipment at **Fletcher's Boathouse** *(4940 Canal Rd., N.W., tel 202/244-0461)*, about 3 miles (4.8 km) beyond Georgetown.

🗺 See also area map pp. 148–149
➤ M & 29th Sts., N.W. (Metro: Foggy Bottom–GWU)
🕐 2 hours
↔ 2 miles (3.2 km)
➤ St. John's Church

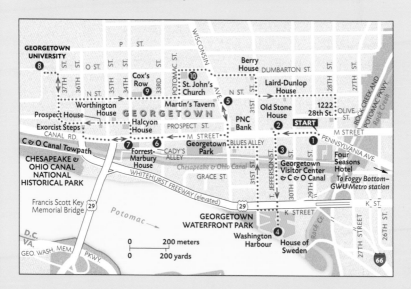

INSIDER TIP:

Washington Harbour is a little bit of a Las Vegas experience with its oversize buildings, luxurious interiors, and restaurants. But instead of gambling, you have the Potomac River.

—KARIN KINNEY
National Geographic Books contributor

185 miles (298 km) up the Potomac to Cumberland, Maryland, where work stopped in 1850. Don't miss the small brick row houses that run along the canal just off Thomas Jefferson Street; they were built after the Civil War as homes for laborers. A few are now Asian takeout restaurants.

Go from the old to the new at the bottom of the hill by crossing K Street under the Whitehurst Freeway; in front of you spreads **Washington Harbour ❹,** a 1980s complex of offices, apartments, shops, and restaurants. A grand fountain in the center becomes a seasonal ice rink. The Harbour offers views of the Potomac, Roosevelt Island, the Kennedy Center, Watergate, and the high-rises of Rosslyn, Virginia, across the river.

The sleek glass box neighboring the Harbour is the **House of Sweden** *(2900 K St., N.W., tours available).* Opened in 2006, it houses Sweden's embassy and business interests.

Next head up 31st Street. On your left you'll pass an alleyway that leads to **Blues Alley** *(1073 Wisconsin Ave., N.W., tel 202/337-4141),* which may look like a dive outside but is actually Washington's swankiest jazz joint. On nights when a big name is in town, you might see 50 people lined up just hoping for no-shows on the reservation list. Definitely arrive early, and expect to pay a hefty amount—well worth it for the intimate setting.

Turn right from the alley onto Wisconsin Avenue and walk up to neighborhood haunt **Martin's Tavern ❺** (see p. 162), then backtrack to M Street. This intersection is the area's busiest; the gold dome on the ornate old Farmers and Mechanics Branch of the PNC Bank serves as a landmark. Turn left heading west on M to the nearly block-long multi-level mall called **Georgetown Park** *(3222 M St., N.W.).*

Step into **Olivia Macaron,** where you can pick up delectable coconut or salted caramel *macarons* for a sweet treat. Erected in 1865, the building sits on a site that also held markets in the 18th century. A little farther down the

---

Shopping & More Shopping in Georgetown

The trendy shops of Georgetown line M Street and Wisconsin Avenue, some tucked into side streets and alcoves. Along with the big name purveyors (think Kate Spade, Puma, Hugo Boss) are independent boutiques with selections that will urge you to splurge. **Hu's Wear** *(2906 M St., N.W., tel 202/342-2020)* carries edgy designer finds handpicked by the owner, while **Sherman Pickey** *(1647 Wisconsin Ave., tel 202/333-4212)* boasts "authentically preppy" merchandise and top-notch service. **Twixt** *(3222 M St., N.W.)* caters to tweens and their parents.

Browse furniture stores—traditional and cutting edge—in Georgetown's design district, Cady's Alley. Shops include **Baker Furniture** *(3330 M St., N.W.),* **Design Within Reach** *(3306 M St., N.W.),* and **Waterworks** *(3314 M St., N.W.).* While there, also visit **Relish** *(3312 Cady's Alley, N.W.)* for perfect-fit jeans.

Appalachian Spring *(1415 Wisconsin Ave., tel 202/337-5780)* offers one-of-a-kind handmade artisanal crafts, from jewelry and spun glass to kaleidoscopes. And stop into **Wines & Spirits** *(3100 M St., N.W.)* to pick up a bottle of fine wine.

Zorro and other revelers make the streets of Georgetown the place to be and be seen on Halloween.

street, you'll come to **Cady's Alley** ❻, the neighborhood's home furnishings hub. Keep going down M Street and just before Key Bridge you'll see the 1788 **Forrest-Marbury House** ❼ (now the Embassy of Ukraine). Here George Washington met with local landowners in 1791 to work out the agreement on the sale of their land to create the new federal city. General Uriah Forrest owned the house then; in 1800–1835 it belonged to William Marbury of the landmark *Marbury* v. *Madison* case, in which the Supreme Court established the doctrine of judicial review.

For a small detour into cinematic history, cross to the north side of M Street and walk west a short distance. Tucked away near a gas station, an eerily familiar 75-step stone stairway stretches upward. Known as the **Exorcist Steps,** the stairs played a prominent role in the 1973 horror classic *The Exorcist.*

Prospect Street has some of Georgetown's most impressive 18th-century houses. For an easier ascent to Prospect, go back east on M and turn left onto 34th Street. At the corner of 34th and Prospect stands the classic Georgian-style **Halcyon House,** built by Benjamin Stoddert, the first secretary of the Navy. A few buildings away is **Worthington House** *(3425 Prospect St., N.W.),* built by prominent lawyer John Thomson Mason. Note the 24-paned windows lining both main floors. Just past 35th Street look for **Prospect House** *(3508 Prospect St., N.W.),* another imposing Georgian, home of a 19th-century shipping merchant. Much of its structure and impressive gardens lie hidden behind a brick wall.

Prospect Street continues past 37th Street, the eastern edge of **Georgetown University** ❽. The Gothic-spired private university is best known for its schools of medicine, law, and foreign service, and its basketball team, the Georgetown Hoyas.

From 37th Street, turn back east on N; across 34th Street is a line of five stately brick town houses known as **Cox's Row** ⑨, built in 1805 by John Cox, Mayor of Georgetown. Down the block, in 1957–1961, Senator John F. Kennedy and his wife, Jacqueline, lived at 3307 N Street, a three-story house with black shutters. On the corner of Potomac and O Streets, Anglican services are still held at **St. John's Church** ⑩, opened in 1804, and designed by William Thornton, first architect of the Capitol.

East of Wisconsin Avenue lie several more blocks of elegant 19th-century houses. Bare brick alternates with stucco facades painted in muted shades. Victorian bay windows and turrets are much in evidence. At the corner of Dumbarton and 31st Streets look for **Berry House,** built in 1810, when the street level was several feet higher. The front door stands unusually far above the street.

Walk one block south to N Street and turn left to see a noteworthy block. On your right is a large brick town house (3038 N St., N.W.), built in 1805 and the longtime home of statesman Averell Harriman and his wife, Pamela. The residence has a lovely arched doorway and odd, shingled dormers.

In a house across the street (3017 N St., N.W.), Jackie Kennedy lived for several months after the assassination of President Kennedy. Almost directly facing it stands the 40-room **Laird-Dunlop House** (3014 N St., N.W.), built in 1799. Robert Todd Lincoln, who was the only son of Abraham and Mary Todd Lincoln to survive into adulthood, lived here from 1918 to 1926. Especially notable is the building's raised fanlight doorway.

If you stroll on to 28th and Olive Streets, you'll come upon one of Georgetown's oldest—and smallest—houses. The tiny wooden cottage at No. 1222 was built sometime before the Revolution, though exactly when is uncertain. A veritable tribute to the past, very little has changed in the building's basic structure.

EXPERIENCE: Find Foodie Hot Spots in Georgetown

Before Adams Morgan and U Street became hip, anyone seeking delectable good times went to Georgetown. Though options have expanded to locations across the city and into the suburbs, Georgetown still reigns supreme as serve-it-up central. If you've a mind to join the fun, be aware that the revelry can be excessive at times, particularly on Halloween. Traffic woes — Key Bridge, the main feeder from Virginia, is a solid jam on weekend evenings—and parking woes don't deter the crowds dining along M Street. Cabbing here makes sense; the fare for two from downtown costs about as much as a movie ticket.

There are food and fun options of all sorts from which to choose. Long-standing favorites include **J. Paul's** (3218 M St., N.W., tel 202/333-3450), with its oyster raw bar; **Clyde's of Georgetown** (3236 M St., N.W., tel 202/333-9180),

featuring vintage decor and afternoon appetizers, and, for pizza, **The Tombs** (1226 36th St., N.W., tel 202/337-6668), near Georgetown University. Located above the Tombs, **1789** (1226 36th St., N.W., tel 202/965-1789) presents elegant formal dinners in a federal-period house decorated with American antiques and Limoges china.

Leopold's Kafe + Konditorei (3315 M St., N.W., tel 202/965-6005) serves its Austrian meals à la carte.

Sushi addicts can find a fix at **Mate** (3101 K St., N.W., tel 202/333-2006), while those with a sweet tooth should visit **Georgetown Cupcake** (3301 M St., N.W., tel 202/333-8448), **Patisserie Poupon** (1645 Wisconsin Ave., N.W., tel 202/342-3248), or, for crepes and coffee, **Café Bonaparte** (1522 Wisconsin Ave., N.W., tel 202/333-8830).

Dumbarton Oaks

An antique Provençal fountain, a miniature Roman amphitheater, and a 16th-century French-style arbor are among the many treasures awaiting you in Dumbarton Oaks's terraced gardens. Spring to fall, the grounds offer an ever changing display that includes early blooming dogwoods, magnolia blossoms, and cherries, peonies and roses, day lilies and chrysanthemums.

In addition to the floral landscape designs at Dumbarton Oaks, a Pebble Garden offers surprise.

Presiding over the gardens is a federal-style house acquired in 1920 by Mildred and Robert Woods Bliss, step siblings and antiquities collectors who married and traveled widely in the Foreign Service. They hired the architectural firm McKim, Mead and White to renovate and enlarge the house for their extensive library and collection of Byzantine and pre-Columbian art. In 1940 they conveyed the property and museum to Harvard University, though they remained actively involved in Dumbarton Oaks until their deaths (Robert in 1962, Mildred in 1969). In 1944 a series of informal conferences held at Dumbarton Oaks laid the foundation for the establishment of the United Nations.

Today the main part of the house functions as Harvard's research institute for Byzantine, pre-Columbian, and garden

Dumbarton Oaks

- △ Map pp. 148–149
- ✉ Garden entrance: 31st & R Sts., N.W.; museum: 32nd St. bet. R & S Sts., N.W.
- ☎ 202/339-6401
- ⏱ Closed Mon., federal holidays, & in inclement weather
- $ Gardens: $$ March–Oct., free in winter
- Ⓜ Metro: Dupont Circle, Foggy Bottom–GWU; Bus: 31–36, Circulator

doaks.org

landscape studies and is not open to the public. Visitors are allowed into the gardens, which have only afternoon hours. The museum, music room, and museum shop are usually open to the public. Check the website for updates.

Visiting

Use the entrance on 32nd Street. Ten-acre (4 ha) formal gardens, designed by landscape architect Beatrix Farrand, spread across a gentle hill and down to a wooded valley. Ornate ironwork and stonework—in the form of gates and balconies, fountains and urns, pillars and stairways—adorn the grounds. Brick paths lined by boxwoods and perennial borders lead from one garden to the

INSIDER TIP:

How is it that fall's yellows, reds, and oranges seem to blaze so bright on (and off) the exquisite trees in Dumbarton Oaks Park?

—SHEILA BUCKMASTER
National Geographic Traveler
magazine editor at large

next, and little trellised bowers offer places to sit and admire the sound of birdsong, scent of flowers, and garden aesthetics.

A self-guided tour brochure, available at the entrance, highlights the gardens and plantings. Inside the gates to the right stands an old katsura tree, its limbs almost touching the

ground. Head up the path to the early 19th-century **Orangery;** a pre–Civil War fig tree climbs its walls. Through here you access the main gardens. Outside, to the right, a huge beech presides over the **Beech Terrace.** Next, steps take you down to the **Rose Garden,** planted with nearly a thousand varieties of roses. Just below are gardens with fountains and a wisteria-draped arbor based on a 16th-century French design.

At the property's edge, a winding walkway skirts the reflecting pool of Lovers' Lane and its small amphitheater. Farther north the garden becomes less formal, with flowering cherry trees, a hillside of golden forsythia, and views of Dumbarton Oaks Park, given by the Blisses to the National Park Service and now part of Rock Creek Park.

Head back uphill to the **Ellipse,** an oval formed by a double ring of hornbeams, pruned to a uniform 16 feet (4.8 m), enclosing a Provençal fountain. Up the steps lies another landscaping masterpiece. The **Pebble Garden** is composed of rounded stones embedded on edge to create a terrace of varying textures; espaliered magnolias and wisteria vines bedeck the walls. Walk on past the pool to the grassy sweep of the **North Vista,** behind the main part of the house.

Filled with natural light, the **museum galleries** display Byzantine and pre-Columbian art objects. The Byzantine collection includes 6th-century ecclesiastical silver and beautiful 14th-century mosaic icons. ■

Dumbarton House

Dumbarton House, originally called Cedar Hill, was built on a hill high above Rock Creek in the first years of the 19th century, when only a few large houses dotted the port of Georgetown. In 1991, the home was meticulously restored and updated with climate and safety features.

Inside the large Dumbarton House, furnishings date primarily from the federal period.

The federal-style brick house's second owner, Charles Carroll, changed its name in 1813 to Belle Vue; he sheltered Dolley Madison here the following year, after she fled the burning White House. In 1915, to make way for the extension of Q Street into Georgetown, the house had to be put on rollers and moved about 100 feet (30.5 m) north.

In 1928, the National Society of the Colonial Dames of America (NSCDA) bought the house, which would become its headquarters, and renamed it Dumbarton House after the Rock of Dumbarton, the tract that once encompassed much of present-day Georgetown. Name aside, the house has absolutely no connection to Dumbarton Oaks (see pp. 155–156), several blocks away.

With great attention to detail, NSCDA restored the house to its early 1800s appearance. The guided 45-minute tour here covers the parlor, dining room, library, breakfast room, and two bedrooms, with such items as a maple sewing work table, silver, ceramics, textiles (including a cloak belonging to Martha Washington's granddaughter), and paintings by artists such as Charles Willson Peale. Under way is a major reinterpretation of the rooms to reflect the home life of its first resident, Joseph Nourse, first register of the United States Treasury. ■

Dumbarton House

- Map pp. 148–149
- 2715 Q St., N.W.
- 202/337-2288
- Closed Mon. & federal holidays
- $
- Metro: Dupont Circle, Foggy Bottom–GWU; Bus: D1–D6

dumbartonhouse.org

Tudor Place Historic House & Garden

Six generations of the Peter family, relatives to George Washington and Robert E. Lee, lived in this handsome neoclassical house. During those years (1805–1983), the country passed through many wars, two of them waged just outside the Peters' door.

Tudor Place

- Map pp. 148–149
- 1644 31st St., N.W.
- 202/965-0400
- House closed Mon.
- $$ (house tour), $ (garden tour)
- Metro: Dupont Circle, Foggy Bottom–GWU; Bus: 31–36, D1–D6, Circulator

tudorplace.org

Martha Custis, daughter of George Washington's stepdaughter, married Thomas Peter, son of Georgetown's first mayor. In 1805 the Peters purchased an 8.5-acre (3.4 ha) city block in Georgetown Heights; to design a home there, they hired William Thornton, architect of the Capitol—the building Martha would watch burn from a window of the house in 1814. The Peters' daughter Britannia inherited Tudor Place in 1854. A Southern sympathizer during the Civil War, she allowed Union officers to board at the house to prevent its becoming a hospital. In 1984 the house was transferred to the Tudor Place Foundation.

The one-hour guided house tour of Tudor Place begins with a look at Thornton's design. On the south lawn, a domed "temple" portico projects from the two-story stuccoed main building, while one-story hyphens connect the two wings, lending symmetry. The curving portico creates a convex wall of windows, which can be lifted to allow breezes to circulate. All the furniture, silver, porcelain, and decorative objects are original, some pieces acquired from an auction at Mount Vernon in the early 19th century. The belongings reflect 180 years of family continuity. The restored Pierce-Arrow automobile out in the garage, for example, was maintained by Armistead Peter III from 1919 until his death in 1983.

The 5.5 acres (1.6 ha) of gardens include a sweeping south lawn, woodlands, and a formal federal-style garden on the house's north side. Among highlights are trees and roses planted in the early 19th century, and an old-fashioned "flower knot" pattern of English boxwoods and pathways. ■

The Tudor Place dining room dazzles with fine silver and china.

Oak Hill Cemetery

Occupying some of the city's finest real estate, this 1849 cemetery rambles over a hill above Rock Creek Park. William Wilson Corcoran, founder of the Corcoran Gallery, bought 15 acres (6 ha) from George Corbin Washington, a great-nephew of the first President, who gave the parcel to the congressionally established cemetery company. James Renwick, architect of the Smithsonian Castle, designed the iron entrance gates and the small English Gothic–style chapel.

A fog-edged day sets the mood for a visit to Georgetown's Oak Hill Cemetery.

At the attractive brick and sandstone gatehouse, you can get a map showing the locations of 68 graves and mausoleums, including those of W. W. Corcoran, John Marbury, Edwin Stanton (Lincoln's secretary of war), Dean Acheson (Truman's secretary of state), and members of the Peter family from nearby Tudor Place (see page opposite). Also buried at Oak Hill is Philip Graham, publisher of the *Washington Post,* as is his widow Katharine, his successor at the *Post* until her death in 2001.

A murky overcast day makes a good time for wandering through this crowded village of the dead, with its elaborate Victorian monuments and obelisks. Winding paths circle knolls that offer views of adjoining Montrose Park, Rock Creek, and the parkway. Springtime sees a rush of bright flowers.

Hiding behind tall trees and high walls, the property at the corner of 28th and R Streets is another Georgetown mansion with a significant past: Evermay was built in the 1790s by Scotsman Samuel Davidson with funds acquired from selling some of his extensive property to the new federal city. Family members lie buried in Oak Hill. ∎

Oak Hill Cemetery

🅰 Map pp. 148–149

✉ 3001 R St., N.W.

☎ 202/337-2835

🕐 Closed funerals, holidays, & in inclement weather

🚇 Metro: Dupont Circle, Foggy Bottom–GWU; Bus: D1–D6

oakhillcemetery dc.org

Famous Denizens of Georgetown

By day, the power of government is exercised in places clustered around Washington's Mall and at both ends of Pennsylvania Avenue. But through the decades, Georgetown has been the residence of choice for political leaders, media heavies, diplomats, legal minds, writers, and society doyennes. In elegant 19th-century houses, a bill that seemed doomed by day may be quietly revived at a dinner party where wine and talk are equally savored.

Washington Post owner Katharine Graham called this house home from 1947 until her death in 2001.

Even Hollywood celebrities have found their way to Georgetown, though at times reluctantly. Elizabeth Taylor, married briefly to Virginia Senator John Warner, has said she thought the couple would live on his hunt country estate in Virginia. Instead, she found herself living in Warner's Georgetown house at 3240 S Street.

As a bachelor, Senator John F. Kennedy lived in a Victorian town house at 1528 31st Street. In fact, John and Jackie first met at a Georgetown dinner party in 1951. He later claimed that he made up his mind at that party that she was "the one," though they dated only sporadically over the next year. He finally proposed, and a year later, he and his bride moved to 3271 P Street. President-elect Kennedy purchased the three-story brick town house at 3307 N Street in 1957, while Jackie was in the hospital giving birth to their first child, Caroline. Tastefully austere, the 1811 house sits on an especially handsome street.

After her husband's death, Jackie Kennedy and her children moved temporarily to 3038 N Street, at the invitation of statesman W. Averell Harriman. (His widow, Pamela, a celebrated hostess and Democratic party activist, later became President Clinton's Ambassador to France.) The former First Lady soon bought the house across the street at 3017 N Street, but departed for New York after only a few months to escape the busloads of gawkers.

At 3014 N stands another grand federal-style mansion with a presidential link. Built in 1799, it was the 40-room home of Robert Todd Lincoln, the 16th President's oldest son, a railroad lawyer who served as secretary of war and minister to Great Britain.

The top ranks of government have always been well represented in Georgetown. Dean Acheson, President Truman's secretary of state, lived in the Georgian town house at 2805 P Street. Here Acheson hosted a farewell luncheon for the President on his last day in office. A four-story town house at 3018 Dumbarton Street is the one-time home of Supreme Court Justice Felix Frankfurter. Later Henry Kissinger, secretary of state under Presidents Nixon and Ford, briefly rented it.

Washington Post owner Katharine Graham, once called "the most powerful woman in America," lived in the mansion at 2920 R Street. Set well back from the street, the home is approached by a semicircular gravel drive—a real Georgetown luxury.

Writers, too, have found Georgetown congenial. In 1922, Sinclair Lewis moved to D.C. from his Minnesota hometown, calling it the perfect place to write, "with neither the country nor lake tempting one out to play,

Senator John F. Kennedy and his wife, Jackie, lived briefly at 3321 Dent Place, N.W., in 1954.

as in Minnesota, nor the noise and phone calls of New York." As soon as he made his fortune with *Main Street,* which later won him the Nobel Prize in literature, he moved to a stately house at 3028 Q Street.

EXPERIENCE: Going Out to Brunch Around Town

Leisurely weekend brunch is a local institution, so it's a good idea to reserve ahead. In Georgetown, neighborhood blue bloods and Europeans gravitate to the eclectic **Peacock Café** *(3251 Prospect St., N.W., tel 202/625-2740).* High on the list of favorites is the cozy **Tabard Inn** *(1739 N St., N.W., tel 202/331-8528)* on a pretty street in the heart of Dupont Circle. It's noted for exotic takes on regional U.S. foods. A brunch specialty: homemade donuts. In the West End area, jazz and a dazzling buffet in the Colonnade Room draw many to holiday brunches at the **Fairmont Hotel** *(2401 M St., N.W., tel*

202/457-5020). Recently opened **Ted's Bulletin** *(1818 14th St., N.W., tel 202/265-8337)* on trendy 14th Street has won over Washingtonians with classic American fare with a twist, such as homemade Pop-Tarts and grown-up milkshakes. Another downtown option is **Brasserie Beck** *(1101 K St., N.W., tel 202/408-1717).* **Perry's** *(tel 1811 Columbia Rd., N.W., tel 202/234-6218),* in bohemian Adams Morgan, has delighted diners for 25 years with a fusion of Asian and cutting-edge American cuisine. More reasons to go: killer views from the rooftop deck and drag queen entertainment on Sunday morning.

More Places to Visit in Georgetown

The Kreeger Museum

Designed by Philip Johnson and Richard Foster and completed in 1967, the modernist travertine house of late philanthropist David Lloyd Kreeger and his wife, Carmen, opened in 1994 as an art museum showcasing the Kreegers' collection of 19th- and 20th-century paintings and sculptures. A chairman of Geico insurance company, Kreeger was famous for his contributions to the city's cultural life, at various times serving as president of the National Symphony, the Washington Opera, and the Corcoran Gallery of Art.

The art collection, which the Kreegers began acquiring in 1959, includes more than 180 works by artists such as Monet, Cézanne, van Gogh, Rodin, Picasso, Miró, Munch, Kandinsky, and Chagall; among Washington artists represented are Gene Davis, Sam Gilliam, and Thomas Downing. Also on display are pieces of traditional African and Asian art. The building's spectacular **Great Hall,** with its 25-foot-high (7.6 m) domed ceiling, was often the scene of concerts; an avid amateur violinist, Kreeger played his Stradivarius with such greats as

INSIDER TIP:

There's no Metro station in Georgetown, but the Circulator bus [dccirculator.com] makes several stops here.

—LUBA VANGELOVA
National Geographic writer

Pablo Casals, Isaac Stern, and Pinchas Zukerman. *kreegermuseum.org* ⓜ Map pp. 148–149 ✉ 2401 Foxhall Rd., N.W., 1.5 miles (2.4 km) NW of Georgetown ☎ 202/338-3552 🕐 Closed Sun.–Mon. & Aug.; by appointment tours Tues.–Thurs.; open visits Fri.–Sat. 💲 $$

Martin's Tavern

Opened by William G. Martin, a Georgetown University sports star who also played professional baseball in the early part of the 20th century, Martin's Tavern has been operating at the southwest corner of N Street and Wisconsin Avenue, N.W., since 1933. Four generations of Martins have managed the restaurant, and many of the staff have been here for years. Stop in for a draft or a meal and imbibe this Georgetown tradition. Wood floors, dark paneling, and a friendly bar create the ambience of a European pub. Among menu offerings are crab cakes, grilled lamb chops, lobster risotto, and daily specials such as meatloaf and corned beef with cabbage. Souvenir cards list some of the politicos and celebrities that have visited or been regulars, including former Secretary of State Madeleine Albright, Elizabeth Taylor, and the Kennedys. Martin's serves lunch and dinner Monday through Friday and brunch on weekends at moderate prices. *martinstavern.com* ⓜ Map pp. 148–149 ✉ 1264 Wisconsin Ave., N.W. ☎ 202/333-7370 🚇 Metro: Foggy Bottom–GWU or Rosslyn, then bus

Mount Zion Cemetery

When Mount Zion Methodist Episcopal Church fathers realized in 1879 that they needed a place to bury members, they leased a parcel of land on the edge of Dumbarton Cemetery, where generations of slaves and freed blacks had been buried. The resulting Mount Zion Cemetery, with its crumbling gravestones, is D.C.'s oldest African-American burial ground. The last burial took place in the 1950s. In 1975 it was designated a national historic landmark. At the back is a brick vault where slaves escaping to the North via the Underground Railroad are said to have hidden. ⓜ Map pp. 148–149 ✉ Q St. bet. 27th St., N.W., & Buffalo Bridge ☎ 202/234-0148 🚇 Foggy Bottom–GWU or Dupont Circle, then bus

An enjoyable melting pot of cultures, cuisines, embassies, and museums beyond hyperkinetic downtown D.C.

Dupont Circle & Beyond

The figures on Dupont Circle's fountain symbolize the wind, sea, and stars.

Dupont Circle & Beyond

At the intersection of three major thoroughfares, the Dupont Circle area is a true Washington gathering place. The energy of the neighborhoods, replete with row houses, cafés, bookstores, restaurants, and galleries spills out to the streets.

Well-situated Dupont Circle marks a key interface between business and residential Washington. The circle, centered on a marble fountain, is in constant motion, with pedestrians passing through and traffic circling around. Yet it is also a place for casual picnics, jackets-off meetings, people-watching, and general loafing. Bicycle messengers form little impromptu gatherings, chess players study their next moves, joggers pound through. In 15 minutes the scene has changed, and a new series of small dramas has begun to unfold.

Starting in the 1870s, the area, then called Pacific Circle, began developing into the most elite neighborhood in Washington. New millionaires with fortunes from mining, steel, railroads, and shipping started putting up ornate beaux arts mansions and attending receptions and musicals in one another's houses, every hostess seemingly intent on outdoing her neighbors. A newspaper reporter in the 1880s wrote that going to lavish parties at Senator William M. Stewart's "Castle" (torn down in 1901) made him feel like Marco Polo at the court of Kublai Khan. This belle epoque lasted only until the 1930s, when the stock market crash and Depression forced many of the wealthy to scale back.

Some mansions were razed, though many were sold to private clubs, organizations, and embassies; surrounding row houses became boarding establishments and apartments. In the 1960s, the area was a haven for counterculturalists, and the circle became a focal point for marches and rallies. Development threatened many of the area's old "palaces" in the 1970s, but the efforts of preservation groups to save the neighborhood resulted in its designation as a historic district. Over the ensuing years Dupont Circle became the core of Washington's gay community. Today the bars, restaurants, shops, and museums attract a stimulating heterogeny of intellectuals, café-society sorts, and experimentalists of all stripes.

A residential zone of about ten blocks lies between the Dupont Circle neighborhood and the Latino enclave to the north, Adams Morgan, a magnet for immigrants, artists, and young professionals. Running eastward from Adams Morgan into the Shaw neighborhood is the U Street corridor, where the black community was drawn beginning in the 1880s. This area possesses a rich legacy of music and culture—Pearl Bailey, Duke Ellington, and other greats once performed at its various theaters and clubs. Deteriorated after the 1968 riots, U Street has in recent years made a compelling comeback, with restored theaters and new clubs, restaurants, and shops. ■

Washington, D.C.

NW   NE

Subject area

SW   SE

Virginia   Md.   Anacostia

Md.

IRVING STREET

HOBART STREET

COLUMBIA   RD.

HARVARD   ST.

GIRARD   ST.

FAIRMONT   ST.

MOUNT PLEASANT

ADAMS MILL RD.

ONTARIO PLACE

LANIER   PLACE

COLUMBIA ROAD

ROAD

FULLER   ST.

MOZART PL.

15TH   STREET

Mexican Cultural Institute

14TH   STREET

13TH   STREET

CALVERT ST.

EUCLID   ST.

CLIFTON   ST.

Duke Ellington Memorial Bridge

Rock Cr.

CONNECTICUT

BILTMORE   ST.

District of Columbia Arts Center

MINTWOOD PLACE

18TH STREET

CHAMPLAIN   ST.

ONTARIO   ROAD

17TH ST.

KALORAMA   ROAD

CRESCENT PL.

16TH   STREET

18th Street

MERIDIAN HILL PARK

BELMONT   ST.

FLORIDA   AVE.

BELMONT PL.

20TH   STREET

19TH   STREET

BELMONT ROAD

ASHMEAD PLACE

ROAD

Meridian International Center

W   ST.

ADAMS MORGAN

WYOMING AVE.

FLORIDA   AVENUE

V   ST.

V   STREET

Howard University & Mary Church Terrell House

HARRISON PLAYGROUND

KALORAMA   AVE.

WYOMING   AVENUE

COLUMBIA ROAD

CALIFORNIA   ST.

U   STREET

SHAW

Ben's Chili Bowl

Lincoln Theatre

KALORAMA

CALIFORNIA   ST.

VERNON ST.

U   STREET

African American Civil War Memorial

23RD   ST.

LEROY PL.

T   STREET

WILLARD   STREET

T   STREET

BANCROFT   PLACE

AVENUE

SWANN   ST.

S   STREET

Whitelaw Hotel

S   STREET

NEW HAMPSHIRE   AVENUE

S   STREET

Thurgood Marshall Center

DECATUR   PLACE

19TH   STREET

18TH   STREET

RIGGS   PLACE

R   STREET

15TH   STREET

14TH   STREET

13TH   STREET

MERIDIAN CIRCLE

R   STREET

FLORIDA

Cosmos Club

CORCORAN   STREET

Scottish Rite Headquarters

Anderson House

The Phillips Collection

MASSACHUSETTS   AVENUE

Dupont Circle

Q   ST.

Q   STREET

Q   ST.

CHURCH ST.

16TH   ST.

CHURCH   ST.

Rock Creek

23RD   ST.

22ND   STREET

P   STREET

DUPONT CIRCLE

Patterson Mansion

Wadsworth House

P   STREET

P   STREET

LOGAN CIRCLE PARK

21ST   ST.

O   STREET

Dupont Circle

MASSACHUSETTS   AVENUE

CONN. AVE.

O   STREET

VERMONT AVENUE

Heurich House Museum

N   STREET

RHODE ISLAND   AVE.

N   STREET

M   STREET

17TH   ST.

M   STREET

SCOTT CIRCLE

M   STREET

THOMAS CIRCLE

MASS. AVE.

0   200 meters

0   200 yards

L   STREET

17TH   ST.

To Metropolitan Club

L   STREET

The Phillips Collection

Visit the well-located Phillips, near Dupont Circle, and you'll see why it's the favorite museum of many Washingtonians and regarded as one of the best small museums in the world. It has an outstanding collection of works by masters of Impressionism and American and European modern art and carries out a stellar program of cultural and educational activities.

Renoir's "The Luncheon of the Boating Party" (1880–1881) is a highlight of the Phillips Collection.

Begun in the 1920s by founder Duncan Phillips (1886–1966), the Phillips Collection was the first modern art museum in the United States. Its permanent holdings include more than 3,000 carefully chosen pieces of art from the late 19th century to the present.

One of the most charming things about The Phillips Collection is the feeling you get of touring a private home as you walk around the museum, which is still located in Phillips's 1897 Georgian Revival brownstone and has been expanded by compatibly scaled additions. The house gives off a comfortable, informal aura, and that effect is exactly what Phillips had in mind when, in a memorial to his recently deceased brother (James Laughlin Phillips) and father (Maj. D. Clinch Phillips), he opened up two rooms of his home in 1921 so that other art lovers could enjoy the works he

The Phillips Collection

🅐 Map p. 165
✉ 1600 21st St., N.W. (corner of 21st & Q Sts., N.W.)
☎ 202/387-2151
🕐 Closed Mon. & federal holidays
💲 Admission to permanent collection included in fee for special exhibits ($$$) but by donation on weekdays
Ⓜ Metro: Dupont Circle; Bus: D1–D6, N2–N6, L1

phillipscollection.org

INSIDER TIP:

When I need a pick-me-up, I park myself in front of "The Luncheon of the Boating Party" at the Phillips and pretend I'm the girl with the dog.

—MELINA GEROSA BELLOWS
National Geographic, Chief Education Officer

and his brother had collected. After Phillips—himself an heir to the Jones and Laughlin steel fortune—married artist Marjorie Acker that same year, the couple began assembling an outstanding collection of Impressionist, Post-impressionist, and Cubist art.

In 1930, Phillips and his family moved to a new home on Foxhall Road and opened up their entire former home to the expanding collection. A new wing was added in 1960, and in the late 1980s it was renovated again. Phillips's son, Laughlin, a founder

of *Washingtonian* magazine, helped guide the growth of the museum through the renovations of the 1980s. In 2006, the museum completed a major expansion that added galleries and other amenities to better serve visitors, students, and scholars. Two-thirds of the new space is belowground, thereby preserving the character of the neighborhood.

The museum's best known piece is Pierre-Auguste Renoir's dazzling work of impressionism, "The Luncheon of the Boating Party," which features a mix of Renoir's friends.

The permanent collection also includes works by Paul Cézanne, Edgar Degas, Paul Klee, Henri Matisse, Claude Monet, Pablo Picasso, Maurice Prendergast, John La Farge, Vincent van Gogh, Jacob Lawrence, Richard Diebenkorn, Elizabeth Murray, and Sean Scully.

A strong patron of emerging artists, Phillips collected works of many artists who had not yet become widely recognized, including Georgia O'Keeffe,

EXPERIENCE: Pursuing Art for Sale

If the Phillips stirs your desire for an original painting of your own, Dupont Circle, with more than two dozen galleries, is the place to shop. In recent years one gallery offered a Toulouse-Lautrec lithograph for $70,000, a Picasso painting for a mere $16,000, and a piece by Miró for less than $5,000. Stop in **Burton Marinkovich Fine Art** *(1506 21st St., N.W.)*, for example, and you can purchase etchings and lithographs by the likes of Frankenthaler, Hockney, Motherwell, and

Diebenkorn. Or check out **Kathleen Ewing Gallery** *(3615 Ordway St., N.W., 2nd fl.)* for vintage and contemporary photography as well as paintings and drawings. Some of the galleries specialize in African art, Inuit sculpture, and English and American crafts. To find your way around, pick up a free gallery guide, available in any of the galleries. A consortium of 25 galleries in the area holds opening receptions on the first Friday most months from 5 to 7:30 p.m.

Urban Playground—Dupont Circle Happenings

Named in honor of Rear Admiral Samuel Francis du Pont, a Civil War naval hero, Dupont Circle is a neighborhood that fans out from a beloved little park of the same name. The circle itself sits where three major avenues intersect, a calm amid the city's fast pace. It's a popular spot for an alfresco lunch, chess games, and a fine farmers market.

Land that served as a brickyard and slaughterhouse after the Civil War is now a magnet for relaxation, fun, and the occasional protest rally. The National Park Service maintains the Dupont Circle park with its benches, grass, and fountain.

A mix of nightclubs and restaurants, embassies and office buildings, museums and historic row houses, shops and cafés gives the area a lively diversity that's reflected in the crowds that gravitate here. You'll find people of all ages and nationalities picnicking in the park, walking their dogs, or just hanging out. This area is also the center of the city's gay and lesbian community. The **Dupont Circle High Heel race,** an annual event since 1985, is the 9 p.m. climax of a drag queen parade along 17th Street, N.W. It takes place on the Tuesday before Halloween.

It's Your Move at Dupont Circle

After ten concrete chess tables were installed in Dupont Circle in 1968, players of every skill level and from all walks of life began coming here to challenge one other. Over the years, a sort of Chess University sprung up, with a number of skilled players giving lessons (the local legend is Tom Murphy). Even if you've just stopped by to observe, you may find yourself expected to pay a couple of bucks; some of the regulars are also experts at hustling. Checkers, anyone?

Market Central

On Sunday mornings check out the popular Dupont Circle **farmers market,** in a parking lot at Massachusetts Avenue and 20th Street, N.W. Operating year-round, rain or shine, it's been named one of the best of its kind in the country by the *Wall Street Journal,* the *Financial Times of London,* and others. During the peak season, more than 40 vendors sell a variety of things fresh, from bread to flowers, pies to pasta, as well as herbal products and artisan soap.

A Magnet for All Sorts of Occasions

When the city got hit with crippling back-to-back blizzards in February 2010—an event dubbed **Snowmageddon**—more than 2,000 bundled-up people converged at the circle for a massive snowball fight organized by a pair of neighborhood 30-something friends. "A whole bunch of people had a whole lot of fun," the *Washington Post* reported.

A few months later folks gathered at Dupont Circle for a **Green Rush** team scavenger hunt to celebrate the 40th anniversary of Earth Day. Speakers, entertainment, and exhibitors turned the circle into a green-for-a-day environment.

During the 2014 World Cup, giant television screens set up in the park drew hordes of soccer fans to outdoor viewing and cheering of the U.S.A. vs. Germany game.

Look for events, including musical performances, online *(washingtondc.com/calendar /washington-dc/dupont-circle).*

Arthur Dove, John Marin, and Milton Avery. The **Rothko Room,** opened in 1960, was designed in accordance with both Mark Rothko's and Phillips's aesthetic preferences and represents a rare bond between artist and patron.

Phillips felt that artists were strongly influenced by their predecessors, and he sought to illustrate that in the museum's collection. A key link between Impressionism and expressionism, he believed, was Pierre Bonnard, and today the museum has one of the largest collections of works by this artist. Phillips also acquired pieces by such 18th-century masters as El Greco, Francisco Goya, and Jean-Baptiste-Simeon Chardin to show how they affected later painters of modern art.

In 2006, the museum launched the Phillips Collection Center for the Study of Modern Art, which brings together scholars from across academic fields to engage in discussion, research, and publishing of modern art. Intersections is a series of thought-provoking contemporary art projects that explore the intersections between old and new traditions.

Visiting

Some of the museum's galleries offer special exhibitions that change regularly, but selections from the permanent collection are always on display. On the first floor, take time to visit the **Music Room,** a perennial favorite, with its dark oak paneling, decorative ceiling, and carved stone and wood mantelpiece. Since 1941, Sunday afternoon concerts

Several large examples of post-1950s art hang in graceful, spare fashion at the Phillips Collection.

(Oct.–May, $$$$) here have been a Washington favorite.

A café and museum shop are located on the main level near the entrance. Behind the café is an **outdoor courtyard,** which features a sculpture by Barbara Hepworth and a specially commissioned work by Ellsworth Kelly. The museum has extended hours on Thursday evenings, and on the first Thursday of the month it hosts Phillips After 5, a lively mix of art, music, and other entertainment. ■

A Walk Through Embassy Row & Kalorama

This approximately 1-mile (1.6 km) stroll offers an impressive glimpse of early 20th-century Washington's affluence and its evolution. Many of the area's grand residences of the wealthy were sold to foreign delegations—for embassies—after the Great Depression.

The Indonesian Embassy boasts 60 rooms behind its elegant beaux arts facade.

The triangle formed by Massachusetts and Connecticut Avenues and Rock Creek holds more than 50 embassies (about one-third of the city's total) plus many other architectural treasures that reflect the glamour of the early 1900s, when this was a fashionable neighborhood for Washington tycoons.

On the northeast corner of 18th Street and Massachusetts Avenue stands the **Andrew Mellon Building ❶**, a beaux arts palace originally built in 1915 as the McCormick apartment building. Long the headquarters of the National Trust for Historic Preservation (now located in the Watergate complex), it will soon become the new home of the American Enterprise Institute. The building's first floor contained two apartments, while five floors above each

---

NOT TO BE MISSED:

Andrew Mellon Building • Heurich House Museum • Islamic Center

---

held an 11,000-square-foot (1,020 sq m) apartment with six bedrooms and 14.5-foot (4.4 m) ceilings. The most famous tenant, Andrew W. Mellon, founder of the National Gallery of Art and a U.S. secretary of the treasury, lived on the top floor from 1921 to 1937. In 1936, he paid $21 million for paintings and sculptures owned by Sir Joseph Duveen, an art dealer leasing the apartment below; at the time, it was the largest art transaction on record.

Now head west toward Dupont Circle, where you can see examples of turn-of-the-20th-century mansions that never became embassies. Housing the Sulgrave Club *(private)*, a sorority of socially prominent Washington ladies, the circa 1900 **Wadsworth House** *(1801 Massachusetts Ave., N.W., sulgraveclub .org)* was the winter residence of landowners Herbert and Martha Wadsworth of upstate New York. It shows how a large building could be designed to fit a triangular lot on the circle. Taking a different approach to the same problem, the Wadsworth's neighbor to the north, the ornate **Patterson Mansion,** fits into its wedge at 15 Dupont Circle with symmetrical wings and a concave front. Formerly a women's social club, the 1903 house was designed by Stanford White for Robert W. Patterson, publisher of the *Chicago Tribune.*

In **Dupont Circle ②** (see p. 168) you can see a striking example of how L'Enfant's city plan works, with grand avenues vectoring out from the central green. In the middle of the

circle is a marble fountain designed in 1921 by Daniel Chester French, who is also known for the giant statue of Lincoln in the Lincoln Memorial. Spilling into a large pool, an upper basin is supported by a central column that is surrounded by three allegorical figures representing the sea, wind, and stars. A block southwest at 1307 New Hampshire Avenue, the **Heurich House Museum ③** (see p. 178) is one of the country's best examples of an intact late Victorian home.

Now head north 1.5 blocks to the **Blaine Mansion** at 2000 Massachusetts Avenue. This brick Victorian mansion was built in 1881 for presidential candidate James Blaine, who lost in 1884 to Grover Cleveland. The curving sweep

> ⓐ See also area map p. 165
> ► Andrew Mellon Building
> 🕐 3–4 hours
> ↔ 1 mile (1.6 km)
> ► The Phillips Collection

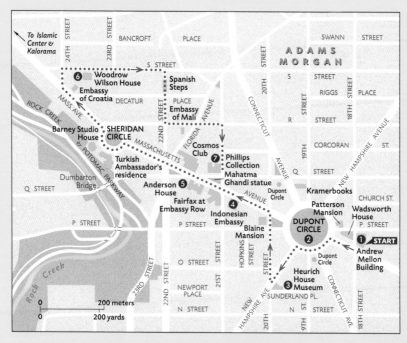

of the **Indonesian Embassy** ④ (2020 *Massachusetts Ave., N.W., embassyofindonesia .org*) has marble columns, arched windows, and a red-tile mansard roof. It was built at the turn of the 20th century by Irishman Tom Walsh, who struck gold in a Colorado mine. He moved to Washington, built his dream house, and became part of the new moneyed class. His daughter, prominent

INSIDER TIP:

Many embassies regularly host cultural open houses and international concerts. Check *washington.org* for information on upcoming events.

—KAREN CARMICHAEL
National Geographic writer

hostess Evalyn Walsh McLean, was the last private owner of the Hope Diamond (now on display in the National Museum of Natural History; see p. 95); in 1951 she sold the mansion to the Republic of Indonesia.

At 2100 Massachusetts Avenue, the building housing the **Fairfax at Embassy Row,** (see Travelwise p. 251), exudes the flair of a European-style hotel. Al Gore lived here when his father was a U. S. senator. The double-winged mansion at 2118 Massachusetts Avenue is the **Anderson House** ⑤ (see p. 178), headquarters of the Society of the Cincinnati. At 2121 Massachusetts Avenue stands the exclusive **Cosmos Club** (*private, cosmosclub.org*), completed in 1902 as the home of Richard Townsend, president of the Erie & Pittsburgh Railroad. The fabulous limestone mansion was sold in 1950 to the club.

A number of embassies edge **Sheridan Circle,** named for Union general Philip H. Sheridan; the 1908 equestrian bronze in the center is by Gutzon Borglum, sculptor of Mount Rushmore. Among the impressive buildings nearby is the **Turkish Ambassador's residence**

(*1606 23rd St., N.W., turkishembassy.org*), built in the 1910s for industrialist Edward Everett. A block south, the 1914 **Dumbarton Bridge—** often called the Buffalo Bridge for its bronze bison—carries Q Street over Rock Creek into Georgetown.

Back on Massachusetts is the **Barney Studio House** (*No. 2306*). The one-time home of philanthropist and socialite Alice Pike Barney, this Spanish mission–style building completed in 1902 was the first house built on the circle. It now houses the **Latvian Embassy.** At the corner of 24th Street you'll see the **Embassy of Croatia** (*2343 Massachusetts Ave., N.W., us.mfa.hr*). In front of the embassy is a large bronze statue of St. Jerome the Priest, sculpted by Croatian artist Ivan Meštrovi. Several blocks farther is the **Islamic Center** (*2551 Massachusetts Ave., N.W., tel 202/332-8343, theislamic center.com*), a mosque richly embellished with tilework, arches, and pillars. In the carpeted sanctuary, shoes and shorts are not allowed and women must cover their heads. The network of streets to the east is the prestigious Kalorama neighborhood, with several embassies and handsome apartment buildings.

Turn up 24th Street, then go east on S Street. Compared to many area houses, the **Woodrow Wilson House** ⑥ (*2340 S St., N.W., tel 202/387-4062, closed Mon., $$*), designed in 1915 by Waddy B. Wood, has a modest appearance. The President spent the last three years of his life in this Georgian Revival brick town house after leaving the White House in 1921; his wife stayed until her death in 1961.

Continue along S Street to 22nd Street and turn right. Washington's version of Rome's Spanish Steps offers a shortcut to **Decatur Place,** a peaceful spot to take a break. Keep heading south on 22nd Street, N.W., and turn right on R Street to the **Embassy of Mali** (*No. 2130, maliembassy.us*), where Franklin Delano Roosevelt once lived. One block away, turn right on 21st Street to end your tour at the **Phillips Collection** ⑦ (see pp. 166–169), one of Washington's most cherished museums.

Adams Morgan

A culturally diverse enclave, Adams Morgan became in the 1980s and '90s the top apartment-and-nightlife nexus for artists and hip young professionals alike. With its international restaurants, funky shops, and rocking nightclubs, the neighborhood sprang to life with a personality all its own, a bastion of bohemian flair in the center of staid Washington. Never mind that this popularity meant there was no longer any place to park—especially on weekend evenings.

The name itself alludes to the neighborhood's melting pot mix: By combining the names of two schools—the mostly white Adams School and the predominantly black Morgan School—local citizens coined the term Adams Morgan in the 1950s for an area that had been part of four neighborhoods. In that same decade, the Spanish-speaking population swelled as an influx of students from Latin America and Mexican professionals added to the existing community of embassy workers.

The early 1960s saw an increase in Cuban immigration, followed by large numbers from South and Central America through the next few decades. The ethnic influence here still tends toward Latin—Spanish is heard on the streets as often as English—but in the smorgasbord of restaurants and shops, you'll find many other cultures, including Ethiopian, Chinese, Thai, Indian, and Vietnamese.

Local Peruvians celebrate Our Lord of Miracles Day in Adams Morgan, a traditionally Hispanic neighborhood.

The heart of Adams Morgan is the intersection of **Columbia Road** and **18th Street.** On the northeast corner a kiosk provides lists of upcoming cultural events. At the intersection's southwest corner is a plaza where vendors set up shop on weekends and sell fresh produce and breads. Most of the area's action—eating, drinking, and dancing—takes place south of the intersection on 18th Street between Columbia Road and Florida Avenue, and along a little branch west on Columbia Road to Belmont Road. That's pretty much it. Part of the neighborhood's appeal is its small size. Although

Adams Morgan

🅰 Map p. 165

✉ Within Columbia Rd., 16th St., & Florida Ave., N.W.

Ⓜ Metro: Dupont Circle (1.5 miles/ 2.4 km S) or Woodley Park– Zoo/Adams Morgan (0.75 mile/1.2 km NW); Bus: 42, 90–92, 96, L2, Circulator

the few attractions here are worth seeing, they do not draw crowds.

Visiting

The three-story, brightly painted brick buildings lining the blocks of 18th Street south of the Columbia Road–18th Street intersection hold most of the ethnic restaurants, bohemian bars, and boutiques. On sultry summer evenings, the sidewalks buzz with people strolling, walking dogs, or

18th St., N.W., tel 202/667-5370).

The **District of Columbia Arts Center** (2438 18th St., N.W., tel 202/462-7833, open afternoons, closed Mon.–Tues.), features the work of emerging artists and holds live performances at night.

Columbia Road on both sides of 18th also has several good restaurants—including **Perry's** (1811 Columbia Rd., N.W., tel 202/234-6218), the place to be and be seen; its rooftop dining

Shoppers examine local wares at a street fair on 18th Street—the heart of Adams Morgan.

sipping and noshing at sidewalk cafés and bars.

Ethnic eateries abound, with exotic cuisine just about routine hereabouts. For some down-home fare, including burgers, grilled cheese, and pulled pork served up with live music seven nights a week, head over to **Madam's Organ Restaurant & Bar** (2461

(great sushi) is one of the city's most pleasant experiences. Along Columbia Road you'll also find Latino grocery stores, outdoor jewelry stands, and vintage clothing and sundries shops.

Daytime Adams Morgan offers different sights to see. For grand interiors, walk down **16th Street.** Just below Columbia Road, the

EXPERIENCE: Sample International Cuisines

Do you prefer Indian or Ethiopian? Thai or Caribbean? Take your pick in the eclectic neighborhood of Adams Morgan, where restaurants specialize in dishes from many regions of the world.

Washington has one of the largest concentrations of Ethiopian restaurants outside Addis Ababa, and **Meskerem** *(2434 18th St., N.W., tel 202/462-4100)* provides a good introduction. The food is served on a communal platter; you pinch off pieces of *injera*—large, floppy pancake-like bread—and scoop up the spicy stews of vegetables and meat. One block away, you can try Nepalese food at **Himalayan Heritage** *(2305 18th St., N.W., tel 202/483-9300). Momo* (dumplings) is a popular choice.

Many locals think **Lauriol Plaza** *(1835 18th St., N.W., tel 202/387-0035)* has the city's best Mexican/Latin cuisine. Try the Cuban-style morsels of pork in hot *criollo* sauce and bitter oranges. **Mezè** *(2437 18th St., N.W., tel 202/797-0017)* serves freshly made Turkish small plates such as *dolma* (stuffed grape leaves) and *köfte* (lamb meatballs). Caffeine aficionados will like **Tryst** *(2459 18th St., N.W., tel 202/232-5500)* and its selection of coffees and teas from around the globe.

Mexican Cultural Institute *(2829 16th St., N.W., tel 202/728-1628, closed Sat.–Sun.),* in a 1911 Italianate house, holds a huge tile-covered solarium, a lively stairwell mural, and ornately furnished salons; rotating exhibits are presented on two floors.

A few blocks farther, **Meridian International Center** *(1624 & 1630 Crescent Pl., N.W., tel 202/667-6800, closed Mon.–Tues.)* promotes international understanding through cultural exchanges. The adjoining houses, with free art exhibits, were designed by John Russell Pope in 1911 and 1921; the 1630 address has antique French furnishings and a courtyard with 40 linden trees.

Pope also designed the glorious 1911 **Scottish Rite Headquarters** *(1733 16th St., N.W., tel 202/232-3579, closed Fri.–Sun.),* just beyond Adams Morgan at S Street; he modeled the building after the Mausoleum at Halicarnassus in Turkey.

INSIDER TIP:

Grab a window seat at one of the communal tables at Tryst *[2459 18th St., N.W.]* and linger over a latte as you observe the Adams Morgan scene.

—LUBA VANGELOVA
National Geographic Traveler
magazine writer

The northwest portion of Adams Morgan, up 18th and onto Adams Mill Road and Calvert Street is more residential, with closely packed houses. Just off Adams Mill is one of the area's many colorful wall murals, this one dating from the 1970s and depicting life in Washington's barrio. If you follow Calvert, you'll come to the **Duke Ellington Memorial Bridge** over Rock Creek *(toward Woodley Park–Zoo/Adams Morgan Metro station).* ■

U Street Corridor

Known as Washington's "Black Broadway" in the early 20th century, U Street was legendary for several decades as the heartbeat of urban African-American life. Intellectuals and professionals shared the streets with families of all economic levels, while the musical genius of Duke Ellington and others fueled a world-famous club scene. Today the area is undergoing a renewal that's once again making it a vibrant community with a lively street life and rich cultural vibe.

American cuisine at its best: Ben's Chili Bowl on U Street

During the Civil War, two military camps and a hospital occupied the area. The surrounding Shaw neighborhood got its name from Robert Gould Shaw, the white colonel of the war's first black regiment (from Massachusetts).

With the rise of nearby Howard University (see sidebar p. 178) in the late 1860s, local residents developed a respect for academic achievement that inspired generations of black leaders. Elegant late Victorian row houses, many still surviving, marked the neighborhood's prosperity. By the 1920s, more than 300 businesses made the U Street area a bustling district of commerce and entertainment. Evenings and weekends, parades of people in their finest attire

flocked to movie theaters, night-clubs, and ballrooms. On Sundays they gathered at the churches, some dating from the Civil War, when the city had a large free-black population.

In the 1930s and '40s, clubs featured such luminaries as Cab Calloway, Pearl Bailey, Sarah Vaughan, Jelly Roll Morton, and native son Duke Ellington. So great was the area's reputation as a musical mecca that patrons included many white people, in a rare exception to Washington's rigid lines of racial segregation. Ironically, desegregation in the 1950s sparked a decline as residents moved to the suburbs. The 1968 riots further devastated the neighborhood, and by the 1970s blight and safety fears kept people away.

Since the 1990s the area has been undergoing a renaissance. A steady influx of businesses has created a mix of cafés, restaurants, boutiques, and nightclubs that's attracting diverse crowds and injecting energy into the neighborhood. **Busboys & Poets** (14th & V Sts., N.W.) is a popular bookstore cum café. For years the **9:30 Club** (815 V St., N.W., 930.com) has been one of the city's hottest concert venues, with a steady lineup of top acts. ∎

EXPERIENCE: Relive Black History—on Foot

The history of African Americans in Washington, from Civil War days until the present, is a richly faceted one that prompts a wide spectrum of emotions. The city is rich in landmarks that help locals and visitors see and understand how African Americans have shaped history.

A group called Cultural Tourism DC (cultraltourismdc.org) offers a self-guided Heritage Trail walk in the U Street (see p. 176) area, free to download. The visitor center next door to Ben's Chili Bowl (see sidebar below) offers printed information. Here are some neighborhood highlights.

If you exit the Metro at the U Street stop, on Vermont Avenue, you'll see the **African-American Civil War Memorial** (1925 Vermont Ave., N.W.). A small nearby museum (at the Thurgood Marshall Center) chronicles the role of the 200,000 "colored troops" who fought alongside Union soldiers.

At 11th and U Streets you'll find **Bohemian Caverns** (bohemiancaverns.com), site of performances by jazz greats such as John Coltrane and Miles Davis. After a nearly 30-year hiatus, the club reopened in 2000.

A block away, the

INSIDER TIP:

Visit the Sunday night Drum Circle in Meridian Hill Park [16th & Euclid Sts., N.W.] to enjoy dance, music, yoga, juggling, tightrope walking, and picnics.

—KENNY LING
Mapmaker & National Geographic contributor

lavishly Italianate 1903 **True Reformer Building** (12th & U Sts., N.W.) was built by African-American architect John Lankford. Down the street, the **Thurgood Marshall Center** (1816 12th St., N.W.) opened in 1853 as the country's first YMCA for blacks. Its patrons over the years included poet Langston Hughes and boxer Joe Louis.

Nearby are two **Duke Ellington houses** (1805 & 1816 13th St., N.W.), where

he lived from ages 11 to 18, absorbing the influences of church choirs, traveling pianists, and local music teachers. The **former Whitelaw Hotel** (1839 13th St., N.W.) opened in 1919 to offer African-American travelers first-class accommodations in segregated Washington. Its restaurant and ballroom were a favored location for elite parties. Big bands also performed in the Colonnade room of the **Lincoln Theatre** (1215 U St., N.W.), which opened in 1922. After renovation, it now offers a range of entertainment. The baroque 1910 **Howard Theatre** (620 T St., N.W.) was the country's first legitimate theater built for blacks.

Meridian Hill Park (16th & Euclid Sts., N.W.), inspired by the 18th-century European gardens, completed in 1936, and also known as Malcolm X Park, is a lively anchor for the area's multicultural community.

Ben's Chili Bowl

When this tiny eatery opened in 1958 at its present location (1213 U St., N.W., tel 202/667-0909), Eisenhower was President and jazz artists often hung out at Ben's after playing local gigs. More recently, Bill Cosby courted his wife here in the 1960s, and Barack Obama stopped by for a half-smoke with chili sauce a few days before his Inauguration. The founder of Ben's, who died in 2009, turned the place into a multimillion-dollar business—and a Washington institution. His obituary revealed that while Mahaboob Ben Ali had created a small empire, he'd never actually tasted one of the dogs he made so famous: He was Muslim and didn't eat pork.

More Places to Visit in Dupont Circle & Beyond

Anderson House–Society of the Cincinnati

This spectacular 1905 mansion serves as the headquarters and museum of the **Society of the Cincinnati,** a patriotic organization whose first president general was George Washington. The house was once the winter residence of diplomat Larz Anderson III, whose wife, Isabel Weld Perkins, inherited $17,000,000 from her grandfather's shipping fortune. After Anderson died in 1937, his widow gave the mansion to the society, of which Anderson had been a member. The 3,800 members descend from officers in the Continental Army or Navy. Its name comes from the Roman senator Cincinnatus.

Among the treasures are walnut choir stalls from 16th-century Italy and a ballroom with Verona marble columns. The Billiard Room holds two temporary exhibits each year, primarily on the history of the Revolutionary War and the society's founding. A 45,000-title research library *(closed Sat.–Sun.)* focuses on the era of the American Revolution. Guided tours offered. *societyofthecincinnati.org* 🅐 Map p. 165 ✉ 2118 Massachusetts Ave., N.W. ☎ 202/785-2040 🕐 Closed Sun.; museum also closed Mon. & a.m. 🚇 Metro: Dupont Circle

Heurich House Museum

Built in 1894 for brewer Christian Heurich, this Romanesque dark stone castle is now a landmark building on the National Register of Historic Places. Heurich, a German immigrant, came to the United States in 1866. He purchased this property just off Dupont Circle in the late 1870s. He lived here and ran a brewery on what is now the site of the Kennedy Center. In 1956 his third wife, Amelia, deeded the house to the organization that became the Historical Society of Washington (since relocated). A guided tour takes you through 11 rooms on three levels. Sumptuous elements include a marble

Howard University

General Oliver Otis Howard (1830–1909) came to Washington after the Civil War and took charge of the new Bureau of Refugees, Freedmen, and Abandoned Lands (better known as the Freedmen's Bureau). Under Howard's leadership, the bureau bought the Barry Farm near what would become the Anacostia neighborhood, in Southeast Washington, and sold off parcels to black families. The Freedmen's Bureau also helped fund and establish educational programs for freed people. In 1867, Howard University *(6th & Bryant Sts., N.W.)* was founded (and named for the general against his wishes) on land purchased by the bureau. It is now the country's leading black university, with an enrollment of more than 10,000 students.

mosaic floor in the main hall and beautifully carved furniture in the dining room. *heurichhouse.org* 🅐 Map p. 165 ✉ 1307 New Hampshire Ave., N.W. ☎ 202/429-1894 🕐 Tours offered Thurs.–Sat. at 11:30 a.m., 1 p.m., & 2:30 p.m. 🅢 $ 🚇 Metro: Dupont Circle

Mary Church Terrell House

The LeDroit Park neighborhood *(S of Howard University)* has been the home of many prominent African Americans since the 1890s. Civic leader Mary Church Terrell, wife of the city's first black municipal judge, lived a long, active life. In 1950, at age 86, she headed a campaign to reinstate antidiscrimination laws that had been written in the 1870s. She lived in a three-story brick house *(326 T St., N.W., private).* Other blacks who lived in this area include poet Paul Laurence Dunbar and Walter Washington, the city's first elected mayor.

From the bucolic (Rock Creek Park) to the divine (Washington National Cathedral)—respite from standard sightseeing

Cleveland Park & Beyond

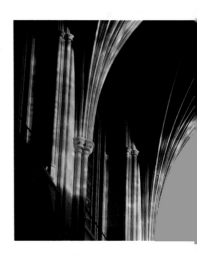

Arches soar inside the vast Washington National Cathedral.

Cleveland Park & Beyond

Just north of Dupont Circle, the leafy neighborhood of Cleveland Park offers a pleasant afternoon of relaxed sightseeing or lounging in a loved-by-locals café. Higher elevations and the nearness of Rock Creek Park provide relief from the downtown heat.

Cleveland Park offers visitors a global smorgasbord of international eateries.

The tony neighborhood of Cleveland Park is named for President Grover Cleveland, who spent the summers of his second administration (1893–1897) at Woodley (*3000 Cathedral Ave., N.W.*) a Georgian mansion built about 1800.

Visitors who venture this far from the Mall usually come for the zoo. It's a fine reason to head this way, made easy by the Metro's Red Line to Cleveland Park or Woodley Park–Zoo/Adams Morgan stations. And maybe a nearby site could land on your list of D.C. favorites.

When the city's trolley tracks were extended across Rock Creek Valley at Calvert Street in the 1890s and then up Connecticut Avenue, the area took on a fashionable cachet. Today Connecticut Avenue is still lined with big apartment buildings (the more ornate ones from the 1920s and '30s) and fine old houses with wide front porches. Indeed, the city's largest hotel, the Marriott Wardman Park (*Woodley Rd. & Connecticut Ave.*), got its start in 1928 as a luxury apartment building called the Wardman Tower. The tower's residents have included Herbert Hoover, Earl Warren, and Clare Booth Luce. Across Calvert Street, the 1930 Omni Shoreham has hosted Inaugural Balls since Franklin Delano Roosevelt took office in 1933. Farther up Connecticut Avenue is the almost pastoral 163-acre (66 ha) Smithsonian's National Zoo. It abuts Rock Creek Park, a delightful preserve of trees, meadows, and cycling paths.

A mile (1.6 km) west of the zoo, Washington National Cathedral towers gloriously on its high hill. Scores of stonemasons labored 83 years to complete this architectural masterpiece. The Hillwood Estate to the north is a jewel box of Russian and French antiques. Afterward, settle in with a cappuccino or a meal at one of the many eateries clustered near the Metro stops along Connecticut Avenue. Shoppers should keep heading northwest to Friendship Heights for the upscale Mazza Gallerie and neighboring high-end retailers. ■

NOT TO BE MISSED:

The always entertaining denizens of the National Zoo **182–184**

Exploring Rock Creek Park by bike, on foot, or in a car **185–186**

Tea or lunch amid the formal Hillwood Estate gardens **187–188**

The views from Washington National Cathedral's Pilgrim Observation Gallery **189–191**

Taking in a film at the classic Uptown Theater—a true movie palace **192**

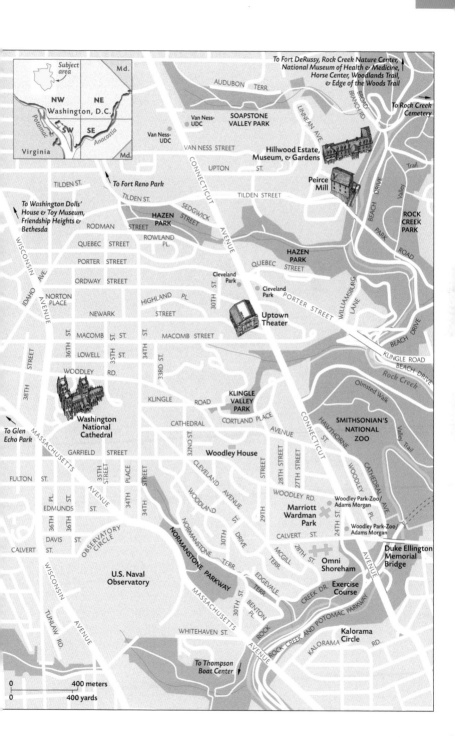

Subject area
NW NE
Washington, D.C.
Md.
SW SE
Virginia
Potomac
Anacostia
Md.

To Fort DeRussy, Rock Creek Nature Center, National Museum of Health & Medicine, Horse Center, Woodlands Trail, & Edge of the Woods Trail

To Rock Creek Cemetery

AUDUBON TERR.

BRANCH RD.
LINNEAN AVE.
BROAD

Van Ness-UDC
SOAPSTONE VALLEY PARK

Hillwood Estate, Museum, & Gardens

VAN NESS STREET
UPTON ST.

Van Ness-UDC

Peirce Mill

Trail

ROCK CREEK PARK

BEACH DRIVE

Valley

To Washington Dolls' House & Toy Museum, Friendship Heights & Bethesda

TILDEN ST.

To Fort Reno Park

TILDEN ST.

TILDEN STREET

HAZEN PARK

SEDGWICK STREET

CONNECTICUT AVENUE

RODMAN STREET

QUEBEC STREET

ROWLAND PL.

HAZEN PARK STREET

QUEBEC STREET

WILLIAMSBURG LANE

PARK ROAD

WISCONSIN AVE.
IDAHO AVENUE

PORTER STREET

ORDWAY STREET

Cleveland Park

Cleveland Park

PORTER STREET

NORTON PLACE

HIGHLAND PL. STREET

30TH ST.

Uptown Theater

BEACH DRIVE

NEWARK

MACOMB ST. ST. ST.

MACOMB STREET

KLINGLE ROAD
BEACH DRIVE

36TH STREET
35TH ST.
34TH ST.
33RD ST.

LOWELL ST.

WOODLEY RD.

Rock Creek

Olmsted Walk

38TH STREET

Washington National Cathedral

KLINGLE ROAD

KLINGLE VALLEY PARK

CATHEDRAL

CORTLAND PLACE

CONNECTICUT ST.

HAWTHORNE ST.

SMITHSONIAN'S NATIONAL ZOO

Valley Trail

To Glen Echo Park

MASSACHUSETTS AVENUE

GARFIELD STREET

32ND ST.

AVENUE

CATHEDRAL AVE.

WOODLEY

FULTON ST.

35TH STREET
35TH PLACE
34TH STREET

Woodley House

CLEVELAND AVENUE

WOODLAND ST.

STREET

28TH STREET
27TH STREET

WOODLEY RD.

Woodley Park-Zoo/Adams Morgan

EDMUNDS ST.

PL.

36TH PL.
36TH ST.

29TH

Marriott Wardman Park

24TH ST.

Woodley Park-Zoo/Adams Morgan

DAVIS ST.

OBSERVATORY CIRCLE

NORMANSTONE PARKWAY

30TH DRIVE

CALVERT ST.

MCGILL TERR.

26TH ST.

Omni Shoreham

Duke Ellington Memorial Bridge

CALVERT ST.

WISCONSIN AVENUE

TUNLAW RD.

U.S. Naval Observatory

NORMANSTONE TERR.

MASSACHUSETTS

31ST ST.

EDGEVALE TERR.

BENTON PL.

Exercise Course

CREEK DR.

AVENUE

Kalorama Circle

WHITEHAVEN ST.

ROCK

AVENUE

ROCK CREEK AND POTOMAC PARKWAY

KALORAMA RD.

To Thompson Boat Center

0   400 meters
0   400 yards

Smithsonian's National Zoo

The National Zoo was conceived as "a home and a city of refuge for the vanishing races of the continent." In 1887, Smithsonian taxidermist William T. Hornaday corralled some of North America's vanishing bison and a few other animals in a small zoo on the Mall. Two years later, Congress set aside acreage along a bend in Rock Creek to create the National Zoo "for the advancement of science and the instruction and recreation of the people."

Prowling among native vegetation, this Sumatran tiger lives in the zoo's Great Cats exhibit.

National Zoo

- Map p. 181
- 3001 Connecticut Ave., N.W.
- 202/633-4888
- Parking: $$$$ per day
- Metro: Cleveland Park, Woodley Park–Zoo/ Adams Morgan; Bus: 96, L1–L2, Circulator

nationalzoo.si.edu

Part of the Smithsonian Institution, the 163-acre (66 ha) biological park opened in 1891 and is home to more than 2,000 animals representing 400 species. Nearly a third of the species—including Asian elephants, cheetahs, Sumatran tigers, giant pandas, western lowland gorillas, and Komodo dragons—are endangered.

The animal enclosures at the National Zoo were designed to re-create natural habitats. Meanwhile, at the zoo's 3,000-acre (1,214 ha) Smithsonian Conservation Biology Institute in Front Royal, Virginia, zookeepers have bred golden lion tamarins, red wolves, and black-footed ferrets for reintroduction to the wild.

Visiting

Given the zoo's 5 miles (8 km) of hilly paths, it's hard to avoid at

On the National Zoo's Asia Trail, kids gravitate to the red pandas—they look like little raccoons, eat bamboo, and are on the threatened-species list.

—DANIEL R. WESTERGREN
National Geographic Traveler
magazine director of photography

least some uphill walking. To minimize your efforts, pick up a map at one of the information stations at either end of the zoo's main east-west thoroughfare, the Olmsted Walk (Frederick Law Olmsted designed the zoo's original layout).

With more than 30 animal exhibit areas to choose from, you may want to hit a few of the highlights and save the rest for another day. Fall and winter are the least crowded seasons at the zoo, but the buildings close early November through March.

If you begin at the visitor center inside the Connecticut Avenue entrance, the **Olmsted Walk** will lead you past the cheetahs, zebras, and other mammals to the **Giant Panda Exhibit.** This indoor-outdoor area features Tian Tian and Mei Xiang, a pair of pandas on long-term loan from China, and their cub Bao Bao (see sidebar right). Within days of arriving in December 2000, the pandas had adapted so well that they were devouring the decorative plantings of ornamental bamboo.

The exhibit outlines efforts to save the panda, whose numbers have seriously dwindled.

Continue downhill and east past the Elephant House to reach the **Small Mammal House,** where the challenge is to spot the golden lion tamarins, pygmy marmosets, two-toed sloths, and three-banded armadillos that occupy the glassed-in jungle.

The **Great Ape House,** next door to the little mammals, is home to gorillas and orangutans. The latter can climb over an aerial pathway called the O Line to **Think Tank,** swinging on vinelike cables attached to a set of towers.

A popular stop nearby, the **Reptile Discovery Center** features Komodo dragons, huge Aldabra tortoises, and spiky matamata turtles among the 70 or so species of reptiles and amphibians

Panda Report

Two giant pandas that have thrilled zoo-goers for the past decade—Mei Xiang and Tian Tian—arrived here in December 2000 from a research center in Sichuan, China, to become part of the Asia Trail exhibit. The male and female pair were on loan from China as part of a research, conservation, and breeding program that has been renewed through 2015. Immediately, they charmed visitors and became one of the zoo's biggest draws.

Mei Xiang and Tian Tian's second off-spring, Bao Bao, was born in August 2013, and huge crowds line up daily hoping for a glimpse of the young female cub.

Today, fewer than 1,600 giant pandas are left in the wild; about 300 live in zoos and breeding centers around the world, such as the National Zoo in Washington.

INSIDER TIP:

At the Think Tank exhibit, which focuses on cognition, visitors can enjoy a tug-of-war with an orangutan or compare their memory with that of the primates.

—KATHERINE BRAZAUSKAS
National Geographic contributor

represented here. Also on hand are multimedia exhibits.

Beyond the center you'll find the **Great Cats,** where Sumatran tigers and African lions roam their terraced exhibits. The playful, rapidly growing lion and tiger cubs are a fun highlight. **Lemur Island** is home to ring-tailed and red-fronted lemurs (red-ruffed lemurs can be found in the Small Mammal House).

Recently added to this area, near Parking Lot D, is a 2-acre (0.8 ha) **Kids' Farm** that was designed to introduce young children to farm animals and the basics of animal care. At the farm's pizza garden kids can explore the growing of pizza ingredients.

Next, head to the warm, humid **Amazonia** exhibit, the zoo's largest and most complex, which simulates a journey through a rain forest; here parrots and other tropical birds flit through kapok and mahogany trees beneath a domed 50-foot-high (15 m) ceiling. After Amazonia, the American Trail features North American species such as beavers, bald eagles, gray wolves, seals, and sea lions. ∎

The endangered golden lion tamarin, a small monkey, is native to coastal Brazil, where its habitat is dwindling. At the zoo they eat fruit, crickets, mealworms, and the occasional stray roach or mouse.

Rock Creek Park

When you need to get away from urban living (or touring), a peaceful Washington park awaits. Rock Creek Park, administered by the National Park Service, runs in a long strand of hilly woods and meadows from the National Zoo to the Maryland border 4 miles (6.4 km) north; tendrils of green branch off into other parts of the city. At 1,739 acres (704 ha)—more than twice the size of New York's Central Park—Rock Creek is one of the nation's largest urban parks.

Bridges, trails, and seasonal glories are among the enticements of this sprawling urban sanctuary.

For some 5,000 years, Algonquin Indians camped in the woods around Rock Creek above its run-in with the Potomac. They gathered fruits and nuts; hunted deer, bear, and elk; and quarried the valley, extracting quartz for tools and soapstone for bowls and other implements. By the early 1700s, the Indians had been displaced by white settlers who'd cleared out more of the forest and built mills along Rock Creek. The only one of these that remains is the 19th-century **Peirce Mill** (*Tilden St. & Beach Dr., N.W.*), whose adjacent barn is open several hours on weekends.

During the Civil War, a ring of 68 forts went up to protect against Confederate attack. You can see some earthworks from **Fort DeRussy** half a mile (0.8 km) north of the nature center. Other fort sites, most long since reduced to picnic and ball-playing areas, include **Fort Bayard Park** (*River Rd. & Western Ave., N.W.*); **Fort Reno Park** (*Chesapeake St. & Belt Rd., N.W.*), occupying the highest point of land in Washington and partially reconstructed; and **Fort Stevens Park** (*13th St., N.W., N of Military Rd.*), the only Washington-area battlement that came under enemy fire.

Rock Creek Park
 Map p. 181
nps.gov/rocr

Rock Creek Nature Center & Planetarium

Map p. 181

5200 Glover Rd., N.W., S of Military Rd.

202/895-6070

Closed Mon.– Tues. & major holidays

Set aside in 1890, Rock Creek Park is the city's playground. About 85 percent of the park is forested; the remainder is mainly meadows and fields. Over the years, Theodore Roosevelt, Ronald Reagan, and other Presidents have availed themselves of the park's walking and bridle trails. Today, people come for the tennis courts, an 18-hole golf course, playing fields, nature center and planetarium, and more than 32 miles (51 km) of trails for jogging, hiking, biking, and horseback riding.

Visiting

Start your visit at the **Rock Creek Nature Center & Planetarium.** Here you can learn about the park's flora and fauna, scope out its cycling and running paths, and pick up a trail map. The center's excellent offerings include a bee colony and astronomy programs.

Two short nature loops— the **Woodland Trail** and the wheelchair-accessible **Edge of the Woods Trail**—have signs identifying trees and plants. Come spring, dogwoods, redbud, and azalea blooms emerge in a gaudy show.

From the nature center, you can also access the park's larger trail network. Some pathways are open to bikes and horses; others allow only foot traffic. Hikers gravitate to the moderate, blue-blazed, 5.6-mile (9 km) **Valley Trail,** which winds along the east side of Rock Creek from Boundary Bridge on the Maryland line down to Bluff Bridge at the park's southern end. Its analogue on the western edge is the strenuous, green-blazed, 4.6-mile (7.4 km) **Western Ridge Trail.**

Just south of the nature center, sign up for a trail ride or lesson at the **Rock Creek Horse Center** (tel 202/362-0117). Much farther south, where Rock Creek joins the Potomac River, **Thompson Boat Center** (tel 202/333-9543) rents canoes, kayaks, and bicycles. ∎

EXPERIENCE: Hiking & Biking Rock Creek Trail

Running north–south, the scenic Rock Creek Trail extends a total of 25 miles (40 km), starting at the Lincoln Memorial in Washington, D.C., and going all the way to Lake Needwood Park in Montgomery County, Maryland. For biking, walking, jogging, or picnicking, the trail can be accessed from the **Rock Creek Park Nature Center & Planetarium.**

The northern trail—the portion that goes beyond D.C. and crosses 14 miles (22.5 km) into Maryland—is entirely on paved roadways. It connects with **Beach Drive,** usually a pulsing commuter artery but pleasant on weekends when sections of it are closed to motor vehicles, giving cyclists an unobstructed ride all the way from the Maryland border south to Broad Branch Road.

Rock Creek Trail's southern route runs alongside Rock Creek and the Potomac Parkway until it reaches Memorial Bridge. Although paved, the path is narrow, windy, and rough in patches. Be on the alert for children, pets, and others. About halfway along this stretch of trail, near Calvert Street and Connecticut Avenue, you'll find a 1.5-mile (2.4 km) exercise course with fitness apparatus.

Hillwood Estate, Museum, & Gardens

A hidden gem, Hillwood was the final home of heiress Marjorie Merriweather Post (1887–1973). With her fabulous collection of imperial Russian and 18th-century French decorative arts, she furnished the house with the idea that it would become a museum after her death. The site opened to the public in 1977, and Hillwood, with 13 acres (5.2 ha) of formal gardens, is now one of the top art collector's house museums in the country.

As the only child of cereal magnate C. W. Post, Marjorie inherited a fortune at age 27 when her father died (just two years after her mother). She and her husband bought a mansion on Fifth Avenue in New York and began furnishing it with the help of renowned art dealer Sir Joseph Duveen, who became Post's mentor. She also educated herself by taking classes on tapestries, porcelain, and furniture at the Metropolitan Museum of Art.

In the course of a long and extraordinary life, Post married and divorced four times and amassed a tremendous collection of European artwork. An astute businesswoman, she also donated millions of dollars to charities and other organizations, including $100,000 to help build the Kennedy Center (see pp. 126–127).

It was after her third divorce, in 1955, that Post purchased Hillwood—a 1926 Georgian house on the woodsy edge of Rock Creek Park. She spent two years renovating and enlarging the house, transforming it into a residence where she could entertain in legendary style. Hillwood parties routinely exceeded 200 guests, the politicians mixing with celebrities in

Frank O. Salisbury painted this elegant portrait of Marjorie Merriweather Post in 1934, when she was 47 years old.

the gardens. At formal dinners, guests ate off Post's antique porcelain; informal dinners sometimes wound down with square dancing in the pavilion.

In the interstices between soirées, Post expanded her art

Hillwood Estate, Museum, & Gardens

- Map p. 181
- 4155 Linnean Ave., N.W.
- 202/686-5807
- Closed Mon., some Sun., & most of Jan.
- $$$
- Metro: Van Ness–UDC; Bus: L1–L2

hillwoodmuseum.org

collection, eventually turning Hillwood into a stunning showcase of decorative and fine arts. Today the museum is best known for its collection of 18th- and 19th-century Russian imperial art—the most comprehensive outside Russia—and for its French decorative art.

Visiting

Get oriented to the museum and gardens with a 15-minute film at the visitor center. You can take a one-hour **guided tour** of the house, usually offered several times a day, or a self-guided audio tour, and then stroll the gardens. There's a café on-site that serves lunch and afternoon tea; call for reservations (tel 202/686-5807).

The imposing exterior of the brick house and the inside customarily prompt a chorus of oohs and aahs. One highlight, the **Russian Porcelain Room,** contains Imperial Glassworks pieces from the 1730s.

More tsarist treasures are on display in the outstanding **Icon Room,** where you can feast your eyes on the diamond wedding crown worn in 1894 by Russia's last empress, Alexandra Fedorovona; two Fabergé Easter eggs (one dates from 1914 and is studded with gold, diamonds, and pearls);

Post's treasures included ornate jewel-studded Russian imperial Easter eggs created by Fabergé.

and Russian Orthodox icons from the 16th century. Post discovered her love of Russian decorative and liturgical art while living in the Soviet Union from 1937 to 1938 with her third husband, U.S. Ambassador Joseph E. Davies.

INSIDER TIP:

Marjorie Merriweather Post created a pet cemetery after her beloved dog died. Every October, dogs and their owners are invited to the Spooky Pooch Parade.

—SUSAN O'KEEFE
National Geographic Traveler
magazine associate editor

The elegant **French Drawing Room** is furnished in the style of Louis XVI, with 18th-century tapestries designed by painter François Boucher and furniture by David Roentgen. Upstairs, Post's bedroom is likewise decorated in Louis XVI style; a display of her clothing and jewelry adds life and personality to the collection.

Equally impressive are the 12 acres (4.8 ha) of lawns and formal gardens and 13 acres (5.2 ha) of native woodlands. A French parterre with a fountain, a circular rose garden, a lunar lawn, a Japanese-style garden, a cutting garden, and an orchid-filled greenhouse round out the grounds. It all makes strolling through Hillwood a delight in any season. ∎

Washington National Cathedral

Dominating the cityscape, Washington National Cathedral is visible from points all over the district. Conversely, its lofty perch on Mount St. Alban gives cathedral visitors a commanding vista of the urban skyline. Officially known as the Cathedral Church of St. Peter and St. Paul, this towering Gothic church is one of Washington's most magnificent architectural achievements.

The idea of a national church featured in Pierre-Charles L'Enfant's Federal City plans. He envisioned a house of prayer for national services, open to all rather than reserved for a particular denomination. It took nearly a century for the idea to gain adequate support. In 1893 the Protestant Episcopal Cathedral Foundation obtained a charter allowing the church to be established.

After the 57-acre (23 ha) site atop Mount St. Alban was selected and public donations were obtained, President Theodore Roosevelt and a crowd of 10,000 were on hand in 1907 for the laying of the foundation stone. The Bethlehem Chapel, named for one of its stones that came from a field near Bethlehem, opened first, in 1912. Services have been held here ever since, even though construction of the building actually took 83 years. President George H. W. Bush dedicated the west towers in 1990.

For half a century, construction of the cathedral was guided by Philip Hubert Frohman, who had dreamed of becoming its architect; he got the job after the two initial designers died in 1917. Obsessed with detail, Frohman once ordered that all the molding

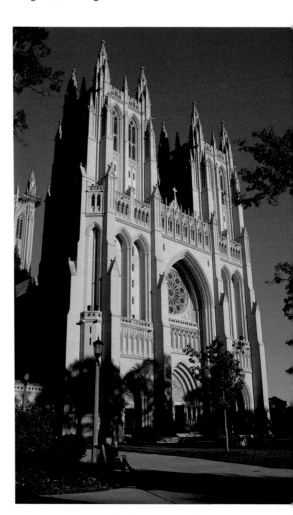

The imposing St. Peter and St. Paul towers on the west facade of Washington National Cathedral bask in the honey-gold sunshine of late afternoon.

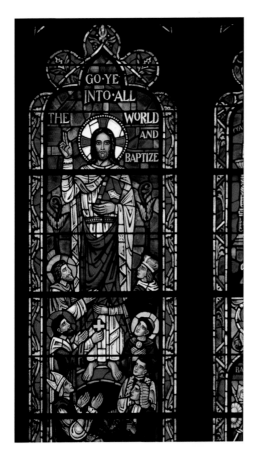

"History of the Baptism" illuminates the south transept.

Washington National Cathedral

 Map p. 181

✉ Massachusetts & Wisconsin Aves., N.W.

☎ 202/537-6200

 Bus: 31–32, 36–37, 96–97, N2–N4

nationalcathedral.org

on the central tower be shifted by one-eighth of an inch (0.3 cm). He died in 1972, at the age of 85, after being struck by a car while walking to work from his home.

Others who dedicated their lives to the cathedral were the many masons, stone carvers, and stained-glass artisans who applied 14th-century skills to modern times. Their legacy includes more than 200 stained-glass windows, 3,000 stone sculptures, and many other artfully crafted works. Most

of the building was constructed of grey Indiana limestone, selected for its endurance without the need for major restoration over time.

Visiting

Half-hour docent-led tours are offered several times at midday *(donation)*, beginning at the west end of the nave. For groups, reservations are required *(tel 202/537-6207 ext. 5)*. You can also wander on your own with an audio tour *($$)*. Tours may be unavailable, however, if the cathedral is being used for a special event; check the website, which also has the schedules of services and musical events.

Stroll outside to admire the flying buttresses, the arches, and some of the **112 gargoyles** whose expressions range from silly to fiendish. In addition to warding off evil, the gargoyles funnel rainwater away from the building during storms. The figures are carved in various shapes: wild boars, mythical beasts, cats, dogs, even caricatures of people who were central to the construction of the cathedral. Binoculars are handy for inspecting the higher ones.

Outside is also the best place to absorb the immensity one of the largest cathedrals in the world, and the second largest in the United States (only New York's St. John the Divine is bigger). The central Gloria in Excelsis Deo tower rises 300 feet (91 m), while the nave measures one-tenth of a mile (0.16 km).

The west entrance central portal features Frederick Hart's spellbinding tympanum sculpture, "Ex Nihilo," in which the act of creation is expressed through half-formed men and women.

Faithful to its Gothic style, the church was built in a cruciform shape. Stand at the crossing and look up; the massive piers rise 98 feet (30 m) to the vaulting overhead. The pulpit, from which Dr. Martin Luther King, Jr., gave his final sermon on March 31, 1968, was carved from stone donated by England's Canterbury Cathedral. The 10,500 pieces of glass in the spectacular **West Rose Window** cast late afternoon rainbows.

Running along the nave are memorial alcoves, or bays. The **Woodrow Wilson Bay** honors the life of the 28th President, the only U.S. President whose final resting place is Washington, D.C. The floor of the **Lincoln Bay** is inset with 33 Lincoln-head pennies—one for each state in the Union at the time of the Great Emancipator's assassination.

About halfway down on the right (south) side, the modernistic **Space Window** has a moon rock embedded in the center lancet.

Scattered throughout, nine chapels vary from the tiny **Good** Shepherd Chapel to the church-size **Bethlehem Chapel** on the crypt level. Especially appealing is the intimate **Children's Chapel,** where every item has been scaled to a size befitting a six-year-old. Also on this level is a store offering books, tapes, cards, and snacks.

For a closer look at the cathedral's towers and gargoyles (and a panoramic view of the city), take an elevator to the **Pilgrim Observation Gallery** on the seventh floor of the St. Peter and St. Paul towers. In nice weather, stroll in the beautifully landscaped **Bishop's Garden,** which was designed by Frederick Law Olmsted. ∎

Bell Appeal

National Cathedral's central tower holds ten peal bells and a 53-bell carillon. It is the only cathedral in North America blessed with both kinds of bells in a single tower.

Each peal bell is mounted on a wheel, from which a rope hangs down to the ringers' chamber. The pull must be smooth and even, so one ringer is assigned to each bell. Weighing 600 to nearly 3,600 pounds apiece (272 kg— 1,632 kg), the bells cannot be rung fast enough for a melody; instead, sequences of notes called "changes" are played. Change ringing is difficult and dangerous: Lose your concentration and you not only sabotage the change but risk injury when the bell's momentum jerks you high off the floor. Peals *(Sun. after a.m. service)* can last from several minutes to the rare "full peal," a three-hour extravaganza of 5,000 changes. The joyous noise can be heard at the White House, 3 miles (4.8 km) away.

More Places to Visit in Cleveland Park & Beyond

National Museum of Health & Medicine

Though it now stresses serious science over sensational spectacle, this museum is not for the squeamish: Exhibits range from preserved human fetuses and a stomach-shaped hair ball to a leg swollen by elephantiasis and a hands-on brain.

Cinematic Magic at the Uptown Theater

The world premiere of the hit science fiction movie *2001: A Space Odyssey* took place at the Uptown on April 2, 1968. Projected on the theater's huge screen that night was the original 2 hour 40 minute version of the film (director Stanley Kubrick then decided to cut 20 minutes from the running time). *2001: A Space Odyssey,* an instant success, ran at the Uptown Theater for 51 weeks.

Other films to enjoy long runs at the Uptown include *South Pacific,* which ran for seven months in 1958, and *West Side Story,* on the Uptown's big screen for nine months in 1961.

The last movie palace within the District of Columbia to screen first-run films, the Uptown Theater still boasts the largest screen in town.

Also on display: the bullet that killed President Lincoln and a tent hospital from Iraq. The collection was begun during the Civil War as a research tool for military medicine and surgery. Today the museum's vast collection of skeletal specimens, organs, and models is employed for research on human anatomy. *medicalmuseum.mil* 🄰 Map p. 181 ✉ 2500 Linden Lane, Silver Spring, MD ☎ 301/319-3300 🚇 Metro: Forest Glen

Rock Creek Cemetery

A mile and a half (2.4 km) east of Rock Creek Park in the Petworth neighborhood, this 86-acre (35 ha) site exudes the feel of an old country parish. Set amid this pastoral glebe, St. Paul's Episcopal (or "Rock Creek") Church is the city's sole surviving colonial church. It was founded in 1719, long before Washington was a city; although the current building dates from 1775, only the walls are original.

Some of the city's finest cemetery memorials reside here. They honor crusading novelist Upton Sinclair, Cabinet members, Supreme Court justices, and National Geographic Society founder Gilbert H. Grosvenor. The cemetery also houses one of the finest works by one of America's greatest sculptors: The Adams Memorial (1890) by Augustus Saint-Gaudens was commissioned by historian Henry Adams to honor his wife, Clover. It depicts a seated figure wearing a heavy cloak, the face obscured by shadows. Mark Twain remarked that the sculpture embodied all of human grief, while Saint-Gaudens himself called his work "The Mystery of the Hereafter" and "The Peace of God That Passeth Understanding." *stpaulsrockcreek.org* 🄰 Map p. 181 ✉ Rock Creek Church Rd. & Webster St., N.W. ☎ 202/829-0585

Uptown Theater

Opened in 1936, the art deco Uptown is Washington's premier movie palace, a blast from the past that underscores the ongoing power of the big screen. Its 850 seats, including a balcony, make it the city's largest remaining cinema theater. A curved screen, 72 feet (23 m) long and 32 feet (9.7 m) high, wraps viewers in movie magic, while a Dolby digital sound system keeps the illusion up-to-date. Almost any movie looks great in a house this thrillingly large. 🄰 Map p. 181 ✉ 3426 Connecticut Ave., N.W. ☎ 888/262-4386 🚇 Metro: Cleveland Park

Discoveries off the beaten path—a museum honoring African Americans, a dazzling basilica, gardens, and more gardens

East & North of the Capitol

Asters flourish at the U.S. National Arboretum.

East & North of the Capitol

It's an area rich in African-American and military history, as well as botanic treasures, marshes, and woods. Architecture lovers will find one of the city's most awe-inspiring buildings here, the nation's largest Catholic church.

Reverend Willie Wilson plays washboard at Union Temple Baptist Church in Anacostia.

The history of this part of the city is tied to its river, the Anacostia, first seen by a European, explorer John Smith, nearly 400 years ago.

NOT TO BE MISSED:

A stroll though the U.S. National Arboretum (especially in the spring blooming season) **196–197**

Basilica of the National Shrine of the Immaculate Conception **198**

Abraham Lincoln's "country" retreat **199**

The Frederick Douglass house at Cedar Hill **200**

Checking out the graves of famous people buried at Congressional Cemetery **201**

Back then the Nacotchtank Indians (whose corrupted name, Anacostan, would be given to this East Branch of the Potomac) lived here. The arrival of white settlers meant the Indians' demise and the spread of tobacco plantations. In 1790 the lower Anacostia became part of the new capital. Soon developments arose on the northwest riverfront—the Washington Navy Yard (1799) and the U.S. Arsenal (1803).

Across the river from the Navy Yard, the city laid out its first whites-only suburb, Uniontown, in 1854. During the Civil War, the military erected several forts east of the river. After the war, the Freedman's Bureau bought nearby 375-acre (151 ha) Barry farm and sold lots to 500 black families. Still the community, renamed Anacostia in 1886, remained mostly white until the 1950s, when whites migrated to the suburbs. By 1970, Anacostia was 86 percent black. The District government and private

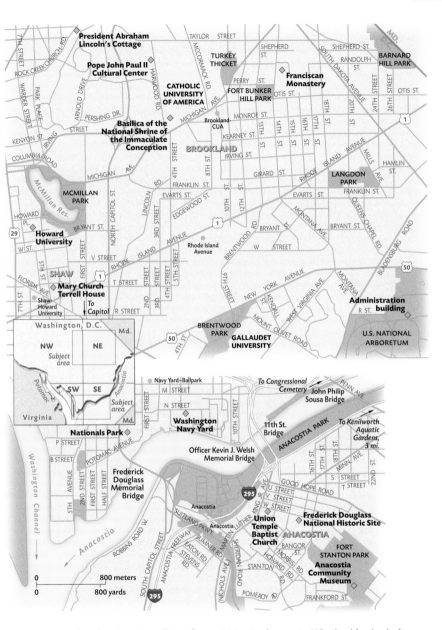

corporations have been investing millions of dollars to develop the Anacostia waterfront.

On the other side of the river, the Northeast quadrant is anchored by the U.S. National Arboretum and the Catholic University of America. Also in this area is Gallaudet University, the premier U.S. school for the deaf.

Sports fans know the area as the site of Langston Golf Course and RFK Stadium, once home to the Washington Redskins football team, now home to D.C. United, the MLS soccer team. ■

U.S. National Arboretum

A little off the beaten tourist path, this delightful oasis of fields, ponds, fountains, gardens, and flowering trees is just the tonic for those in need of some outdoor beauty. Established by an act of Congress in 1927, the National Arboretum is run by the Department of Agriculture as a living museum and a research and education facility. The arboretum's 446 acres (180 ha) include 9.5 miles (15 km) of gentle roadways that wind past a dozen garden areas.

Children create their own floral tableau beneath a flowering "Tonto" crape myrtle at the arboretum.

U.S. National Arboretum

- Map p. 195
- 24th & R Sts., N.E., or 3501 New York Ave., N.E.
- 202/245-2726
- Closed Tues.–Thurs.
- Bus: B2

usna.usda.gov

A pleasure any time, the arboretum is especially beautiful in spring, with 15,000 multicolored azaleas and blossoming dogwoods, cherries, and crab apples blushing on the hillsides. In summer, delicate flowers and high grasses stipple meadows, while daylilies and crape myrtles take to the heat with ease, and water lilies bloom in the koi pool near the administration building. Fall enriches the color palette with the vivid yellows of hickory and tulip poplar and the wine reds of sweet gum and dogwood. The late flowers of witch hazel and spider lilies fan the flames. In the cold quiet days of winter, the bright red berries of holly glisten like little beads, and dwarf conifers and other evergreens are sometimes rimed with ice. Ornamental grasses and dry leaves chatter in the breeze.

Visiting

On the way to the administration building from the New York Avenue entrance, you'll notice

The Story of the Anacostia River

Since the arrival of Europeans nearly 400 years ago, the Anacostia watershed has been used, overused, and abused. Runoffs from big farms in the 18th century silted the river, and urban growth has troubled the waters ever since. In the early 20th century, efforts to reshape the waterway and "reclaim" the adjoining swamps for development nearly killed the Anacostia.

Fortunately, the tide is turning for the Anacostia River. Government agencies as well as several citizen groups, such as the Anacostia Watershed Society, are working to protect this valuable ecosystem, a vital part of the country's largest estuary—the Chesapeake Bay.

In recent years, hundreds of tons of debris have been cleaned up, and more than 13,000 trees have been planted. In the city, the river's watershed is essentially sidewalk and street drains, which means that unfiltered trash too often finds its way into the river. With an eye on the future, the Anacostia Watershed Society has enlisted thousands of city youths to help clean up the river.

beehive-shaped **brick kilns.** When the brickyard, dating from 1909, shut down in 1972, the acreage and buildings were sold to the arboretum. At the administration building, you'll find maps and a list of gardens in bloom.

Next to this building, the **National Bonsai & Penjing Museum** has an outstanding collection of miniature trees from Japan, China, and North America. Breezes lilt through feathery Japanese maples and paths meander among bonsai pavilions.

Across the drive, the 2.5-acre (1 ha) **National Herb Garden** features some 800 varieties of herbs. Standing like unexpected ruins in a nearby field are 22 sandstone Corinthian columns, removed from the Capitol's east central portico in 1958 when the Senate side of the building was enlarged. Take the guided 35-minute open-air tram tour (*weekends, seasonal, $*) which starts near the R Street entrance. Or drive or bike to most gardens by looping the outer roads.

Heading southwest from the administration building, you come to the **National Boxwood Collection**—around 150 types on 5 acres (2 ha). Adjoining perennials include irises, peonies, and daylilies. Continue to the **Azalea Collections,** which peak in late April. To the east, on Crabtree Road, is **Fern Valley;** a half-mile (0.8 km) wooded path winds past wildflowers, a meadow, prairie, and a stream.

At the arboretum's far eastern end are the well-loved **Asian Collections,** with flora planted on a hillside so that from strategically placed benches you have glimpses of a pagoda and views down to the Anacostia River. To the north, the **Gotelli Collection** of dwarf and slow-growing conifers is considered among the world's best.

The setting of the **Dogwood Collections** nearby offers a fine view of the Anacostia River. South of the Asian collections, the glossy **hollies and magnolias** are striking in all seasons. ∎

Basilica of the National Shrine of the Immaculate Conception

The blue dome and 329-foot-tall (100 m) campanile of the National Shrine preside over the skyline of Northeast Washington. Built along Byzantine and Romanesque lines, the National Shrine is the country's largest Roman Catholic church. One of the most impressive pieces of architecture in a city renowned for its monuments, it rivals the great sanctuaries of the world.

The National Shrine is one of the world's ten largest churches. Its dome and bell tower punctuate the skyline.

Basilica of the National Shrine of the Immaculate Conception

🅰 Map p. 195

✉ Michigan Ave. & 4th St., N.E.

☎ 202/526-8300

🚇 Metro: Brookland–CUA; Bus: 80, H1–H4

nationalshrine.com

The idea of giving Washington a magnificent Catholic church in the manner of Old World cathedrals was first proposed in 1846. In 1913, the rector of the Catholic University of America presented Pope Pius X with plans for building a shrine to the Blessed Virgin Mary on the campus. With the Pope's support, work began in 1920; the building was dedicated in 1959. In 1990, John Paul II designated the shrine a basilica because of its significance as a national center of worship.

You can take a free group tour or pick up a floor plan near the entrance and wander on your own. More than 70 chapels and oratories circle the perimeter of the crypt level and upper church. Enter on the upstairs level, where the grandiose **Great Upper Church** soars to a height of 100 feet (30.5 m). Natural light floods the vast interior, stained glass casts rich color on walls and floors, and mosaics and candles sparkle in almost every niche and dome. Notice the swirling cosmos and the Creation depicted above the east transept and, in the west transept, the people rising toward a cloud-enthroned Jesus. The chancel dome holds a huge mosaic titled "Christ in Majesty." A soothing contrast is the trickling fountain of the **Mary Queen of Ireland chapel.**

Stairs lead to the **crypt level,** where marble walls and pillars adorn **Memorial Hall,** honoring the shrine's donors. Also on this level, the **Crypt Church** was modeled on Roman catacombs. The cathedral offers six Masses and five hours of Confession daily. ∎

President Abraham Lincoln's Cottage

It was in a handsome "country cottage" on a hill, about 3 miles (5 km) from the center of the city, that President Abraham Lincoln and his family spent most of June–November in 1862, 1863, and 1864, in retreat from the heat. Most days, Lincoln would commute to his office via horse, passing temporary shelters housing former slaves who had escaped to freedom.

The 10,000-square-foot (930 sq m) home was built in 1842 as the summer house of George Washington Riggs, a prominent banker. In 1851, he sold the property to the government; later that year, Congress passed legislation that established the home as a place for retired or disabled soldiers.

After a $15 million renovation by the National Trust for Historic Preservation, the cottage, located on the Armed Forces Retirement Home campus in Northwest Washington, was opened to the public for the first time in 2008. Now you can walk the grounds where Lincoln pondered difficult decisions surrounding the Civil War.

Far from a log cabin, the 34-room house served as the setting for important meetings; it's also where Lincoln drafted the Emancipation Proclamation. Admission is by guided tour only, and tickets are required. ∎

President Abraham Lincoln's Cottage

- 🅐 Map p. 195
- ✉ Rock Creek Church Rd. & Upshur St., N.W.
- ☎ 202/829-0436
- 💲 $$
- Ⓜ Metro: Georgia Ave.–Petworth (1 mile/1.6 km away); Bus: H8

lincolncottage.org

H Street Corridor

The H Street Northeast area, just beyond Union Station and the U.S. Capitol, got hit hard by the rioting that occurred after Rev. Martin Luther King, Jr., was assassinated in 1968. Recovery was slow in coming, but today the neighborhood offers one of the hippest club scenes in Washington D.C.

In 2003, the city adopted a plan to develop the H Street Corridor as an arts and entertainment zone to drive social and economic revitalization. Philanthropist Jane Lang spearheaded renovation of a 1930s art deco movie theater into the **Atlas Performing Arts Center** (1333 H St., N.E., atlasarts.org). It opened in 2006, providing 60,000 square feet (5,575 sq m) of space for theater, dance, choral, and orchestral groups. An influx of new businesses is expected to follow the installation of a streetcar line, currently in the final stages of construction. Clubs and coffee shops have already sprung up, many with unvarnished decor and eclectic themes, such as the **Rock & Roll Hotel** (1353 H St., N.E., rockandrollhoteldc.com) for indie and punk music; **H Street Country Club** (1335 H St., N.E., thestreet countryclub.com) with Mexican food and indoor miniature golf; and the Irish pub/Jewish deli **Star and Shamrock** (1341 H St., N.E., starandshamrock.com). **Dr. Granville Moore's** (1238 H St., N.E., granvillemoores.com), a spot named for the physician whose name is still above the door, specializes in mussels and Belgian beer. If you want to try the dining scene, there's **Ethiopic** (401 H St., N.E., ethiopicres taurant.com) and **Dangerously Delicious Pies** (1339 H St., N.E., dangerouspiesdc.com).

Frederick Douglass National Historic Site

Situated among the row houses of Anacostia, Cedar Hill—former home of abolitionist Frederick Douglass—was built in the 1850s atop a grassy knoll. The 21-room tan brick house offers a commanding view of Washington from its gracious front porch. A visit to this National Park Service site provides a fascinating glimpse into the life and work of the "sage of Anacostia," the most prominent African-American orator of the 19th century.

The Douglass house contains many of the early civil rights leader's personal effects.

Frederick Douglass National Historic Site

Map p. 195

✉ 1411 W St., S.E.

☎ 202/426-5961 or 877/444-6777 for tour reservations

💲 $

🚇 Metro: Anacostia, then Bus B2

nps.gov/frdo

Frederick Douglass was born a slave in Maryland's Talbot County in 1818, son of a black mother and a white father, possibly his owner. Sent to Baltimore as a servant, he taught himself to read; at 20 he escaped to New York, then Massachusetts, where he lectured for the Massachusetts Anti-Slavery Society. To elude slave hunters after publishing his autobiography, in 1845, he fled to Europe. The purchase of his freedom by friends allowed him to return two years later. He began the *North Star* newspaper and kept working for the rights of blacks and women.

After the Civil War, he moved to Washington, D.C. Appointed U.S. marshal of the District in 1877, he bought 9-acre (3.6 ha) Cedar Hill. Cedar Hill was originally a farm estate with chicken coops, barn, and carriage house. He expanded it to 15 acres (6 ha) and enlarged the house by seven rooms. After his 1895 death, his widow, Helen, preserved Cedar Hill, which was later turned over to the National Park Service.

The guided 30-minute tour begins with a 17-minute film. Among items on display is a Lincoln cane given to Douglass by the President's widow. After the film, you climb the hill (via steep steps) to the **Victorian house.** Inside, the tastefully appointed parlors, library, and dining room look much as they did in Douglass's time—some 70 percent of the furnishings are original.

Upstairs, Douglass's bedroom is replete with a 19th-century bootjack and pair of shoes tucked by a chair. To see the different styles of his two wives, peek into their separate bedrooms.

Outside, you will find the **Growlery** (a reconstruction), the private study to which Douglass often retreated. ∎

More Places to See East & North of the Capitol

Anacostia Community Museum

Located in Fort Stanton Park, site of a Civil War fortification, this Anacostia museum opened in 1967 as a neighborhood museum devoted to the interpretation of the African-American experience, particularly in Washington, D.C.

Now part of the Smithsonian Institution, the museum offers a changing program of exhibits, music, art, dance, storytelling, and poetry. One of the exhibits, for example, focuses on black baseball teams in D.C., from Reconstruction to the second half of the 20th century.

Other exhibits have included retrospectives on black photographers, such as New Orleans's Jules Lion and inventors such as Benjamin Banneker, who helped plan the capital city. In addition, the museum has staged exhibits covering topics as diverse as African-American quilts, black churches, the antebellum South, the civil rights movement, Malcolm X, the 1920s renaissance, and the meaning and celebration of the Kwanzaa and Juneteenth holidays. *anacostia.si.edu* Map p. 195 ✉ 1901 Fort Pl., S.E. ☎ 202/633-4820 Ⓜ Metro: Anacostia, then Bus W2–W3

Congressional Cemetery

Founded by residents of Capitol Hill in 1807, this cemetery came to be reserved for members of Congress who died in office. Beginning in 1839, sandstone monuments were created for every member of Congress. (Fewer than 90 of the monuments have bodies buried beneath them; the rest honor people who are buried elsewhere.) Congress stopped the practice in 1877 after a furious debate, in which Senator George Hoar of Massachusetts argued that being buried under one of the massive monuments added "a new terror to death." Among the cemetery's famous residents are Capitol architect William Thornton (1828), Civil War photographer Mathew Brady (1916),

Marine Corps bandmaster John Philip Sousa (1932), and J. Edgar Hoover (1972), director of the FBI. Visitors can stroll the hilly grounds; a map is available at the entrance. *congressionalcemetery.org* Ⓜ Map p. 195 ✉ 1801 E St., S.E. ☎ 202/543-0539 Ⓜ Metro: Potomac Avenue

Franciscan Monastery

If a trip to the Holy Land is on your must-do list, this working monastery near the National Shrine of the Immaculate Conception offers a more accessible alternative. Tours are offered hourly, and you can wander the gardens freely. Built in 1899 to educate missionaries, the monastery contains full-scale reproductions of such sacred places as the Grotto of Lourdes, the Grotto of Gethsemane, the Tomb of the Virgin

A monk leads a tour down into the catacombs of the Franciscan Monastery.

Mary, and the Holy Sepulchre of Christ. The Byzantine-style church is laid out in the shape of a Crusader's cross, with chapels in the four corners. Especially memorable are the Roman-style catacombs down below. In spring the gardens grace the monastery with flowering rose bushes, dogwoods, and cherry trees. *myfranciscan.org* ⚠ Map p. 195 ✉ 1400 Quincy St., N.E. ☎ 202-526-6800 🚇 Metro: Brookland–CUA

Kenilworth Aquatic Gardens

A cool feast of water lilies and lotuses floats on the waters of the Kenilworth Aquatic Gardens, on the east bank of the Anacostia River. Started in 1880 by Civil War veteran Walter B. Shaw, this lovely 14-acre (5.6 ha) sanctuary—now managed by the National Park Service—is in full bloom in the middle of the summer. Garden tours are offered mornings on weekends during summer months.

A **visitor center** near the gardens' parking lot has exhibits on the area. With 40 ponds and a 335-yard (306 m) boardwalk extending into marshes, the gardens offer fine opportunities for viewing birds and

other wildlife, such as osprey, snapping turtles, and muskrats.

The 0.7-mile (1.1 km; one way) **River Trail** offers a closer look at 77-acre (31 ha) Kenilworth Marsh, which borders the gardens and is rich in bird and plant life. Here American bittern, long-billed marsh wrens, and spotted salamanders live in a cattail-fringed wetland.

The best time for seeing wildlife and catching night-blooming lilies is in the early morning. The gardens are open 7 a.m.–5 p.m. *nps.gov/keaq* ⚠ Map p. 195 ✉ 1550 Anacostia Ave., N.E. ☎ 202/426-6905 🚇 Metro: Deanwood, then walk across Kenilworth overpass to Douglas St. & Anacostia Ave.; Bus: V7

Washington Navy Yard

Authorized in 1799, the Washington Navy Yard occupies land set aside by George Washington for the federal government. The Greek Revival arched gate at the main entrance was designed in 1804 by Benjamin Latrobe, one of the U.S. Capitol's architects. Early on the Navy Yard became a major shipbuilding facility, turning out vessels that ranged from 70-foot (21 m) gunboats to 246-foot (75 m) frigates. Burned in the War of 1812, the yard was rebuilt and played a major role in the city's defense during the Civil War; President Lincoln was a frequent visitor to the site. After the eight conspirators involved in his assassination were captured, they were taken to the yard and held aboard ship.

The Navy Museum near the U.S.S. *Barry* (see sidebar left), houses an impressive array of artifacts dating from the Revolutionary War. See the website or call for information on arranging a visit. *history.navy.mil* ⚠ Map p. 195 ✉ 11th & O Sts., S.E. (weekdays); 6th & M Sts., S.E. (weekends) ☎ 202/433-4882 (Navy Museum), 202/433-3377 (U.S.S. *Barry*) 🕐 Call for hours 🚇 Metro: Eastern Market, Navy Yard–Ballpark

---

Tour a Navy Ship

The U.S.S. *Barry*, permanently docked at the Washington Navy Yard, offers a chance to experience the tight quarters and self-contained operations of life aboard a military destroyer. Before it was decommissioned in 1982, the *Barry* supported U.S. airborne landings in Beirut, Lebanon, in 1958; helped quarantine Cuba in 1962 after Soviet missiles were installed on the island; and earned battle stars for its service during the Vietnam conflict. Today the ship is open for free self-guided tours Thursday through Saturday (but is closed during the winter). Guided tours can be arranged on request *(tel 202/433-3377)*.

On the Virginia side of the Potomac, from Alexandria to Arlington, lots more of the country's past

Across the Potomac

Welcome to Alexandria: A pineapple door knocker symbolizes hospitality.

Across the Potomac

The Northern Virginia region just beyond Washington proper is an exciting, densely populated mix of historic sites, residential neighborhoods, restaurants, and shops. Arlington and Alexandria especially have much to offer residents and visitors alike. Both bustling communities originally belonged to the District of Columbia, which once straddled both sides of the Potomac River.

Theodore Roosevelt Memorial Bridge connects Washington with the Virginia burbs.

Though Virginia took back roughly a third of the city in 1846, the fortunes of the reclaimed areas remain tied to Washington. Separated by the Crystal City high-rises around Ronald Reagan Washington National Airport, the communities of Arlington and Alexandria are connected by the Metro system and highly scenic George Washington Memorial Parkway.

NOT TO BE MISSED:

Already a tobacco port, Alexandria got its official start in 1749 as a 60-acre (24 ha) town site. Both George Washington, who lived 9 miles (14.5 km) south at Mount Vernon, and Robert E. Lee considered it their hometown. Alexandria has prospered of late with the sprucing up of its waterfront and the restoration of 18th-century town houses. Now a tony residential area, the town draws a steady stream of visitors to its bars, restaurants, and shops. Historical sites give insight into the lives of Washington, Lee, and other prominent locals.

One of the nation's smallest counties, with no incorporated cities or towns, Arlington did not exist as a separate entity until after 1846, when the land was returned from Washington to Virginia. Today it is home to Arlington National Cemetery and the Pentagon. The moving Marine Corps War Memorial, Theodore Roosevelt Island, the string of Potomac River parks along the parkway, and the restaurants along the Ballston/Clarendon corridor are other good reasons for venturing to the Virginia side of the river. ■

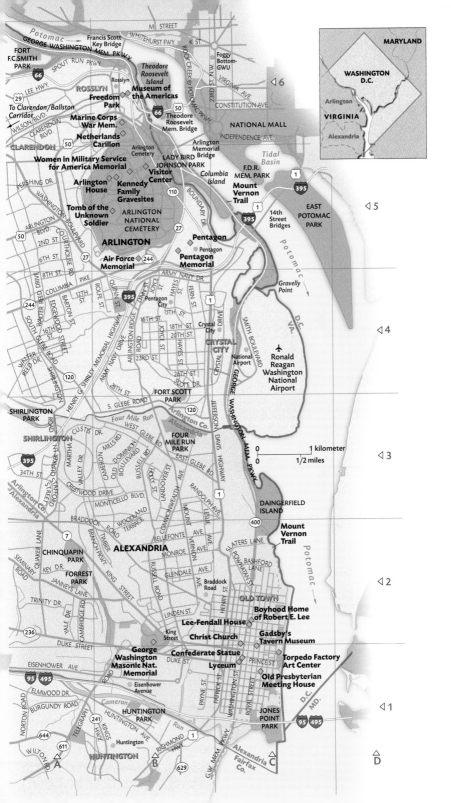

Arlington

Originally part of the area surveyed for the nation's capital, the land on the west bank of the Potomac River was returned to the Commonwealth of Virginia by the U.S. Congress in 1846. Sites with historic resonance abound, along with 86 miles (138 km) of hiking and biking trails.

Hundreds of thousands of servicemen and women lie buried beneath Arlington's green expanses.

Arlington National Cemetery

 Map p. 205 B5

✉ Virginia side of Arlington Memorial Bridge, off Va. 110

☎ 703/607-8000

🕐 Changing of the Guard, every hour Oct.–March, every half hour April–Sept.

💲 $ (parking fee), $$ (tourmobile)

🚇 Metro: Arlington Cemetery

arlingtoncemetery .mil

Arlington National Cemetery

Rows of white headstones on rolling hills, the Changing of the Guard at the Tomb of the Unknowns, the eternal flame at John F. Kennedy's grave: These enduring images immediately bring to mind the nation's most famous national cemetery.

The nearby mansion atop the hill is Arlington House, once the home of Robert E. Lee and his wife, Mary. Lee's father-in-law— George Washington Parke Custis, the first President's adopted grandson—built the Greek Revival mansion in 1802–1817; it anchored a 1,100-acre (445 ha) plantation. Lee and his wife lived

here on and off for 30 years while traveling between U.S. Army posts.

Soon after Lee left to fight for the Confederacy in 1861, the federal government confiscated the estate. In 1864, the mansion and 200 acres (91 ha) were set aside for a national cemetery at the urging of Union Quartermaster Gen. Montgomery Meigs. Later that year, his son was killed in the war; a high-relief tomb effigy of him lying slain by the side of the road is one of the cemetery's most distinctive memorials.

Despite the objections of Meigs, Confederate soldiers were allowed burial in the Arlington cemetery, but without any official observances. In 1900

Congress finally designated a Confederate section of the cemetery, and in 1914 the **Confederate Memorial** was dedicated by President Woodrow Wilson.

As for the Lee family's fate, Lee's son, G. W. C. Lee, sued the government after the Civil War for confiscating the land. The Supreme Court ruled that he should be paid the market value, $150,000.

The 624-acre (252 ha) cemetery is now the final resting place for more than 400,000 service people. With 135–150 funerals conducted every week, the cemetery is expected to be filled by 2060, at which time it may expand onto other government-owned land. For burial here, a service person must have died on active duty, retired from active duty service, or been awarded a high military decoration; the cremated remains of any veteran with an honorable discharge can be placed in the Columbarium. For a funeral with full military honors, a flag-draped casket is accompanied by an honor guard. After three rifle volleys, "Taps" is played. The honor guard then presents the folded flag to the next of kin.

Visiting: Entering the cemetery via Memorial Drive, you'll see the semicircular building of the **Women in Military Service for America Memorial.** Dedicated in 1997, it honors the nearly two million women who have served since 1776. Begin your tour in the visitor center, which has exhibits, a 12-minute film, and a map of the cemetery. You can stroll on your own among the quiet, tree-shaded pathways or board a tourmobile, which stops at major points of interest.

From behind the visitor center, head up the pathway to find the **gravesite of President John F. Kennedy.** At his funeral in 1963, his widow, Jacqueline, lit an eternal flame that continues to flicker even in the rain. She and their two infant children also are interred here. The site offers a grand view of familiar monuments across the river in Washington. Nearby, white wooden crosses mark the **graves of Senators Robert F. Kennedy and Edward M. Kennedy.**

INSIDER TIP:

Two Presidents are buried at Arlington National Cemetery: William Howard Taft (1930) and John F. Kennedy (1963).

—LARRY PORGES
National Geographic Travel Books editor

The best view of Washington, however, is farther up the hill at **Arlington House.** The Union Army used the house as a defense post headquarters. After the war, the cemetery superintendent lived and worked here for many years. In 1955 it was officially designated the Robert E. Lee Memorial.

Restored to its antebellum appearance, the house looks much as it did during the Lee years.

Arlington House

- Map p. 205 B5
- Arlington National Cemetery
- 703/235-1530

nps.gov/arho

Marine Corps War Memorial

 Map p. 205 B6

 N. Marshall Dr., just N of Arlington Cemetery

☎ 703/289-2500

🚇 Metro: Arlington Cemetery or Rosslyn

nps.gov/gwmp

Though many heirlooms in the 15 rooms were looted, about a third of the furnishings are original. In the slave quarters and museum out back are exhibits on the Lee and Custis families.

About a half-mile (0.8 km) walk south of the house, adjacent to the amphitheater, the **Tomb of the Unknowns** holds the remains of unidentified servicemen, one each from the two World Wars and Korea (the Vietnam veteran's

---

Restaurants & Shops Along Arlington Corridor

This busy commercial and residential area, served by several stops along Metro's Orange Line, has become a popular destination for dining and shopping. The **Market Common at Clarendon** (*2800 Clarendon Blvd.*) has a walkway that will deliver you to chain stores as well as small shops and coffee hangouts. Close-by restaurants include **Cava Mezze** (*2940 Clarendon Blvd., tel 703/276-9090*), which features fresh ingredients in its Greek small plates, and **Le Pain Quotidien** (*2900 N. Clarendon Blvd., tel 703/465-0970*) for casual munching on quiche and pastry. Other good choices are **La Tasca** (*2900 Wilson Blvd., tel 703/812-9120*) for tapas and Italian fare and **Ray's the Steaks** (*2300 Wilson Blvd., tel 703/841-7297*) for hand-carved beef.

---

remains were removed in 1998 when they were identified). A 24-hour guard patrols this symbolic site, carrying an M-14 rifle with a ceremonial bayonet. The sentinel takes 21 steps on the plaza (symbolic of a 21-gun salute), then turns to face the tomb for 21 seconds. Among those buried at Arlington are polar

explorer Richard Byrd, boxer Joe Louis, 229 sailors from the U.S.S. *Maine* (sunk in Havana harbor in 1898), and the city designer of Washington, Pierre-Charles L'Enfant, whose grave lies in front of the mansion. Another is Gen. John J. Pershing, commander of the American Expeditionary Forces in World War I, who lies buried among those with whom he served. Section 60, one of the cemetery's active burial sections, is the final resting place for more than 800 service members killed in Iraq and Afghanistan.

Marine Corps War Memorial

Located a short distance from Arlington National Cemetery, the Marine Corps War Memorial (or Iwo Jima Memorial) depicts an actual event. There were, however, two flag raisings. On February 23, 1945, four days into a vicious struggle for control of Iwo Jima, a detachment of U.S. Marines made it to the top of Mount Suribachi and raised a small American flag. Later that day, after the slopes had been cleared of enemy resistance, five Marines and a Navy hospital corpsmen raised a larger flag—inspiring the iconic image that won news photographer Joseph Rosenthal a Pulitzer Prize. The Marines' capture of the island three weeks later was a key victory in the Pacific campaign. Sculptor Felix de Weldon, then on duty with the U.S. Navy, was so moved by the image he later cast it in bronze. The statue was dedicated in 1954.

Air Force Memorial

The sleek stainless-steel spires of the Air Force Memorial, completed in 2006, soar skyward from a promontory near the Pentagon. The novel design is by architect James Ingo Freed, who drew his inspiration from the "bomb burst" formation of Air Force jet maneuvers. Three spires—the tallest reaches 270 feet (82 m)—represent the three core values of the Air Force (integrity, service before self, and excellence) and its three divisions (active, guard, and reserve). In granite beneath each spire is the Air Force star.

The Air Force Memorial's three steel spires stretch to the sky.

Pentagon & Pentagon Memorial

No one today can look at this massive headquarters without recalling the tragedy of September 11, 2001, when a hijacked jetliner crashed into the building's south side, now rebuilt. Millions of dollars in donations were collected to construct a memorial park to honor the 184 civilian and military victims of that incident.

One of the world's largest office buildings, the 6.5-million-square-foot (603,870 sq m) **Pentagon** was built in just 16 months during World War II to combine the offices of the War Department under one roof. The number five has no particular significance; the building originally conformed to a five-sided site, and since President Roosevelt liked the unique shape, it was kept.

Today the Pentagon is a city unto itself, housing 23,000 military, civilian, and support personnel working to protect national interests. On weekdays, enlisted members from the military services conduct 60-minute tours along more than a mile (1.6 km) of corridors, where military art, model planes, and portraits of military leaders are on display. Out of sight are the top-secret War Room and other situation rooms. Reservations are mandatory for Pentagon tours and should be made online at least two weeks in advance.

The adjacent 2-acre (0.8 ha) **Pentagon Memorial** occupies a site near where American Airlines Flight 77 hit the Pentagon. In an open competition, the winning design for the memorial was submitted by a pair of young architects, Julie Beckman and Keith Kaseman. It features lighted reflecting pools, maple trees, and rows of steel benches—one bench for each of the victims.

Air Force Memorial

- 🅰 Map p. 205 B5
- ✉ 1400 block of Columbia Pike
- ☎ 703/979-0674
- 🚇 Metro: Pentagon or Pentagon City, then a mile (0.6 km) walk

airforcememorial.org

Pentagon & Pentagon Memorial

- 🅰 Map p. 205 B5
- ✉ I-395 & Jefferson Davis Hwy. (Va. 110)
- ☎ 703/697-1776
- 🕐 Closed Sat.–Sun. & federal holidays
- 💲 $ (parking fee Pentagon City)
- 🚇 Metro: Pentagon

pentagontours.osd.mil

Theodore Roosevelt Island

 Map p. 205 B6

✉ Potomac River, 0.25 mile/0.4 km N of Theodore Roosevelt Bridge via George Washington Memorial Pkwy. N (no vehicle access southbound)

☎ 703/289-2500

🚇 Metro: Rosslyn

nps.gov/this

The 125 benches are arranged so that visitors will see the names of the victims and the Pentagon at the same time; the benches dedicated to the 59 airline passengers are oriented toward the flight path. Each bench bears the name of one victim, organized on an age line (ranging from 3 to 71).

The site can be approached from the Pentagon's south parking lot and nearby Metro station or from public parking lots at Pentagon City.

Theodore Roosevelt Island

An arcadia of wooded paths and bird-filled marshes, this 91-acre (37 ha) island opposite the Kennedy Center is a favorite lunchtime retreat for office workers. Some 2.5 miles (4 km) of trails are just right for walking, running, bird-watching, and general relaxing from city stresses.

In 1967, the island was turned into a memorial to the charismatic, conservation-minded U.S. President. Many people heading over the footbridge for a walk

INSIDER TIP:

Leave your wheels behind. Neither cars nor bicycles are allowed on Theodore Roosevelt Island, a place of green in the Potomac River.

—JONATHAN TOURTELLOT
National Geographic fellow

are surprised to find, tucked in the middle of the woods, a rather grandiose **memorial** featuring a 17-foot-high (5 m) bronze of Roosevelt, fountains, and several enormous granite tablets inscribed with his words.

After a look at the memorial, you can choose between wooded or river-edged paths. One of the most delightful areas is the **boardwalk** through the swamp and marsh on the island's east side. Along here, herons stalk prey among cattails and pickerelweed, while bald cypresses and gnarled oaks suggest a pre-Washington landscape. ■

An island and statue honor President Theodore Roosevelt.

Cruising the George Washington Memorial Parkway

Offering peerless views of the capital city, this stunning roadway lends the perfect excuse for a leisurely drive. Ambling along the Potomac River between Mount Vernon and the American Legion Bridge, it links historic sites, riverside parks, and overlooks.

Beginning south of Alexandria at **Mount Vernon** (see pp. 224–226), the parkway (nps .gov/gwmp) winds north through maples, oaks, beeches, and tulip poplars, chosen when the parkway was designed in the 1930s to give it the look of the Virginia countryside. Two miles (3.2 km) on sprawls **Fort Hunt Park,** preserving batteries that guarded the river approach to the city, 1898–1918. Look across the river to see its mate, **Fort Washington** (1824). Ahead, a right turnoff leads to **River Farm** (tel 703/768-5700, closed Sun.), once part of George Washington's estate. Beyond **Belle Haven Marina** spreads a wide upriver view— birders congregate here. For a closer look, stroll **Dyke Marsh** (Belle Haven Marina), a 240-acre (97 ha) bird haven.

Within **Old Town, Alexandria** (see pp. 214–216), the parkway becomes Washington Street. Two blocks beyond King Street rises **Christ Church** (see pp. 212–213), on the left. Beyond town you'll spot **Daingerfield Island,** site of a small marina and restaurant with a view.

Just north of Ronald Reagan Washington National Airport you'll see the **Washington skyline** and its parade of monuments: the Capitol, Jefferson Memorial, Washington Monument, and Lincoln Memorial. Beyond the 14th Street Bridge rises the **Navy and Marine Memorial.** Farther, you'll pass through the **LBJ Memorial Grove** and **Lady Bird Johnson Park** (see sidebar below). About a quarter mile (0.4 km) beyond Roosevelt Bridge is the turnout for **Theodore Roosevelt Island** (see p. 210). The road passes beneath Key Bridge, with **Georgetown University**'s spire looming across the river. The road then climbs above the Potomac. About 1.5 miles (2.4 km) beyond **Turkey Run Park,** the parkway ends at I-495 and the **American Legion Bridge.**

INSIDER TIP:

Pull off at Gravelly Point in Arlington and watch jetliners take off and land—seemingly just above your head. Ronald Regan National Airport is that close.

—BARBARA NOE
*National Geographic Travel Books
senior editor*

Lady Bird's Legacy

Thousands of daffodils, hundreds of red tulips, and groups of golden willows and dogwood trees—that's just part of the plantings at **Lady Bird Johnson Park,** a 17-acre (7 ha) site on Columbia Island, across the Potomac River from Washington. During her 1960s White House years, the First Lady took up the task of beautifying the landscapes of both the nation and its capital (among those efforts was the planting of wildflowers along blighted patches of highway). The nearby memorial to her husband, Lyndon Baines Johnson, is a granite sculpture set in a grove of trees. Access the parking lot near both parks from the northbound lanes of the George Washington Parkway, between Memorial Bridge and the 14th Street Bridge.

Alexandria

With its brick sidewalks, federal town houses, and quaint shops and restaurants, Alexandria's Old Town reminds many people of Georgetown. No coincidence here, since both arose as tobacco ports in the mid-1700s, a mere eight river miles (13 km) from one another.

Local color: King Street's panoply of shops and restaurants fills centuries-old row houses.

Christ Church

Map p. 205 C2

✉ 118 N. Washington St.

☎ 703/549-1450

🚇 Metro: King St.; Bus: 10A

historicchrist church.org

Scotsman John Alexander, for whom Alexandria is named, purchased much of present-day Alexandria in 1669 from an English ship captain for 6,000 pounds (2,720 kg) of tobacco. Incorporated in 1749, the town thrived as a foreign port of entry. Strolling along Old Town's beautifully preserved wharf today, it's easy to visualize how Alexandria must have looked when tall-masted brigs and schooners docked at the piers, mariners bustled about, and captains strutted cobbled lanes. Slaves and grain as well as tobacco added to the early prosperity of this genteel Southern town.

The Civil War, however, changed all that. As a buffer for Washington, only 100 miles (160 km) north of

the Confederate capital of Richmond, Alexandria was occupied and soon overrun with Union forces. The fortified town became a crossroads for men and supplies—hundreds of thousands of soldiers tramped through on their way to postings and battles, and train after train rolled in with the wounded. Warehouses, churches, hotels, even large houses were requisitioned for use as military stations and hospitals. After the war, the small-town atmosphere was all but gone. As Washington grew, Alexandria deteriorated. In 1946 the City Council moved to protect the 18th- and 19th-century row houses, making Old Town the nation's third officially designated historic district.

Today, Old Town is a delightful place to stroll (see pp. 214–216). Especially on weekend evenings, crowds pack the restaurants and pubs, enjoying the vibrant nightlife against its historical backdrop.

Christ Church

This historic church has sat behind its iron-gated fence on Washington Street since before Alexandria was established. Completed in 1773 in Georgian country style, it has a brick exterior and whitewashed interior. The Palladian chancel window is unusual for its time.

George Washington was one of the first to buy a pew here, now marked by a silver plaque (No. 60). Tradition says that on the lawn he first declared to friends his intent to fight the war of American independence. Robert E. Lee was confirmed here on July 17, 1853 (marked by another silver plaque, on the chancel), and he worshiped here with his family.

The tree-shaded **burying ground** was used for Alexandrians until 1808; the earliest tombstone is dated March 20, 1791. Look for one of the latest tombstones, for actress Anne Warren. Her 1808 epitaph reads in part: "The unrivaled excellence of theatrical talents was surpassed by the mighty virtues ... which adorned her private life." Docents lead **tours** daily; meet at the church's front door.

Gadsby's Tavern Museum

Consisting of a 1785 tavern and a 1792 hotel, Gadsby's Tavern was colonial Alexandria's center of social, political, and business life. Balls, meetings, performances, and receptions once enlivened its rooms, earning it praise as the finest public house in America. Restored as a museum and restaurant, the tavern appears just as frequent visitor George Washington might have seen it. A 30-minute **guided tour** shows the taproom where patrons dined on whatever fare happened to be served that night—perhaps ham and cheese "pye" or cream of County Surrey peanut soup. You learn that the drink of choice was rum, sometimes mixed with fruit juice and imported sugar. You also see the dining room, ballroom, and assembly room, where local groups met. In the third-floor communal bedchambers, the beds and floors were shared by as many travelers as could fit the space. ■

Gadsby's Tavern Museum

- 🅰 Map p. 205 C1
- ✉ 134 N. Royal St.
- ☎ 703/746-4242
- 💲 $
- 🕐 Closed Mon.–Tues. Nov.–March
- Ⓜ Metro: King St.; Bus: AT2–AT5

gadsbystavern.org

EXPERIENCE: Follow the Trail to Mount Vernon

Running along the Virginia side of the Potomac River, the **Mount Vernon Trail** extends nearly 18 miles (29 km) from Theodore Roosevelt Island to George Washington's estate. Walkers, joggers, and rollerbladers are a common sight, but there are other activities you can enjoy.

The best plan for biking to Mount Vernon is to start from Old Town Alexandria. Rent a hybrid or mountain bike from **Big Wheel Bikes** (2 Prince St., tel 703/739-2300), then head south on the Mount Vernon Trail for 10 miles (16 km; note: It's somewhat hilly, especially as you approach the tail end). When you reach Mount Vernon, you can park your bike and tour the estate and gardens (see pp. 224–226).

For a vigorous walk and great views of the monuments, start at **Theodore Roosevelt Island** (see p. 210). Travel south along the path to **Gravelly Point;** roundtrip, you'll cover about 4 miles (6.4 km).

Gravelly Point Park attracts people straining to film the drama of giant planes landing and taking off at National Airport. Take a blanket and picnic if you like, but the deafening roar overhead isn't conducive to conversation.

The **Washington Sailing Marina** (tel 703/548-9027, washingtonsailingmarina .com), 1.5 miles (2.4 km) south of the airport, is a favored spot for small sailboat racing. The marina offers weekend sailing lessons, and its **Indigo Landing Restaurant** (tel 703/548-0001) serves up seafood year-round.

Old Town by Foot

Strolling is the best way to enjoy Old Town's colonial ambience, allowing you plenty of time to study the architectural details of historic row houses, admire postage-stamp gardens, visit historic buildings once frequented by Thomas Jefferson, George Washington, and Robert E. Lee, poke into specialty shops, and simply see what there is to see. The walk outlined here can be done in a couple of hours—more if you linger.

Along the Potomac River: The wharf offers pleasant waterfront views and breezes.

Begin in the heart of the historic core at the two-story, yellow-frame **Ramsay House Visitor Center** ❶ *(221 King St., tel 703/746-3301)*, a reconstruction of the 1724 home of town founder William Ramsay. Across Fairfax Street, **Market Square** holds a Saturday morning market that dates from 1753, making it one of the country's oldest.

From the visitor center, walk south on Fairfax Street. About half a block down on the right, the **Stabler-Leadbeater Apothecary Museum** ❷ *(105–107 S. Fairfax St., tel 703/746-3852, closed Mon.–Tues. Nov.–March, $)* operated from 1792 to 1933. George Washington, James Monroe, and Robert E. Lee all knew these walls, stocked with all kinds of goods, including medical supplies. Preserved intact, the shop contains original potions, herbs, mortars, and journals.

NOT TO BE MISSED:

**Torpedo Factory Art Center
• Christ Church • Gadsby's
Tavern Museum**

Go back to King Street and turn right. On the river, the **Torpedo Factory Art Center** ❸ *(105 N. Union St., tel 703/838-4565, torpedo factory.org)* holds 80-odd studios where you can watch artisans sculpt, paint, weave, and more. A museum of local archaeological artifacts is on the third floor. Built in 1918, the factory turned out torpedo shell casings and other weaponry for both World Wars (look for the torpedo on the ground floor); the federal government used the building for storage until the city of

Alexandria bought it in 1969. The art center, opened in 1974, was incorporated into a major waterfront development a decade later. Out back, you can stroll along the docks or relax on a bench and enjoy the fresh air.

Walk south on Union and make a right on Prince Street. Known as **Captain's Row,** this cobblestoned block is lined with sturdy federal town houses, many of which were owned by ship captains in the 18th century. Cross Lee Street, and on the right stands the 1851 pink stucco Greek Revival **Athenaeum** *(201 Prince St., tel 703/548-0035, nvfaa.org),* which once functioned as a bank; with the onset of the Civil War, the bank closed and documents were hidden until after the war, when customers were reimbursed. Now owned by the Northern Virginia Fine Arts Association, the Athenaeum features a contemporary art gallery. A little farther up the block, William Fairfax,

an original trustee of Alexandria, lived at **207 Prince Street,** and next door at **209 Prince** lived Dr. James Craik, the surgeon-general who was with George Washington throughout the Revolutionary War, and who attended him at his death in nearby Mount Vernon.

At Fairfax Street, turn left and head south across Duke Street to the **Old Presbyterian Meeting House** *(321 S. Fairfax St., tel 703/549-6670, opmh.org).* Built in 1774, the church has an unadorned interior; in the churchyard lies the Tomb of the Unknown Soldier of the American Revolution.

▲ See also area map p. 205
► Ramsay House Visitor Center
🕒 3 hours, without stops
⟺ 2 miles (3.2 km)
► Carlyle House

Green Christmas boughs adorn town houses on Old Town's quaint, historic Queen Street.

Proceed back up Duke Street to Washington Street, the main north-south thoroughfare, and head north. On the street's west side, the Greek Revival–style **Lyceum** *(201 S. Washington St., tel 703/838-4994),* built in 1839 as a cultural center and library, now has history exhibits.

At the intersection of Washington and Prince stands the bronze **Confederate Statue,** a memorial to the town's Confederate dead. Created by Casper Buberl and erected in 1889, the defeated-looking veteran faces south. A block north you're back at **King Street,** Old Town's main commercial avenue with a busy assortment of restaurants, bars, and boutiques. Antique shops pack the stretch to the west.

The monument rising on the hill a mile (1.6 km) or so west is the grandiose **George Washington Masonic National Memorial** *(King St. & Callahan Dr., tel 703/683-2007, gwmemorial.org),* with views of Alexandria and Washington from the ninth-floor observation deck. The guided one-hour tour *($$)* lingers a bit much on Masonic history, but is worthwhile for the collection of Washington memorabilia, including his family Bible and leather field trunk.

Back at Washington and King Streets, the next block north holds historic **Christ Church ④** (see pp. 212–213). Three blocks farther north on Washington, the **Lee-Fendall House ⑤** *(614 Oronoco St., tel 703/548-1789,*

leefendallhouse.org, closed Mon.–Tues., $) was built in 1785 by lawyer Philip Fendall, who married an aunt of Robert E. Lee. Family heirlooms on display include portraits, letters, and books.

Across Oronoco Street is the **Boyhood Home of Robert E. Lee** (No. 607), where George Washington once dined and which the Marquis de Lafayette visited. The house was recently bought by private owners and is not open to the public.

Head back down Washington and make a left on Cameron. To get a feel for how early Alexandrians dined, stop by the **Gadsby's Tavern Museum ⑥** (see p. 213). Then walk east to Cameron and Fairfax Streets and end your stroll at the Georgian Palladian-style **Carlyle House** *(121 N. Fairfax St., tel 703/549-2997, carlylehouse.org, closed Mon., $$),* built in 1753 by Scottish merchant John Carlyle. British Gen. Edward Braddock convened a meeting here in 1755 with five colonial governors to discuss the financing of the French and Indian War. Interesting tours showcase the lifestyles of an 18th-century Virginia family and their servants and slaves.

Alexandria—National Harbor by Water Taxi

Go by water from the Old Town, Alexandria, historic waterfront downriver to National Harbor—and vice versa. Water taxis *(potomacriverboatco .com, $$)* make the 20-minute trip (one way) several times a day year-round. Along the Maryland banks of the Potomac, National Harbor *(nationalharbor.com)* is a mix of hotels, restaurants, and shops, including the Gaylord National Resort and Convention Center, a Swarovski crystals shop, and the nation's first Peeps store (yes, those marshmallow chicks and bunnies). Among the special events along the National Harbor are a summer clambake and Oktoberfest.

A wealth of historic sites worth a peek even without the capital city nearby, plus a surprising on-the-water metropolis

Excursions

Even the grass seems to stand tall at the U.S. Naval Academy in Annapolis.

Excursions

With riverside parklands and cobble-laned villages, colonial plantations and busy harborfronts nearby, Washington is blessed with an abundance of easy escapes within an hour's drive away.

Kids learn to curtsy at Gunston Hall in Virginia.

Among the most accessible destinations is the Chesapeake & Ohio National Historical Park, which preserves the ruins of a 19th-century canal and its towpath. Beginning in Georgetown and paralleling the Potomac River for more than 180 miles (290 km) north,

---

NOT TO BE MISSED:

---

it's especially popular with walkers, bikers, and campers. Great Falls—its most distinctive feature and probably the most spectacular natural attraction between the Blue Ridge and the Chesapeake Bay—is only 5 miles (8 km) beyond the Beltway (I-495). Great Falls Park on the Virginia side of the river is also a popular place to view the falls.

One of the area's newest additions is the Udvar-Hazy Center, the National Air and Space Museum annex near Washington Dulles International Airport in Northern Virginia. The hangarlike facility houses notable aircraft too large to fit in the downtown museum, including the *Enola Gay* and a supersonic Concord.

You'll find history that goes even further back on the Potomac River south of Washington. More than 250 years ago, Virginia colonists established vast plantations and manor houses, such as Mount Vernon, the home of George Washington, and Gunston Hall. Built by the slaves of early citizens, these historic houses, and the younger Woodlawn, stand today as tributes to the quality workmanship and to the tireless efforts of preservationists.

Annapolis, some 30 miles (48 km) east of D.C. at the point where the Severn River spills into the Chesapeake Bay, is equally well preserved. The Maryland state capital is a charming, history-steeped, seafood-proud water town. It's easy to fill a day exploring the town's colonial center and admiring the sailboats.

To the north, Baltimore, with its vibrant Inner Harbor, sits on the Patapsco River off the Chesapeake Bay. Boasting a world-class aquarium, stellar museums, and the only Civil War–era vessel still afloat today, this popular, newly revitalized city makes for another good waterside excursion. ∎

Vienna

50

236

645

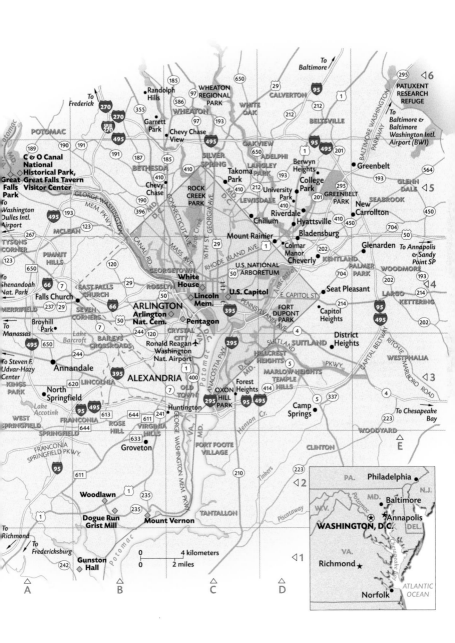

Chesapeake & Ohio Canal and Great Falls

Snaking 184.5 miles (297 km) northwest from Georgetown to Cumberland, Maryland, the Chesapeake & Ohio Canal National Historical Park is one of the longest, skinniest parks in the National Park system. The most dramatic section is certainly the Great Falls area, just north of Washington, where the Potomac River hurls over steep, ragged rocks in a spectacular series of thundering falls before flowing through narrow Mather Gorge.

A kayaker hones his technique in the holes and waves below Great Falls.

C & O Canal National Historical Park

🗺 Map p. 219 A5

✉ Georgetown Visitor Center, 1057 Thomas Jefferson St., N.W.

☎ 202/653-5190

✉ Great Falls Tavern Visitor Center, 11710 MacArthur Blvd., Potomac, MD

☎ 301/767-3714

💲 $

nps.gov/choh

President John Quincy Adams broke ground for the C & O Canal on July 4, 1828. It was considered a Great National Project that would link Georgetown in Washington with Pittsburgh on the Ohio River. Plagued with problems from the start, however, including stiff competition by the new Baltimore & Ohio Railroad, the canal only made it as far as Cumberland, Maryland.

Thousands of laborers toiled for 22 years to carve the trench, sometimes out of pure rock. A feat of engineering, its 74 lift locks raise it 605 feet (184 m) in elevation from beginning to end.

Mule-drawn barges hauled coal, hay, fertilizer, and cement from the Appalachian Mountains into Washington until 1924. Today, you can board a mule-powered canal boat in Georgetown and ride through a working lock (April–Oct., $$).

In the early 1950s, Supreme Court Justice William O. Douglas led a movement to preserve the abandoned canal. The C & O was designated a national historical park in 1971.

You can bike or hike the 14-mile (22.5) towpath stretch from Georgetown to Great Falls, a lovely stretch offering pretty river views; or you can drive, via MacArthur Boulevard, to the Great Falls Tavern section of the national historical park. The white stucco building overlooking the canal houses the **visitor center.** Built in 1831, the structure served as a lodge for travelers and boatmen for nearly a century. Exhibits tell about the canal's history.

To see the falls—and perhaps bald eagles—head a short way downstream on the towpath to the trail leading to **Great Falls Overlook.** A combination of boardwalk and bridges, the trail links the two sections of Olmsted Island, ending at roaring Great Falls as it narrows and tumbles 76 feet (23 m) over craggy boulders. Back on the towpath, continue downstream. Before the stop-lock bridge, pick up the **Billy Goat Trail,** a wild, 2-mile (3.2 km) romp over jagged rocks high on the river's edge, along Mather Gorge. In spring, trout lilies, jack-in-the-pulpits, and bluebells sprinkle the forest floor, and goose honks and songbird trills fill the air. Often kayakers play in the rapids below and rock climbers scale the gorge wall. The trail ends farther down the towpath, allowing an easy 1.25-mile (2 km) walk back to the visitor center.

The 4.2-mile (6.7 km) **Gold Mine Loop** behind the visitor center winds through post oaks and river birches to the Maryland Mine. Now in ruins, it operated from 1867 to 1939.

Great Falls Park

On the Virginia side of the falls, a short distance as the crow flies but some 12 miles (19 km) by car, is 800-acre (323 ha) Great Falls Park. Learn about local flora and fauna, kayaking, and rock climbing at the **visitor center.** Nearby overlooks provide fine views of the wide river. The blue-blazed **River Trail** heads downstream for about a mile and a half (2.4 km), edging the bluff above Mather Gorge. Here you'll find the ruins of the **Patowmack Canal,** started by George Washington in 1786 and closed in 1830 after work on the C&O had begun; five locks raised or lowered boats the height of the falls. A 2.2-mile (3.5 km) trail takes you past the ruins of **Matildaville,** a town that served the needs of the canal industry. ∎

Great Falls Park

🅰 Map p. 219 A5

✉ Intersection of Georgetown Pike (Rte. 193) & Old Dominion Dr., Mclean, VA

☎ 703/285-2965

💲 $

nps.gov/grfa

EXPERIENCE:
Trekking the C&O Canal Towpath

The C&O Canal towpath, part of the 830-mile-long (1,335 m) Potomac Heritage National Scenic Trail, begins in southern Maryland at the confluence of the Potomac River and Chesapeake Bay, passes though Washington, then extends northwest to Cumberland, Maryland, and on to Pittsburgh, Pennsylvania. Local groups manage sections of the trail. The **Allegheny Trail Alliance** (atatrail.org) has info on hiking and biking. You can plan side trips to attractions such as **Fallingwater** (fallingwater.org), Frank Lloyd Wright's landmark in southwest Pennsylvania, and **Fort Stevens** (nps.gov/cwdw/historyculture/fort-stevens.htm), site of the only Civil War battle fought within Washington, D.C.

Steven F. Udvar-Hazy Center

This annex of the National Air and Space Museum (see pp. 77–83), located near Washington Dulles International Airport in Northern Virginia, was built to house additional aircraft and space artifacts too large and numerous to fit into the downtown building. But the splendid hangarlike facility, named the Steven F. Udvar-Hazy Center for its major donor, hardly plays second string to the more established museum when it comes to attractions.

Aircraft is displayed high and low at the Smithsonian National Air and Space Museum's facility.

Steven F. Udvar-Hazy Center

✉ 14390 Air & Space Museum Pkwy., Chantilly, VA (S of Dulles Airport's main terminal, near Rtes. 28 & 50)

☎ 703/572-4118

🕐 Closed Christmas Day

💲 Entrance free, parking $$$

airandspace.si.edu/visit/udvar-hazy-center

Planning for the annex began in the early 1980s. In 1998, the Smithsonian and the Metropolitan Washington Airports Authority signed a long-term lease for the center's 176-acre (71 ha) site, which lies south of Dulles Airport's main terminal, in Chantilly, Virginia. The Steven F. Udvar-Hazy Center opened in December 2003—timed to coincide with the 100th anniversary of the Wright brothers' first powered flight.

The center continues adding to the items on display, which have grown to more than 300 aircraft and large space objects and nearly 2,000 smaller artifacts. In 2010, the center opened the huge Mary Baker Engen Restoration Hangar, where visitors can witness specialists at work on the restoration and preservation of planes and other flight-related artifacts.

Visiting: You enter the facility on the second level of the museum. Pick up a map inside the entrance to see the layout of the building, which is arranged according to different types, eras, and uses of flight, such as military, sport, general, and commercial. Begin your tour in the far southwestern corner of the building, with a display on helicopters and vertical flight.

The cavernous **Boeing Aviation Hangar** that makes up the core of the Udvar-Hazy Center rises ten stories high and extends as long as three football fields. The objects are displayed on three levels, with elevated walkways allowing a closer look at suspended aircraft.

Among the featured aircraft are the Boeing B-29 Superfortress *Enola Gay,* which dropped the first atomic bomb; an Air France Concorde, the first supersonic airliner; a sleek, black Lockheed SR-71A Blackbird, the fastest airplane in the world; the Boeing "Dash 80" prototype of the 707, America's first commercial jet airliner; and the de Havilland Chipmunk aerobatic airplane.

Other interesting objects in this hangar include engines, hang gliders and ultralights, and experimental flying machines. The exhibit on sport aviation, for example, explains how designers of home-built aircraft often used the most advanced ideas in aerodynamics, propulsion, and structures. Check out the flight suits and other artifacts of giants in aviation such as Charles Lindbergh, Amelia Earhart, James Doolittle, Roscoe Turner, and "Hap" Arnold. Displays of aircraft models, aerial cameras, and "balloonamania" —popular culture items from the 18th century—add further interest.

After you've covered the immense aviation hangar, head to the adjoining building, which houses the **James S. McDonnell Space Hangar.** The centerpiece here is the restored space shuttle *Discovery.* You can also view displays on satellites, missiles, rockets, Mars probe equipment, space capsules, and other equipment used in human space flight, such as the mobile quarantine unit used by the returning crew of the Apollo 11.

Circling back to the entrance area, visit the nearby **observation tower** to watch overhead traffic at Dulles Airport. Also in this area is an **IMAX theater** *(fee).* Near the main stairs in the aviation hangar, you can climb inside a **simulator** to ride on a variety of history's greatest flying machines—from the Sopwith Camel to the F-5 Tiger—or take a 3-D journey around the International Space Station *(fee).*

On your way out, take a closer look at the **Wall of Honor,** running along the entryway. The memorial bears the names of hundreds of people who have contributed to aviation and space exploration. ■

Potomac River Plantations

In the 18th and early 19th centuries, landowners built magnificent plantation houses along the Potomac south of present-day Washington, D.C. Three—Mount Vernon, Woodlawn, and Gunston Hall—lie within easy reach of the city. A visit to any one of these mansions, each carefully preserved in period detail, immerses you in the early slave-holding aristocratic life.

Washington enlarged Mount Vernon—once a modest 1.5-story farmhouse—to its present size.

Mount Vernon

🅜 Map p. 219 B2

✉ S end of George Washington Memorial Pkwy., Mt. Vernon, VA

☎ 703/780-2000

🚇 Metro: Huntington, then bus

💲 $$$

mountvernon.org

Mount Vernon

The stately Georgian-style home of George Washington sits on 500 acres (202 ha) of smartly kept grounds overlooking the Potomac. George Washington moved to Mount Vernon, home of his elder half brother Lawrence, when he was in his teens; he acquired the estate from Lawrence's widow in 1754 at the age of 22. As commander in chief of the Continental forces, Washington rarely saw his home between 1775 and 1783. He then spent the next six years farming, expanding the plantation to nearly 8,000 acres (3,237 ha). After serving as the country's first President

(1789–1797), he had only a couple of years left to enjoy his beloved home before his death.

The Mount Vernon Ladies' Association purchased the estate from a Washington relative in 1858 and continues to own and operate it. Both the Confederate and Union Armies considered the estate neutral ground during the Civil War.

Visiting: Even if you've been to Mount Vernon before, a return visit is a must because a large-scale expansion of educational facilities was completed in October 2006. Today, you could easily spend an entire day here learning about

Washington during every stage of his life, through a dizzying array of films, museum displays, tours (including a visit to his nearby distillery; see sidebar p. 227), and interactive programs.

Visitors enter the estate through an **Orientation Center.** Audio-tour equipment is available if you want to get more information while wandering the 45-acre (18 ha) grounds on your own. A 20-minute film depicts pivotal moments in Washington's life as a citizen, soldier, and statesman.

The biggest attraction remains the famous red-roofed mansion and its gardens, pasture, and woodlands. The wood exterior of the mansion looks like stone; sand thrown onto wet paint created this impression. All details of the house's appearance, down to the exact color of the interior, are authentic to the period.

Inside, many of the furnishings are original to the house; others, 18th-century duplicates. Docents are on hand to provide information about each of the 12 rooms. The large two-story green dining room, painstakingly reinterpreted to appear as it did in the Washingtons' lifetime, was used for many different functions; it held chairs and sideboards, but formal tables were installed only when the family entertained. Washington's study sits at the other end of the house. Various personal artifacts displayed here, including a telescope and an 884-volume library, reflect his varied interests.

A small staircase connects the study to the master bedroom on the second floor. This simply decorated bedroom contains the four-poster bed in which Washington died in 1799. After his death, his wife, Martha, could not bear to stay in the room; she moved to another room, on the third floor.

Back on the first floor, before you step onto the piazza, note the framed key hanging on a wall in the passageway. It's the key to the Bastille's west portal, which the Marquis de Lafayette sent to Washington as a gift in 1790. The piazza, looking east over a lawn that dips toward a deer park, offers a grand view of the Potomac River.

INSIDER TIP:

At Mount Vernon's reconstructed Blacksmith Shop, you can watch and listen as period-style tools and hardware are handcrafted.

—DIANA PARSELL
National Geographic writer

On the house's west side, explore the **formal grounds** and **outbuildings.** The smokehouse, kitchen, washhouse, servant's hall, and other buildings suggest how much work it took to run a large, profitable 18th-century estate. Walled upper and lower gardens flank the bowling green.

Circle around the fruit garden and nursery to the iron-gated brick **tomb** that holds the remains of George, Martha, and other

Slave Quarters

Blacksmith Shop

Entrance

Upper Garden

Woodlawn

🅰 Map p. 219 B2

✉ 9000 Richmond Hwy. (U.S. 1), 3 miles W of Mount Vernon

☎ 703/780-4000

🕐 Closed Tues.– Thurs. & Dec.–Feb.

💲 $$

woodlawn1805.org

members of the family. A nearby memorial marks the estate's slave burial ground. Downhill is the site of a wharf where George Washington staged the transport of his goods to Alexandria.

Most of Mount Vernon's historic artifacts are now housed in the **Museum and Education Center,** tucked beneath a pasture just inside the main gate, to preserve the estate's pastoral quality. Two dozen galleries and related activities offer insight into numerous aspects of Washington's family and professional life. You can see, for example, a scenario of the dinners Washington held every Thursday at 4 p.m. for invited members of Congress and other government officials.

The greatest treasure in the museum is the 1785 terra-cotta bust of Washington that French sculptor J. A. Houdon made from a life mask. The center also has three life-size figures of Washington—at ages 19, 45, and 57—that were based on forensic research.

On-site dining facilities and shops at Mount Vernon have been expanded. If time allows, visit the re-creation of a 16-side barn and the 4-acre (1.6 ha) demonstration farm that depicts planting and crop experiments.

Woodlawn

George Washington gave Nelly Custis, his step-granddaughter, and Maj. Lawrence Lewis, his nephew, 2,000 acres (809 ha) of his estate in 1799 as their wedding present and asked William Thornton, first architect of the U.S. Capitol, to design a house for them. Thornton completed the late Georgian/ early federal–era two-story mansion in 1805. Typical of the period, the house is arranged symmetrically according to a five-part Palladian plan. There is no "front" or

Mount Vernon
Estate & Gardens

Labels on map: Washington's Tomb · Slave Memorial · Wharf · Mansion · George Washington Pioneer Farm Site · Lower Garden · Fruit Garden & Nursery

"back," rather two formal facades for approach by land or river.

The Lewis family and more than 90 slaves lived on the estate for more than 40 years. The family sold the estate in 1846 to a Quaker community, which used the house as a nucleus for their growing abolitionist organization. The National Trust for Historic Preservation acquired the house and some of the land in 1951; the estate now comprises about 120 acres (48.5 ha). The house is furnished much as it was during the Lewises' occupation, with some furnishings that the Lewises brought over from Mount Vernon.

Tours are offered on the hour from noon until 4 p.m. Inside, the refined **first-floor interior** includes a dining room, a family sitting room, and a parlor. The ceilings reach 13.5 feet (4 m) high—the parlor excepted, which is a foot higher, in keeping with

the grand proportions of the space. The second floor is divided into four graciously appointed chambers. In honor of its first patron, Woodlawn's **reception area** features a bust of Washington commissioned by Nelly Custis Lewis; it stands on a pedestal at 6 feet 2 inches (188 cm), the general's actual height.

Outside is a **formal garden** with lilacs, azaleas, and roses.

George Washington's Distillery & Gristmill

Washington had the largest distillery in early America, which provided revenue for Mount Vernon. From April through October, you can watch whiskey-making demonstrations. Adjacent to the distillery is a 1771 water-powered gristmill where cornmeal for use in the distillery was ground and where wheat was ground into flour for export. The site is about 3 miles (4.8 km) south of Mount Vernon, on Route 235.

Gunston Hall

 Map p. 219 B1

✉ 10709 Gunston Rd., Mason Neck, VA, 20 miles S of Washington, off I-95 & US 1

☎ 703/550-9220

$ $$

gunstonhall.org

From the riverside portico you can make out the Potomac, although silting over the past two centuries has pushed the river back. On the eastern horizon, tall trees block your view of Mount Vernon.

Before leaving Woodlawn, you can also walk over to view the 1940 **Pope-Leighey House** *(tel 703/780-4000).* This Frank Lloyd Wright–designed house was moved in 1964 from Falls Church, Virginia, to save it from destruction. The low-ceilinged, flat-roofed dwelling is a classic example of Wright's Usonian style.

Gunston Hall

The farthest south of the three plantation houses, Gunston Hall anchors 550 magnificently lush acres (222 ha), with tree-lined lanes, formal gardens, and farm animals.

INSIDER TIP:

At Gunston, you can walk a 1-mile [1.6 km] trail through the woods to the river. You might spot deer, herons, and geese along the way.

—DIANA PARSELL
National Geographic writer

It was once a 5,500-acre (2,225 ha) tobacco and corn plantation. Its owner was Virginian George Mason (1725–1792), a lesser known but brilliant patriot and statesman.

Mason tried to quit public life after his wife's death in 1773, but the fledgling country would need him in the years ahead. Mason penned the 1776 Virginia

Declaration of Rights, advocating religious tolerance and freedom of the press. Thomas Jefferson picked up, in some cases almost word for word, the same sentiments for the Declaration of Independence. Mason holds distinction as one of three delegates who refused to sign the Constitution in 1787. In passionate orations, he maintained that the Constitution gave the government too much power, a sentiment that helped pave the way for the Bill of Rights.

Begin your tour at the **visitor center,** which holds several interesting exhibits, including assorted family objects; an 11-minute film presents Mason as a paradoxical man. Although an ardent supporter of human rights and intellectually opposed to slavery, Mason had up to 90 slaves and could not reconcile his desire to end slavery with a means to ensure the continued prosperity of his plantation.

In the two-story Georgian **brick house,** designed in 1755 by indentured servant and soon-to-be-prominent architect William Buckland, each room has its own distinctive style. The Chinese-style formal parlor and the neoclassic, Palladian-style dining room, with arches and painstaking embellishments, are works of art. The rooms are furnished with family and period pieces.

In the **gardens,** a boxwood allée, likely dating from Mason's time, runs between formal plantings to the brow of a hill that provides a glimpse of the distant Potomac River. ■

Annapolis

Yachts, midshipmen in crisp uniforms, streets lined with colonial architecture, and restaurants serving world-famous crab cakes: The colorful port of Annapolis, less than an hour's drive east of Washington, offers big-time history in a small-town setting.

Ego Alley in the heart of Annapolis is the place to show off your boat.

Puritans escaping persecution first settled at the strategic mouth of the Severn River, just off the Chesapeake Bay, in 1649. Named the Capital of the Proprietary of Maryland in 1694, the settlement grew to become one of the Colonies' most sophisticated towns by the eve of the American Revolution. As bales of tobacco flowed out of its port, in flowed European luxuries to adorn beautiful Georgian homes and their elegant inhabitants.

Annapolis's political high point occurred between November 1783 and August 1784, when it served as the fledgling nation's working capital. After the capital was moved to Trenton, New Jersey, in 1784, however, the city dozed for two centuries. The U.S. Naval Academy came in 1845, turning Annapolis into a sort of company town that catered to its guest institution. In the 1960s, interest in historic preservation brought about new life, as taverns, shops, restaurants, and museums moved into restored structures.

Today, Annapolis showcases more than a dozen architectural styles spanning three centuries; some 1,300 buildings—all meticulously maintained—predate 1900. Much of the small city's charm owes to the fact that it preserves its 1695 radial street plan, which gives the highest elevations to the church (St. Anne's) and state (State House)—and offers many vistas of the picturesque waterfront. ∎

Annapolis

🅜 Map p. 219 E4

Visitor Information

✉ Annapolis & Anne Arundel County Conference & Visitors Bureau, 26 West St.; seasonal information booth at City Dock

☎ 410/280-0445 or 888/302-2852

🚍 Free downtown Circulator trolley; inquire at visitors bureau

visitannapolis.org

Walking Around Annapolis

The narrow streets and brick sidewalks in the historic center of Annapolis will enchant you. Plan to spend at least half a day strolling around and visiting its sights. With limited street parking available, your best bet is to leave your car in one of the garages near the visitor center.

The Maryland State House (1779) anchors the city's captivating downtown.

Start your stroll at the friendly, information-packed **visitor center** ❶ *(Annapolis & Anne Arundel County Conference & Visitors Bureau, 26 West St., tel 888/302-2852).* Just to the east, Church Circle features the Romanesque **St. Anne's Episcopal Church** ❷ *(tel 410/267-9333, stannes-annapolis.org),* built in 1858–1859. The church still has the communion silver set sent by King William III in 1696. Standing at the intersection of Church Circle and Main Street, the venerable 1772 **Maryland Inn** *(tel 410/263-2641, historicinnsofannapolis.com)* features wood balconies and an award-winning restaurant, the Treaty of Paris.

Proceed six blocks down Main Street, attractively lined with two-story brick and wood buildings harboring boutiques, restaurants, galleries, and bars. At the end of the street

NOT TO BE MISSED:

City Dock • U.S. Naval Academy
Chapel • Hammond-Harwood House

is Market Space and its busy waterfront, the **City Dock** ❸. This heart of the town bustles with cafés, shops, and restaurants. The number of yachts moored here attests to Annapolis's standing as one of the East Coast's great sailing centers; visiting boaters often cruise down the narrow waterway fronting the dock to show off their boats (hence its local name, Ego Alley). Stop by the dockside **Market House** for a sandwich and join a life-size bronze of *Roots* author Alex Haley by the water's edge, where

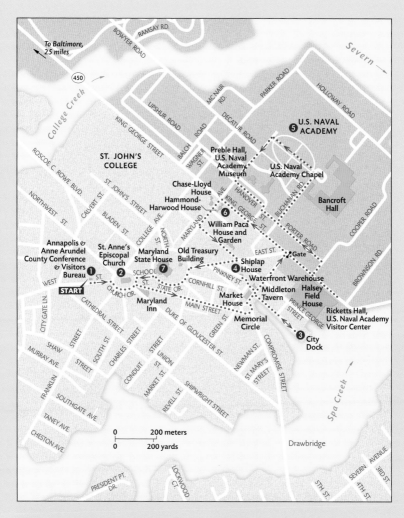

he sits telling a story to a group of children on the same spot where his ancestor, Kunta Kinte, arrived in 1767 on a slave ship. For another dining option, head across Market Space to **Middleton Tavern** (tel 410/263-3323, middleton tavern.com), a cozy place dating from 1750 that welcomed the likes of George Washington, Thomas Jefferson, and Benjamin Franklin.

Just up Pinkney Street, step into the **Waterfront Warehouse** (ca 1815) to see the scale model of the waterfront as it was in the 1700s. A few doors up, **Shiplap House** ④

Ⓜ	See also area map p. 219
▶	Visitor center
🕘	4 hours
↔	1.8 miles (2.9 km)
▶	Maryland State House

(18 Pinkney St.) dates from 1715. Now go back down Pinkney and turn left on Randall; in two blocks turn right for the gates to the **U.S. Naval Academy** ⑤ (usna.edu, tours available by reservation) and follow signs to the visitor center.

Sandy Point State Park

For a change from the cobblestones of Annapolis, drive to this Chesapeake Bay park *(9 miles/14.4 km E of Annapolis on U.S. 50, tel 410/974-2149, $)*. The sandy beach is great for swimming, as well as for views of the Bay Bridge. You can rent rowboats and motorboats, and 5 miles (8 km) of trails wind through woods and marshes.

Established in 1845, the academy is now a 338-acre (136 ha), four-year coed college. Flanking the tree-dotted central green to the southeast is the enormous beaux arts **Bancroft Hall,** one of the world's largest dormitories. The nearby copper-domed **U.S. Naval Academy Chapel** features a long, shiplike nave; don't miss the lavishly displayed marble tomb of Revolutionary War naval hero John Paul Jones in the crypt. Just to the northwest, Preble Hall houses the **U.S. Naval Academy Museum**, containing one of the world's finest collections of model warships. (Note: Visitors are allowed within the academy only on foot and must show a photo ID at the gate.)

Back at the gate turn northwest on King George Street, then southwest on Maryland Avenue. The 1774–1775 **Hammond-Harwood House** ❻ *(19 Maryland Ave., tel 410/263-4683, hammondharwoodhouse.org, closed Mon., limited winter hours, $$)* is on the left. This national historic landmark house, considered by many to be the finest example of Georgian architecture in colonial America, was the last project of architect William Buckland, once an indentured servant, who also designed Gunston Hall (see p. 228). Continue down Maryland Avenue to Prince George Street and turn left to the Georgian **William Paca House and Garden** *(186 Prince George St., tel 410/267-7619, $$)*, built in 1765. Paca was a signer of the Declaration of Independence and a three-term governor of Maryland. The house and gardens have been meticulously restored to their colonial glory.

A block west on East Street is State Circle, where the Old Treasury Building and the **Maryland State House** ❼ *(State Circle, tel 410/946-5400, msa.md.gov)* sit. Completed in 1779, the state house is the nation's oldest continuously used capitol building. Two events of importance took place in its old Senate Chamber during the nine months when Annapolis served as the new country's working capital: George Washington resigned his commission as commander in chief of the Continental Army on December 23, 1783, and, three weeks later, Congress ratified the Treaty of Paris, ending the Revolutionary War. Return to your starting point via School Street and Church Circle.

The U.S. Naval Academy Band stays crisply in line—and in tune.

Baltimore

Only 40 miles (64 km) north of Washington, Baltimore would appear to have very little in common with the District. Baltimore's brick buildings, puffing factories, older ethnic neighborhoods, and heavy ship traffic give it more of a "real city" feel. But it also has its share of world-class museums, and the city's Inner Harbor, a showcase of urban revitalization, ranks as one of the East Coast's top travel destinations.

The Inner Harbor has led Baltimore into the limelight of urban revitalization.

Strategically placed at the mouth of the Patapsco River at Chesapeake Bay, the Inner Harbor has long been a major port for coal and grain. Also considered an urban eyesore, it was targeted for demolition and renewal as far back as 1963. Buildings began coming down in the late 1960s, and the first skyscrapers appeared in the early '70s. Restaurants, tourist attractions, and Oriole Park at Camden Yards followed thereafter, contributing to the harbor's vitality.

Today, a promenade lined with shops and restaurants edges the waterfront and offers a delightful stroll past the harbor's various museums. Water taxis will ferry you from sight to sight if you'd rather ride than walk.

On the harbor's north side, at Pier 3, the seven-story **National Aquarium** *(tel 410/576-3800, $$$$$)* is Baltimore's biggest visitor draw. Inside, bottlenose dolphins perform feats in a 1.2-million-gallon (4.5 million L) oceanarium; an Atlantic coral reef teems with colorful tropical fish; and sharks and manta rays glide through a pool that you cross on bridges.

The submarine U.S.S. *Torsk* and the lightship *Chesapeake* are moored alongside the aquarium. They, along with the Coast Guard cutter *Taney* and Seven Foot Knoll

Baltimore

⚑ Map p. 219 D6

Visitor Information

✉ Baltimore Visitor Center, 401 Light St.

☎ 877/BALTIMORE

baltimore.org

Baltimore Museum of Art

✉ 10 Art Museum Dr.

☎ 443/573-1700

🕐 Closed Mon.–Tues.

artbma.org

Walters Art Museum

✉ 600 N. Charles St.

☎ 410/547-9000

🕐 Closed Mon.–Tues.

thewalters.org

Fort McHenry National Monument and Historic Shrine

✉ 2400 East Fort Ave.

☎ 410/962-4290

💲 $$

nps.gov/fomc

Lighthouse on Pier 5, form the **Historic Ships in Baltimore Maritime Museum** (tel 410/539-1797, historicships.org, $$).

The last Civil War–era vessel still afloat, the **U.S.S. Constellation** is moored at Pier 1 (tel 410/539-1797, $$). Climb aboard to learn about her past. Launched in 1854, she has caught slave traders off the coast of Africa, blockaded ports during the Civil War, and acted as a relief flagship of the U.S. Atlantic Fleet in World War II. Walk past the cruise ship docks toward the harbor's south side and the **Maryland Science Center** (601 Light St., tel 410/685-5225, $$$), which has exhibits, an IMAX theater, and a planetarium.

INSIDER TIP:

The Baltimore-based Morgan State University Choir [msuchoir .org] has performed as far afield as China. A hometown concert is a special occasion.

—SHEILA BUCKMASTER
National Geographic Traveler magazine editor at large

Located inland, on the harbor's north side, is the interactive **Port Discovery** (35 Market Pl., tel 410/727-8120, closed Mon. in winter, $$$), catering to kids with interactive exhibits and activities.

Impressionism lovers will not want to miss the Cone Collection—works by Matisse, Picasso, and others—on display at the **Baltimore Museum of Art.** The **Walters Art Museum** offers a broad look at more than 55 centuries of art, including Roman sarcophagi, Asian ceramics, Old Master paintings, and art deco jewelry.

Fort McHenry sits southeast of the harbor. During the War of 1812, as American forces valiantly defended the fort against the British, a young lawyer named Francis Scott Key felt inspired to pen some words as he saw its flag still waving in the early dawn light. A tour of the monument to American freedom is not easily forgotten.

The heart of Baltimore is its historic **Charles Street district.** A stroll down the 12-mile (19 km) strip will take you past Mount Vernon Place, where you can check out Baltimore's Washington Monument (it predates the one in Washington) and climb 228 steps to the top for a great view of the city. Window-shop for collectibles before choosing among the restaurants that serve up crab cakes, steamed shrimp, and oysters.

Also worth a trip: the **B & O Railroad Museum** (901 West Pratt St., tel 410/752-2490). Its locomotive and rolling stock collection dates from 1830 to the present, while its small object collection includes pocket watches, lanterns, and dining car china.

At the end of the day, consider a jaunt to **Fells Point,** where the city took root in the early 1700s. Located east of the Inner Harbor, a short cab ride away, this waterfront district's brick row houses, congenial pubs, and snug restaurants have an enduring charm. ∎

Travelwise

Eero Saarinen designed the Dulles
International Airport terminal.

TRAVELWISE

PLANNING YOUR TRIP

When to Go

Climate

Until well into the 20th century, Washington was, because of its reputation for heat and humidity (plus the mosquitos that thrive in these conditions) classified as a hardship post for British diplomats. It is true that July and August in the capital are frequently hot and steamy, but Washington has relatively brief winters and often long and lovely springs and falls. Rain is fairly evenly divided throughout the year (an average of 3.31 inches/8.4 cm per month), except for afternoon thundershowers in June, July, and August.

The busy season for tourism starts in April with spring school vacation, when busloads of schoolchildren from all over visit the museums, monuments, and U.S. Capitol. Spring is also the time of the annual cherry blossoms display around the Tidal Basin; when the blossoms are at their peak, the area around the monuments is packed. Summer, of course, is family vacation time.

The average high and low temperatures are as follows:

January—44°F/30°F
February—46°F/29°F
March—54°F/36°F
April—66°F/46°F
May—76°F/56°F
June—83°F/65°F
July—87°F/69°F
August—85°F/68°F
September—79°F/61°F
October—68°F/50°F
November—57°F/39°F
December—46°F/32°F

What to Bring

Heavy winter coats are usually essential only in December, January, and February, but a light coat or jacket can come in handy in the cooler spring or fall months. Government buildings and museums have miles of corridors with marble floors, and there's lots of great city walking, so comfortable shoes are a must.

HOW TO GET TO WASHINGTON, D.C.

By Plane

Washington is served by three major airports: Ronald Reagan Washington National Airport (DCA) in Virginia, about 4 miles (6.4 km) from the city center; Washington Dulles International Airport (IAD), 26 miles (42 km) west of Washington; and Baltimore/Washington International Thurgood Marshall Airport (BWI), 25 miles (40 km) northeast of Washington. All three airports are served by SuperShuttle (tel 800/BLUEVAN, supershuttle.com).

Ronald Reagan Washington National Airport is the closest airport to the city and also the most convenient: Washington's Metro system has a station right there. Taxi fare to downtown Washington is about $20.

Dulles International Airport is served by its own Washington Flyer taxi fleet (tel 703/661-6655, washfly.com), with 24-hour service to and from the airport. Taxi fare to downtown Washington is about $60. Washington Flyer also operates coach service (tel 888/WASHFLY) connecting Dulles to the West Falls Church Metro station for $10 one way. The best way to get to and from BWI Airport is by SuperShuttle

or train. Both MARC's Penn Line (tel 800/325-RAIL) and Amtrak (tel 800/872-7245) provide frequent service between Union Station in downtown Washington and BWI's own rail station; a free shuttlebus connects the rail station and the airport terminal.

Airport Information

For general airport information: Reagan National (tel 703/417-8000), Dulles (tel 703/572-2700), and BWI (tel 410/859-7100); Dulles and Reagan share a website (metwashairports.com).

Airlines

The Washington, D.C., metropolitan area is served by the following:
Aeroflot 888/686-4949, aeroflot.ru/cms/en
Air Canada 888/247-2262 aircanada.com
Air France 800/237-2747, airfrance.com
Air Tran 800/247-8726, airtran.com
Alaska Airlines 800/252-7522, alaskaair.com
American Airlines 800/433-7300, aa.com
ANA 800/235-9262, fly-ana.com
Avianca 800/284-2622, avianca.com
British Airways 800/247-9297, britishairways.com
Brussels Airlines 866/308-2230, brusselsairlines.com
Copa Airlines 800/359-2672, copaair.com
Delta Air Lines 800/221-1212, delta.com
Emirates 800/777-3999, emirates.com
Frontier Airlines 800/432-1359, flyfrontier.com

Icelandair 800/223-5500,
icelandair.com

JetBlue Airways 800/538-2583,
jetblue.com

KLM 800/225-2525,
klm.com

Korean Air 800/438-5000,
koreanair.com

Lufthansa 800/645-3880,
lufthansa.com

SAS 800/221-2350,
flysas.com

Saudi Arabian Airlines 800/
472-8342, saudiairlines.com

South African Airlines
800/722-9675, flysaa.com

Southwest Airlines 800/435-
9792, southwest.com

Spirit 801/401-2200,
spirit.com

Sun Country Airlines 800/359-
6786, suncountry.com

United Airlines 800/241-6522,
united.com

US Airways 800/428-4322,
usairways.com

Virgin Atlantic 800/862-8621,
virgin-atlantic.com

By Train

Amtrak *(tel 800/872-7245,
amtrak.com)* trains arrive at
Washington's spectacularly
refurbished Union Station on
Capitol Hill. The station, which
has shops, restaurants, and a
downstairs food court is worth a
visit for its own sake.

Although locals use the train
mostly as a fast, convenient way
to get to New York on the Acela
and Northeast Regional trains,
Washington is a major rail hub,
and it is connected by train to
most U.S. destinations with rail
service. The Metro station at
Union Station provides easy access
to the rest of the city and beyond.

GETTING AROUND
By Metro
The Washington Metropolitan
Area Transit Authority operates

the bus and subway systems in
the metropolitan area. Metrorail
stations are marked by large columns with brown "M" signs.

The clean and efficient rail
network makes it very easy to get
around the region, but mainte-
nance and repairs required from
the growing number of riders
means there may be occasional
delays or outages on some sections of the system. In such cases
bus transfer between stations
is usually available. Metro posts
regular updates about operating
status *(wmata.com).* Most suburban
stations have lots for all-day parking, but go early because they fill
up fast.

Metro farecards are purchased
at vending machines in the stations or online. Fares range from
roughly $1.70 to $5.75 one way,
based on distance and time of
day. (Plastic SmarTrip cards, for
extended travel and easy bus
transfer, are also available at CVS
pharmacy locations in the D.C.
area.) Fare information is available
near the ticket machines.

Metrorail opens at 5 a.m. on
weekdays and 7 a.m. on weekends.
It closes at midnight Sunday
through Thursday. On Friday and
Saturday nights, it runs until 3 a.m.

Metro route information: tel
202/637-7000, wmata.com.

By Bus
Metrobus service covers the
city and the suburbs, with some
lines running 24 hours. The
fare for any destination within
Washington is $1.70 or $3.85
for express service. Exact fare
is required. For route and fare
information, call 202/637-7000.
For just $1 per ride, the DC
Circulator bus service operates
daily in central Washington, with
frequent stops. The five routes
extend from Dupont Circle to
Rosslyn; Georgetown to Union
Station; Union Station to Navy

Yard; Woodley Park to McPherson Square; and Potomac Ave.
to Skyland. Visit dccirculator.com
for route schedules and maps.

By Taxicab
Cabs in Washington are plentiful
and fairly inexpensive. It's usually
possible to hail a cab on a major
street. They run on a meter system, and there are surcharges for
each extra passenger, rush hour,
and baggage. Information on surcharges is posted in every cab.

By Bicycle
In 2008, the District of Columbia
became the first jurisdiction in
North America to launch a bike-
sharing system. Capital Bikeshare
has grown exponentially since
then, with more than 1,800 bikes
offered at 200 stations throughout the District and in Arlington,
Alexandria, and Montgomery
County. The distinctive bright-
red bikes can be found at most
Metro stations and at convenient locations downtown and
along the National Mall. Regular
users can buy a daily, monthly, or
annual membership online, while
visitors can use a credit card at
any Bikeshare station kiosk to
purchase a 24-hour pass for $7
or a 3-day pass for $15.

By Car
Visitors should consider the possibility that a car will be more
of an annoyance than a convenience. Parking is difficult, and
parking garages are expensive.

Should you find on-street
parking, check the signs, since
many streets become no parking
zones during rush hour. If your
car is not where you left it, call
202/541-6083 for information
on its location.

Some streets are two-way
most of the time, but during rush
hour become one way—including

Rock Creek and Potomac Parkway and 17th Street, N.W.

Car Rentals

Washington's airports are served by the following national car rental companies:

Alamo 800/462-5266,
alamo.com

Avis 800/331-1212,
avis.com

Budget 800/527-0700,
budget.com

Dollar 800/800-4000,
dollar.com

Enterprise 800/264-6350,
enterprise.com

Hertz 800/654-3131,
hertz.com

National 800/227-7368,
nationalcar.com

Thrifty 800/847-4389,
thrifty.com

Negotiating the City

When seeking a site, first check the quadrant address, which indicates where it lies vis-à-vis the Capitol. Are you looking for N.W., N.E., S.W., or S.E.? The city is laid out in these four quadrants, with the Capitol Building in the center. North Capitol, South Capitol, and East Capitol Streets radiate from this nucleus, separating the quadrants (the Mall runs west from the Capitol Building).

Be advised that many District addresses can be found in more than one quadrant (for instance, there is a 400 M St. in N.E., S.E., S.W., and N.W.—four different D.C. locations).

After locating the quadrant, note that there are three types of streets in Washington. First are the numbered streets—those that run in a north-south direction from the Capitol. First Street, for instance, is located one block east or west of North or South Capitol Street, respectively.

The second street type is the lettered or named streets laid out in an east-west direction. Starting from East Capitol Street or the Mall, the streets run through the alphabet (with the exceptions of J, X, Y, and Z). The ones nearest the Capitol are one-syllable words; when the alphabet has been run through, they become two syllables, then three. As such, you can tell how far a certain street is from the Capitol by the letter with which it begins and how many syllables it contains.

Finally, the avenues that are named after states run diagonally across the grid.

PRACTICAL ADVICE
Communications
Newspapers

Washington, D.C., is a city of news. Most national and international news agencies have Washington bureaus. The Washington-based daily newspapers are the *Washington Post* and the *Washington Times.* For upcoming local events, check the Weekend section of the *Washington Post,* published on Fridays.

Also of interest is the free weekly publication, the *Washington City Paper,* published on Thursdays. It provides an up-to-date listing of what's happening in the clubs and theaters around town.

Radio

WMAL (AM 630)
Talk shows and breaking news
wmal.com

WTOP (FM 103.5)
News and all-talk format
wtop.com

WAMU (FM 88.5)
Public radio programming
wamu.org

WPFW (FM 89.3)

Pacifica news, jazz
wpfw.org

WCSP (FM 90.1)
C-SPAN and public affairs
c-span.org

WETA (FM 90.9)
Classical music
weta.org

WKYS "Kiss" (FM 93.9)
Urban, hip hop
kysdc.com

WIAD "Fresh" (FM 94.7)
Contemporary rock
947freshfm.cbslocal.com

WPGC (FM 95.5)
Hip hop, R&B.
wpgc.cbslocal.com

WHUR (FM 96.3)
Urban contemporary, black culture
whur.com

WASH (FM 97.1)
Soft-rock music
washfm.com

WMZQ (FM 98.7)
Country music
wmzqfm.com

WIHT "Hot" (FM 99.5)
Contemporary rock
hot995.com

WBIG (FM 100.3)
Oldies
wbig.com

WWDC (FM 101.1)
Rock
dc101.com

WRXQ (FM 100.7)
Classic rock
wrxq.com

WMMJ "Majic" (102.3)
R&B and urban oldies
mymajicdc.com

WKIK (FM 102.9)
Country music
country1029wkik.com

WJZW (FM 105.9)
"Smooth" jazz
smoothjazz1059.com

Telephone

Local and long-distance information, 411
Toll-free directory information, 800/555-1212

The area code for Washington, D.C., is 202; for Maryland, 240, 301, 410, and 443; and for Northern Virginia, 703 and 571. When in Virginia or Maryland, you must dial the area code with the number, even for local calls.

The prevalence of cell phones has limited the availability of public telephones; some are available in public areas, such as Metro stations. Local calls cost 50 cents.

Crime

Crimes of all sorts have been on the decrease in the last few years in Washington, but precautions are advised.

Don't wander onto deserted or ill-lighted streets or parks, particularly at night. If you're uncomfortable in a neighborhood, leave.

Stay with the crowds. There's safety in numbers.

If someone tries to rob you, give the robber whatever he or she asks. Your life is more valuable than your belongings.

Keep your wallet in a front trouser pocket—less vulnerable to pickpockets than rear pockets or breast pockets.

Women should keep their purses close—especially in restaurants. Don't carry large amounts of cash.

Leave credit cards you don't plan to use at home. Don't leave valuables in your car. The trunk is more secure than the space under the seats.

Money Matters

Banks and automatic teller machines (ATMs) are located throughout the city, and most major attractions and shopping centers also have them.

Check with your home bank to find out which system accepts your card. Credit cards, debit cards, and traveler's checks are accepted almost everywhere; make sure you have an official I.D. with you as some places require it before you can make a transaction.

ATM Locations

MasterCard/Cirrus, 800/424-7787
Visa/Plus, usa.visa.com/atm-locator

National Holidays

New Year's Day
Martin Luther King, Jr., Day (3rd Mon. in Jan.)
President's Day (3rd Mon. in Feb.)
Easter Sunday
Memorial Day (last Mon. in May)
Fourth of July
Labor Day (1st Mon. in Sept.)
Thanksgiving Day (4th Thurs. in Nov.)
Christmas Day

Places of Worship

With more than 2,000 established places of worship in the Washington, D.C., area, you will be able to find a service of your choice. Check with your hotel concierge or the local Yellow Pages for a listing of times and locations. The *Washington Post* and the *Washington Times* also publish listings of services in the religion sections in their Saturday editions.

Sales Tax

Taxes will increase the cost of your purchased goods by 5.75 percent, your hotel bill by 14.5 percent, your restaurant bill by 10 percent, and your rental car bill by 10 percent.

Security

Security has become a major issue in many places worldwide, but is especially a concern in and around Washington's public areas and government buildings. Streets are sometimes closed down with or without notice, and may be blocked off by concrete barriers.

Government buildings are generally open to the public, but they may close for security reasons with little or no notice. Be flexible, and call ahead.

Metal detectors are standard equipment in most public buildings. Be prepared to have your belongings scanned and searched. If you have a pacemaker or other medical device that might be affected, let the guards know. And do not carry anything that could be considered a weapon and might be confiscated—for example, Grandpa's pocketknife.

Tipping

Leave at least 15 percent of the bill at restaurants (20 percent at upscale places). Taxi drivers should receive 10 to 15 percent, bartenders 10 percent, hairdressers 15 percent, porters at least a dollar a bag, valet parking attendees $2 or more, and doormen a couple of dollars every time they whistle you a cab. Tip the hotel concierge or restaurant maître d' at your discretion, depending upon services performed.

Travelers With Disabilities

D.C. is a very accessible place for travelers with disabilities.

The Washington Metropolitan Area Transit Authority also publishes a free pamphlet on Metro's bus and rail system accessibility for the elderly and physically disabled. Call 202/962-1100 to order the guide, or visit Metro's website at wmata.com.

Smithsonian museum buildings are accessible to wheelchair visitors. Find detailed information online at si.edu or call 202/633-2921.

Visitor Information

The best source of visitor information is Destination D.C. (washington.org), Washington's official tourism site. It publishes a free visitors guide twice a year with comprehensive listings of attractions and events. Order it or download it online.

EMERGENCIES

Health Care
Useful Numbers

- Emergencies (police/fire/ ambulance), 911
- Washington, D.C., Police (non-emergency), 311
- Metro Transit Police (emergency), 202/962-2121
- U.S. Park Police (emergency), 202/610-7500
- Travelers Aid, 202/371-1937
- International Visitors Information Desk (offers multilingual information and assistance; located at Dulles), 703/572-2536

Lost Credit Cards
American Express,
    800/327-2177
Diners Club, 800/234-6377
Discover Card, 800/347-2683
MasterCard, 800/307-7309
Visa, 800/847-2911

ANNUAL EVENTS

January
Martin Luther King, Jr.'s Birthday Mid-January. Lincoln Memorial (tel 202/619-7222). National Park Service rangers

lay wreaths at the Martin Luther King, Jr. National Memorial and at the Lincoln Memorial, where King delivered his "I Have a Dream" speech on August 28, 1963.

Presidential Inauguration January 20, every fourth year. After the swearing-in on the Capitol steps, a parade follows down Pennsylvania Avenue to the White House.

February
Chinese New Year Parade Late January or early February, depending on the moon. Chinatown, H St., N.W. (bet. 5th & 8th Sts., tel 703/851-8777). Colorful parade with firecrackers, drums, and traditional dragon dancers.

Abraham Lincoln's Birthday February 12. Lincoln Memorial (tel 202/619-7222). A reading of the Gettysburg Address and a wreath-laying at the memorial.

George Washington's Birthday February 22. Wreath-laying ceremonies at Mount Vernon (tel 703/780-2000) and at the Washington Monument (tel 202/619-7222).

March
Blossom Kite Festival Late March or early April (tel 202/357-3030, nationalcherry blossomfestival.org). Professional and amateur kitemakers and kite flyers compete for prizes at a contest on the Washington Monument grounds in a public event organized by the National Cherry Blossom Festival.

April
National Cherry Blossom Festival Late March to early April. (tel 877/442-5666, nationalcherryblossomfestival.org). The city celebrates with three

weeks of performances, exhibitions, and activities. The Cherry Blossom Parade is usually held on the first or second Saturday in April. For up-to-date information on when the blossoms will peak, call or check the website.

Filmfest DC Two weeks of international and American films, shown at local theaters and other auditoriums around the city (tel 202/274-5782, filmfestdc.org).

White House Easter Egg Roll Monday after Easter (tel 202/456-7041). This annual event dates back to 1878 during the Rutherford B. Hayes Administration. Children (chosen by lottery), ages 12 and under, have a chance to play on the South Lawn of the White House. This fun event includes storytelling, music, and costumed characters.

White House Gardens & Grounds Tour A chance to get beyond the gates and tour the lovely spring gardens of the White House's South Lawn (tel 202/456-7041).

May
Georgetown Garden Day 2nd Sat. in May (georgetowngarden tour.com). Walk around the private gardens of some beautiful, historic homes.

Evening Parade Friday nights, May–Aug. U.S. Marine Barracks (8th and I Sts., S.E., tel 202/433-4073, www.barracks.marines.mil). The evening begins with an outdoor concert by the United States Marine Band. Following that is a demonstration of precision marching by Marine Drum and Bugle Corps, and the Marine Corps Silent Drill Platoon.

Memorial Day Celebrations Events on Memorial Day

weekend include ceremonies at the Vietnam Veteran's Memorial (tel 202/619-7222), the Tomb of the Unknowns at Arlington National Cemetery (tel 703/607-8000), and a concert by the National Symphony Orchestra on the West Lawn of the Capitol (tel 202/619-7222).

June
Dupont-Kalorama Museum Walk Weekend 1st full weekend. Dupont Circle neighborhood (dkmuseums.com). Visit several museums and enjoy interactive tours, textile-weaving demonstrations, workshops, and concerts.

July
Smithsonian Folklife Festival Late June/early July. On the National Mall (tel 202/633-6440, festival.si.edu). A popular annual two-week celebration of folk cultures—American and foreign— with music, food, storytelling, art exhibits, handicraft demonstrations, and special evening entertainment.

Fourth of July Celebrations The National Independence Day Parade takes place at 11:45 a.m. on Constitution Ave. between 7th and 17th Sts., N.W. The **National Symphony Orchestra,** with guest stars and soloists, performs at 8 p.m. on the West Lawn of the Capitol. The **Fourth of July fireworks** show starts at about 9 p.m. over the Washington Monument grounds (tel 202/619-7222).

Screen on the Green Late July to August. On the Mall (tel 877/262-5866, hbo.com/screenonthegreen). Roll out a blanket on the Mall's lawn and enjoy the popular annual film series shown under the stars, with weekly screenings of Hollywood classics and family favorites like The Karate Kid.

September
Labor Day Concert The National Symphony Orchestra closes its summer season with a concert on the West Lawn of the Capitol (tel 202/619-7222).

DC Blues Festival The annual festival (dcblues.org) closes out the summer with free performances and workshops at the Carter Barron Amphitheater in Rock Creek Park.

Virginia Wine Festival Sample Virginia's emerging wines along with music, food, and entertainment (virginiawinefest.com).

Kalorama House and Embassy Tour Get inside looks at some of the grand period mansions and stately homes in this neighborhood just northwest of Dupont Circle (tel 202/387-4062).

Washington National Cathedral Open House The National Cathedral (Massachusetts & Wisconsin Aves., N.W., tel 202/537-6200) holds its annual open house, with special tours, tower climbs, and entertainment.

October
Waterford Homes Tour and Craft Exhibit First full weekend (waterfordfoundation.org/waterford-fair). A celebration of colonial and Civil War–era America along the streets of a charming town. Music, food, home tours, and crafts (this is Virginia's oldest juried crafts fair). Waterford, VA, 47 miles (75 km) northwest of Washington.

Marine Corps Marathon Thousands of runners take part in this annual marathon (tel 800/RUN-USMC, marinemarathon.com). It starts at 8 a.m. at the Iwo Jima Memorial in Arlington, VA, and

follows a course through Washington past monuments on the Mall.

November
Veterans Day Celebrations Events honoring the service of U.S. military veterans occur November 11 at Arlington National Cemetery (tel 703/607-8000) and various memorials throughout the area.

Washington Craft Show Washington Convention Center (tel 203/254-0486). A juried show of American crafts, including basketry, ceramics, fiber decorative and wearables, furniture, glass, jewelry, leather, metal, mixed media, paper, and wood.

December
Pageant of Peace/Lighting of the National Christmas Tree On the Ellipse south of the White House (tel 202/208-1631). The official kickoff of the Christmas season in Washington, with concerts and a Christmas tree from each of the states.

Washington National Cathedral Christmas Services Massachusetts and Wisconsin Aves., N.W. (tel 202/537-6200). Christmas Eve services; passes are required for admission.

FURTHER READING
The best book on Washington architecture is E. J. Applewhite's Washington Itself. Applewhite, a former CIA officer, has a keen eye for buildings and an ear for the details of history.

Fiction lovers should check out Margaret Truman's murder mysteries set in and around Washington, D.C. President Truman's daughter wrote dozens of suspense novels, including Murder in the White House and Murder at the Watergate.

Hotels & Restaurants

When it comes to travel, where you sleep and eat can make all the difference. Washington, a city that regularly hosts guests from all nations, offers a panoply of hotel and restaurant selections in all price categories and styles.

Hotels

Washington hotels vary from the luxurious and very expensive—the Four Seasons in Georgetown and the Mandarin Oriental near the Mall being good examples—to the basic and still fairly expensive, such as the large downtown hotels that cater mostly to the convention and meeting trade. Small and charming is harder to find, but the new boutique hotels opened by the Kimpton Group are a hopeful sign.

Because every major business in the country is affected by government legislation and regulations, Washington hotels cater to business travelers on expense accounts. That means high prices during the week, when businesses are paying the tab, but it also means weekend bargains for leisure and family travelers.

Hotels in the city are expensive, so some visitors prefer to stay in less expensive places in suburban Virginia and travel into the city each day. Many hotels routinely offer rates cheaper than their posted rack rates, and many properties offer discounts through organizations such as AAA or AARP.

Most Washington hotels are nonsmoking establishments.

Restaurants

For many years, Washington was thought to hold little interest as a restaurant city. But a number of distinguished chefs running national-class restaurants now make Washington their home. Michel Richard at Central and Todd Gray at Equinox are at the top of the class, but their students, many of whom have stayed in Washington and opened their own restaurants, continue to enrich Washington dining, as do other top chefs who continue to come and open restaurants.

In addition to this wonderful but pricey dining, the Washington area has long been an attractive place for exiles to begin new lives. Refugees from Vietnam opened fine restaurants in the Virginia suburbs. Washington has more Ethiopian restaurants than any other city in the country. Thailand, India, Pakistan, and Malaysia have all given the city fine restaurants.

Unless otherwise noted, all restaurants are open daily and air-conditioned.

As of January 2007, smoking is prohibited in all bars and restaurants.
L=lunch
D=dinner

Credit Cards

Many hotels and restaurants accept all major credit cards. Smaller ones may accept some or none, as shown in their entry. Abbreviations used are: AE American Express, D Discover, DC Diners Club, MC MasterCard, and V Visa.

Organization

Hotels and restaurants are listed by chapter area, then by price category, then alphabetically. Hotel restaurants of note have been bolded in the hotel entries and indicated by a restaurant icon beneath the hotel icon (if they're unusually special, they are treated in a separate entry within the restaurant section).

PRICES

HOTELS
An indication of the cost of a double room in the high season is given by $ signs.

$$$$$	Over $225
$$$$	$175–$225
$$$	$125–$175
$$	$85–$125
$	Under $85

RESTAURANTS
An indication of the cost of a three-course meal without drinks is given by $ signs.

$$$$$	Over $75
$$$$	$50–$75
$$$	$35–$50
$$	$15–$35
$	Under $15

▓ CAPITOL HILL

HOTELS

⊞ THE HOTEL GEORGE
🍴 $$$$$
15 E ST., N.W.
TEL 202/347-4200 OR
800/576-7866
FAX 202/347-4213
hotelgeorge.com
A completely renovated building (from 1928), the George is a Kimpton hotel with striking decor, convenient to Capitol Hill offices and attractions. The restaurant **Bistro Bis** (see p. 243) offers quality contemporary French bistro fare. Cigar-friendly Billiard Room.
ⓘ 139 🅿 🎦 ⊗ All major cards
🚇 Union Station

⊞ HYATT REGENCY WASHINGTON ON CAPITOL HILL
$$$$
400 NEW JERSEY AVE., N.W.
TEL 202/737-1234 OR
800/223-1234
FAX 202/737-5773

⊞ Hotel 🍴 Restaurant ⓘ No. of Guest Rooms 🔲 No. of Seats 🅿 Parking ⊕ Closed

washingtonregency
.hyatt.com
This large convention hotel
occupies a full city block on
Capitol Hill. The hotel is cen-
trally located to offer access
to museums, monuments,
and government buildings.
ⓘ 836 🅿 🏊 🛎 🚅 All major
cards 🚇 Union Station

🏨 **LIAISON CAPITOL**
🍴 **HILL HOTEL**
$$$$
415 NEW JERSEY AVE., N.W.
TEL 202/638-1616
FAX 202/638-0707
affinia.com
This boutique hotel, located
between Union Station and
Capitol Hill, opened in 2008.
It features a rooftop bar and
seasonal pool. The **Art and
Soul** restaurant's chef Art
Smith creates modern ver-
sions of Southern food.
ⓘ 343 🏊 🛎 🚅 All major
cards 🚇 Union Station

🏨 **PHOENIX PARK**
🍴 **HOTEL**
$$$$
520 N. CAPITOL ST., N.W.
TEL 202/638-6900 OR
877/237-2082
FAX 202/393-3236
phoenixparkhotel.com
Named after the park in
Dublin, this hotel has a
European ambience. The
adjoining **Dubliner Pub**
offers good pub cooking
and Irish entertainment.
ⓘ 149 🅿 🛎 🚅 All major
cards 🚇 Union Station

🏨 **WASHINGTON COURT**
HOTEL
$$$$
525 NEW JERSEY AVE., N.W.
TEL 202/628-2100
FAX 202/ 879 7993
washingtoncourthotel.com
Completely renovated in
2009, this hotel has a dramatic four-story atrium lobby
and billiards in the Federal
City bar.

ⓘ 265 🅿 🛎 🚅 All major
cards 🚇 Union Station

🏨 **CAPITOL HILL HOTEL**
$$$
200 C ST., S.E.
TEL 202/543-6000
FAX 202/547-2608
capitolhillhotel-dc.com
Tucked behind the Library
of Congress on the House
side of the hill, Capitol Hill
Hotel offers kitchenettes in
every suite.
ⓘ 153 🅿 🚅 All major cards
🚇 South Capitol

RESTAURANTS

🍴 **BISTRO BIS**
$$$$
THE HOTEL GEORGE
15 E ST., N.W.
TEL 202/661-2700
bistrobis.com
Chef owner Jeffrey Buben
serves contemporary French
bistro fare in this sleek Capi-
tol Hill hangout. Consistently
rated one of Washington's
best restaurants.
🍴 115 🅿 🚅 All major cards
🚇 Union Station

🍴 **BIDWELL**
$$$–$$$$
UNION MARKET
1309 5TH ST., S.E.
TEL 202/547-0172
bidwelldc.com
A cornerstone of the newly
opened Union Market
artisanal food emporium,
Bidwell proudly sources its
ingredients responsibly, with
literal roof-to-table cuisine:
Much of the restaurant's
produce comes from aero-
ponic planters on the roof
of Union Market. Chef John
Mooney's signature dishes
feature Southern flavors,
especially his gin and tonic
salmon, crispy deviled eggs,
and suckling pig.
🍴 120 🕐 Closed Mon.
🚅 All major cards 🚇 NoMa–
Gallaudet U

🍴 **GRANVILLE MOORE'S**
$$$
1238 H ST., N.E.
TEL 202/399-2546
granvillemoores.com
This delightfully rustic Ameri-
can/Belgian gastropub is a
mainstay of the newly transformed H Street corridor and
a favorite local watering hole.
Slip into one of the wooden
booths for Belgian-style beers
and a plate of *moules-frites*.
🍴 90 🕐 Closed Mon.–Fri. L
🚅 AE, MC, V 🚇 Union
Station, then trolley

🍴 **JOHNNY'S HALF SHELL**
$$$
400 N. CAPITOL ST., N.W.
TEL 202/737-0400
johnnyshalfshell.net
Formerly a beloved neighbor-
hood seafood bar in Dupont
Circle, Johnny's has relocated
to a new setting to spotlight
chef Ann Cashion's Southern-
accented seafood. Also open
for breakfast and lunch, with
jazz on Saturday night.
🍴 270 🕐 Closed Sun. 🚅 All
major cards 🚇 Union Station

🍴 **THE MONOCLE**
$$$
107 D ST., N.E.
TEL 202/546-4488
themonocle.com
Its position as the closest
restaurant to the Senate side
of the Capitol means that
there's no better place for
sighting politicos. Run by the
Valanos family for more than
50 years, the Monocle serves
an all-American menu of
burgers, steaks, and seafood.
🍴 110 🕐 Closed Sat.–Sun.
🚅 AE, DC, MC, V 🚇 Union
Station

SOMETHING SPECIAL

🍴 **MONTMARTRE**
$$$
327 7TH ST., S.E.
TEL 202/544-1244
montmartredc.com
This charming bistro offers

consistently good French fare in a simple, inviting space. The braised rabbit is a signature dish, and other menu selections might include truffle-perfumed pasta, veal kidneys, and monkfish. The outdoor patio is popular in warm weather.

🍴 50 🕐 Closed Mon. 🚫 AE, DC, MC, V 🚇 Eastern Market

🍴 BANANA CAFÉ

$$

500 8TH ST., S.E.

TEL 202/543-5906

bananacafedc.com

This cheerful Latin American and Cuban restaurant has a bar and dining room on the main level and a piano bar above. Order from a small selection of tapas to start, but then dive into the Cuban specialties. Don't miss the mango margaritas.

🍴 100 🚫 All major cards 🚇 Eastern Market

🍴 MATCHBOX CAPITOL HILL

$$

521 8TH ST., S.E.

TEL 202/548-0369

matchboxcapitolhill.com

Wood-fired pizzas with blistery crusts and imaginative toppings are a big draw at this spacious and trendy spot, which also features dishes such as bacon-wrapped shrimp with grits. Sister locations are in Chinatown (713 H St., N.W.) and U St. (1901 14th St., N.W.).

🍴 150 🚫 All major cards 🚇 Eastern Market

🍴 MOMOYAMA

$$

231 2ND ST., N.W.

TEL 202/737-0397

This hole-in-the-wall sushi spot tucked away on a side street near the Capitol is popular with government workers on their lunch breaks, offering fresh sashimi and *nigiri*

for excellent value. Creative rolls blend unexpected flavors, such as the house special Momoyama roll with tuna, salmon, and avocado with scallions and caviar. Try a generously portioned bento boxes for a satisfying lunch.

🍴 22 🕐 Closed Sat.–Sun. 🚫 AE, MC, V 🚇 Judiciary Square

🍴 ZEST

$$

735 8TH ST., S.E.

TEL 202/544-7171

zestbistro.com

A neighborhood bistro opened in December 2009 by longtime residents of Capitol Hill, Zest offers a light and airy setting for good, well-priced food such as hanger steak, spinach risotto, and lamb shank.

🍴 88 🚫 AE, MC, V 🚇 Eastern Market

🍴 GOOD STUFF EATERY

$

303 PENNSYLVANIA AVE., S.E.

TEL 202/543-8222

goodstuffeatery.com

This family-run, nontraditional burger joint has been a hit among Capitol Hill staffers ever since it was launched in 2008 by "Chef Spike" Mendelsohn, who worked in Napa Valley and New York City restaurants before coming to D.C. The handcrafted burgers, fries, shakes, and salads are all made with top-quality ingredients.

🍴 100 🕐 Closed Sun. 🚫 All major cards 🚇 Capitol South

■ THE MALL

HOTELS

🏨 MANDARIN ORIENTAL
🍴 $$$$$

1330 MARYLAND AVE., S.W.

TEL 202/554-8588

FAX 202/554-8999

mandarinoriental.com /washington

This super-luxury hotel opened in 2004 near the southeastern end of the Mall, overlooking the Tidal Basin and the Jefferson Memorial. The marble baths, lacquered furniture, silk furnishings, and extensive spa services make for a soothing stay. Chef Eric Ziebold of the hotel's Asian-inspired City Zen (see below) has been named one of America's "best new chefs."

ⓘ 400 🅿 📺 🍽 🚫 All major cards 🚇 L'Enfant Plaza

🏨 L'ENFANT PLAZA HOTEL

$$$$

480 L'ENFANT PLAZA, S.W.

TEL 202/484-1000

FAX 202/646-5060

lenfantplazahotel.com

Close to the Smithsonian museums, this hotel is attractive to both business and leisure travelers. Dining options include a seafood-dominated brasserie and a brewpub. Due to reopen in 2015 after a renovation.

ⓘ 370 🍽 🏊 📺 🚫 All major cards 🚇 L'Enfant Plaza

RESTAURANTS

🍴 CITY ZEN

$$$$

1330 MARYLAND AVE., S.W.

TEL 202/787-6148

mandarinoriental.com /washington/fine-dining/ city-zen

City Zen, at the Mandarin Oriental Hotel in Southwest D.C., is a local favorite for a special night out. Chef Eric Ziebold, formerly of Napa's famed French Laundry, overhauls the menu each month with modern American cuisine, such as veal sweetbreads with swiss chard and black bass accented with squash blossoms. Options include a three-course prix fixe menu, a six-course chef's tasting menu, and a six-course vegetarian tasting menu. Choose from more than 700 wines.

75 P Valet Closed Sat.–Mon. AE, DC, MC, V Smithsonian

CAFÉ DU PARC
$$$–$$$$

1401 PENNSYLVANIA AVE., N.W.
TEL 202/942-7000
cafeduparc.com
Located in the Willard Intercontinental Hotel, this elegant bistro blends traditional French fare with a modern vibe. Sidewalk seating with a view of Pershing Park across Pennsylvania Avenue offers an excellent spot to unwind while sightseeing. Start off with coffee and a croissant or a full breakfast buffet, or enjoy an afternoon lunch of the cafe's famed French terrines or mussels *à la mariniere*.

202 (84 in winter) P Valet at Willard Hotel All major cards Federal Triangle, Metro Center

OLLIE'S TROLLEY
$$–$$$

425 12TH ST., N.W.
TEL 202/347-6119
olliestrolleydc.com
This colorful family-owned restaurant has been a D.C. institution for more than 30 years. Located just blocks from the National Mall, the menu of burgers, crab cakes, fish sandwiches, and milkshakes is a sure hit with kids after a day spent exploring the Smithsonian museums. Don't skip the famous Olliefries, tossed in the secret house blend of 26 herbs and spices.

30 Cash only Metro Center

NATIONAL GALLERY OF ART CAFÉS
$

6TH ST. & CONSTITUTION AVE., N.W.

TEL 202/737-4215
The Garden Café offers light lunch fare, while the large Cascade Café, in the concourse between the two buildings, has a varied cafeteria menu. The Sculpture Garden Pavilion Café serves pizzas, sandwiches, desserts, wine, and beer. Check out the weekend jazz brunches, and for a treat, don't miss the great gelato at the Espresso Bar.

Archives–Navy Memorial, Smithsonian

■ WHITE HOUSE & AROUND

HOTELS

FAIRMONT HOTEL
$$$$$

2401 M ST., N.W.
TEL 202/429-2400 OR
866/540-4505
FAX 202/457-5010
fairmont.com
/washington
Built around a garden courtyard, the Fairmont is in the West End area of town near Georgetown. Rooms are luxurious, service is attentive. The fitness center, with pool, is one of the most complete and popular in the city. **Juniper** offers good modern American cooking, while the **Collonade** serves an elaborate holiday brunch.

415 P All major cards Foggy Bottom–GWU

THE HAY-ADAMS HOTEL
$$$$$

800 16TH ST., N.W.
TEL 202/638-6600 OR
800/853-6807
FAX 202/638-2716
hayadams.com
Built on the site where President Lincoln's secretary John Hay and John Adams's grandson Henry Adams lived. The hotel is

just across Lafayette Square from the White House. The **Lafayette** dining room and guest rooms on the south side offer great views of the Executive Mansion.

145 P All major cards Farragut West, McPherson Square

JW MARRIOTT HOTEL
$$$$$

1331 PENNSYLVANIA AVE., N.W.
TEL 202/393-2000 OR
800/393-2503
FAX 202/626-1357
marriott.com
Centrally located and connected to the shops and boutiques of National Place, the JW Marriott is a convenient hub for exploring the city.

738 P AE, DC, MC, V Metro Center

PARK HYATT
$$$$$

24TH & M STS., N.W.
TEL 202/789-1234
FAX 202/419-6795
parkwashington.hyatt
.com
Located in Washington's West End, just three blocks from Georgetown, the Park Hyatt is comfortably modern. The lobby is decorated with an impressive collection of art. Rooms are large and luxurious. The distinguished restaurant, **Blue Duck Tavern** (see p. 247), serves chef Sebastien Archambault's accomplished modern American cooking and a lavish weekend brunch.

216 P All major cards Foggy Bottom–GWU

RITZ-CARLTON HOTEL WASHINGTON, D.C.
$$$$$

1150 22ND ST., N.W.
TEL 202/835-0500
FAX 202/835-1588
ritzcarlton.com
The elegant guest rooms of this luxury hotel offer a nice

Elevator   Air-conditioning   Indoor Pool   Outdoor Pool   Health Club   Credit Cards   Metro

ambience in a neighborhood setting, with a courtyard view. The hotel's **Westend Bistro** has emerged as one of D.C.'s top-rated restaurants under chef Devin Bozkaya.

ⓘ 300 🅿 🚇 All major cards 🚊 Foggy Bottom–GWU

🏨 SOFITEL
🍴 LAFAYETTE SQUARE
$$$$$
806 15TH ST., N.W.
TEL 202/730-8800
FAX 202/730-8500
sofitel.com

Housed in an 1880s building, this well-located hotel, near the White House, has the restrained elegance of its parent, the French Accor chain. **ICI Urban Bistro,** the hotel's restaurant, serves French cuisine, and **Le Bar** lounge is a popular meeting place.

ⓘ 237 🅿 🚇 🚊 All major cards 🚊 McPherson Square

🏨 THE ST. REGIS
🍴 $$$$$
923 16TH ST. AT K ST., N.W.
TEL 202/638-2626 OR
888/627-8087
FAX 202/638-4231
stregiswashingtondc.com

The posh St. Regis, located near the White House and museums, is built in Italian Renaissance style with fine plasterwork ceilings, antiques, and ornate chandeliers. The hotel underwent an extensive renovation in 2008.

ⓘ 182 🅿 🚇 🚊 All major cards 🚊 Farragut North

🏨 THE WESTIN
GEORGETOWN
$$$$$
2350 M ST., N.W.
TEL 202/429-0100
FAX 202/429-9759
westin.com
/washingtondc

This low-key hotel, located between Georgetown and the White House, is known for its friendly, attentive service.

Comfortable rooms and great location offer good value.

ⓘ 263 🅿 Valet 🚇 🚊 🚊 All major cards 🚊 Foggy Bottom–GWU

🏨 WILLARD INTER-
🍴 CONTINENTAL HOTEL
$$$$$
1401 PENNSYLVANIA AVE., N.W.
TEL 202/628-9100 OR
866/487-2537
FAX 202/637-7326
washington.intercontinental
.com

A Willard Hotel has been located on this site since 1850. Abraham Lincoln stayed here before his Inauguration; Julia Ward Howe wrote the "Battle Hymn of the Republic" here. The hotel has been luxuriously updated. **Café du Parc** features French bistro cuisine and exquisite pastries. The **Round Robin Bar** is one of the city's most popular gathering places.

ⓘ 335 🅿 🚇 🚊 All major cards 🚊 Metro Center

🏨 W WASHINGTON D.C.
🍴 $$$$
15TH ST. & PENNSYLVANIA
AVE., N.W.
TEL 202/661-2400
FAX 202/661-2405
wwashingtondc.com

Italian Renaissance meets modern cool in this newly refurbished hotel (formerly Hotel Washington) with amenities that include a Bliss spa and the rooftop POV bar, with a fabulous view of Washington. **J&G Steakhouse** offers in-house dining.

ⓘ 317 🚊 All major cards 🚊 Metro Center

🏨 AVENUE SUITES
$$$
2500 PENNSYLVANIA AVE., N.W.
TEL 202/333-8060 OR
202/338-3818
avenuesuites.com

Located just over Rock Creek from Georgetown, this hotel

has fully equipped suites that feel like private apartments, in a great location for city walks.

ⓘ 124 🅿 🚇 🚊 All major cards 🚊 Foggy Bottom–GWU

RESTAURANTS

🍴 EQUINOX
$$$$
818 CONNECTICUT AVE., N.W.
TEL 202/331-8118
equinoxrestaurant.com

Chef Todd Gray has received numerous culinary awards for his innovative takes on American cuisine. A commitment to seasonal ingredients and sustainable farming has won this restaurant, renovated in 2010, a strong local following.

🪑 90 🕐 Closed Sat.–Sun. L 🚊 AE, DC, MC, V 🚊 Farragut West

🍴 MARCEL'S
$$$$
2401 PENNSYLVANIA AVE., N.W.
TEL 202/296-1166
marcelsdc.com

Chef Robert Wiedmaier's

Belgian-influenced French cooking is both sophisticated and robust. You can choose from three- to seven-course meals, or have lighter fare from the pre-theater menu.
🛏 120 🅿 Valet 🕐 Closed L 💳 AE, DC, MC, V 🚇 Foggy Bottom–GWU

🍴 OVAL ROOM AT LAFAYETTE SQUARE
$$$$
800 CONNECTICUT AVE., N.W.
TEL 202/463-8700
ovalroom.com
Just across Lafayette Square from the White House, the Oval Room is a favorite lunch spot for senior executive branch staffers. Chef Tony Conte has won critical acclaim for a menu of innovative modern American cuisine with Mediterranean influences.
🛏 125 🅿 Valet 🕐 Closed Sat. L & all Sun. 💳 AE, DC, MC, V 🚇 Farragut West

🍴 BLUE DUCK TAVERN
$$$
24TH & M STS., N.W.
TEL 202/419-6755
blueducktavern.com
One of Washington's very best restaurants, the Blue Duck Tavern has a handsome wood and blue burlap interior that showcases chef Sebastien Archambault's celebration of regional and artisanal American foods. The menu features simple but exquisitely prepared dishes such as ricotta cheese dumplings, braised pork cheek, and pan-roasted sweetbreads.
🛏 100 💳 All major cards 🚇 Foggy Bottom–GWU

🍴 CENTRAL MICHEL RICHARD
$$$
1001 PENNSYLVANIA AVE., N.W.
TEL 202/626-0015
centralmichelrichard
.com
This low-key restaurant has

Washingtonians flocking to its affordable takes on the innovative mastery of chef Michel Richard. The fare is French bistro with a twist, with such dishes as country pâté, bacon and onion tart, and scallops with sweet corn and mushrooms.
🛏 140 🅿 Valet 🕐 Closed Sat.–Sun. L 💳 AE, D, MC, V. 🚇 Metro Center, Archives–Navy Memorial

🍴 OLD EBBITT GRILL
$$$
675 15TH ST., N.W.
TEL 202/347-4800
ebbitt.com
Large, casual, and always crowded, the Old Ebbitt Grill feeds Washingtonians and out-of-towners with a menu that ranges from burgers to grilled fish in a historic saloon environment. There's no better place in town for oysters.
🛏 500 🅿 Valet 💳 All major cards 🚇 Metro Center

🍴 RIS
$$$
2275 L ST., N.W.
TEL 202/730-2500
risdc.com
Esteemed local chef Ris Lacoste, trained in French cuisine, fulfilled a longtime dream in opening this cozy restaurant that features homey food with a deft touch, such as chicken pot pie, cider-glazed pork chops, and pasta with ramps.
🛏 180 💳 All major credit cards 🚇 Foggy Bottom–GWU

■ DOWNTOWN

HOTELS

🏨 GRAND HYATT WASHINGTON
$$$$$
1000 H ST., N.W.
TEL 202/582-1234
FAX 202/637-4781

grandwashington.hyatt
.com
Located near the Washington Convention Center and Verizon Center, this large hotel features a parklike atrium, cigar bar, and several dining options.
🛏 897 🅿 🏊 💪 💳 All major cards 🚇 Metro Center

SOMETHING SPECIAL

🏨 HOTEL MONACO
🍴 $$$$$
700 F ST., N.W.
TEL 202/628-7177 OR
800/649-1202
FAX 202/628-7277
monaco-dc.com
This luxury Kimpton boutique hotel is housed in the architecturally stately 1839 Tariff Building in Penn Quarter, within steps of the Verizon Center, Washington Convention Center, and 7th Street arts scene. The distinctive rooms with 15-foot (4.5 m) ceilings feature neoclassical furnishings and vivid colors. The **Poste Moderne** restaurant is a brasserie offering modern American cuisine.
🛏 183 🅿 💪 💳 AE, D, MC, V 🚇 Gallery Place–Chinatown

🏨 JEFFERSON HOTEL
🍴 $$$$$
1200 16TH ST., N.W.
TEL 202/448-2300
FAX 202/448-2301
jeffersondc.com
Regarded by many as Washington's finest small hotel, the Jefferson—with many touches inspired by the third President—is even more exquisite after an extensive renovation. Dine at the **Plume** restaurant, and don't miss breakfast or lunch in the gorgeous and sunny **Greenhouse**.
🛏 95 🅿 🕐 💳 All major cards 🚇 Farragut West

🏨 MARRIOTT AT METRO CENTER
$$$$$
775 12TH ST., N.W.
TEL 202/737-2200 OR
800/393-2510
FAX 202/824-6106
marriottmetrocenter
.com
Conveniently located at the flagship station of the city's Metro system, the Marriott at Metro Center is attentive to both business and vacation guests.
🛈 459 🍽 📶 🀰 All major cards 🚇 Metro Center

🏨 RENAISSANCE MAYFLOWER HOTEL
$$$$$
1127 CONNECTICUT AVE., N.W.
TEL 202/347-3000 OR
800/228-7697
FAX 202/776-9182
marriott.com
Once the home to many members of Congress, the Mayflower has been the site of many Inaugural Balls. The gracious lobby runs an entire city block from Connecticut Avenue to 17th Street. The bar is a favorite gathering spot.
🛈 657 🅿 📶 🀰 All major cards 🚇 Farragut North

🏨 HENLEY PARK HOTEL
🍴 $$$$
926 MASSACHUSETTS AVE., N.W.
TEL 202/638-5200 OR
800/222-8474
henleypark.com
A Tudor-style hotel in the tradition of Europe's finest hotels and one of D.C.'s most charming. Dozens of gargoyles and lead windows grace its exterior. The **Tavern** restaurant offers very good new American fare. Located near the Convention Center.
🛈 96 🅿 📶 🀰 All major cards 🚇 Mount Vernon Square, Gallery Place–Chinatown

🏨 LOEWS MADISON
$$$$
1177 15TH ST., N.W.
TEL 202/862-1600 OR
800/424-8577
loewshotels.com
/madison-hotel
Cozy and noted for its attentive service, the Madison offers a great location for exploring D.C. sights as well as the Dupont Circle area.
🛈 365 🅿 📶 🀰 All major cards 🚇 McPherson Square

🏨 MORRISON-CLARK
🍴 INN
$$$$
MASSACHUSETTS AVE.
& 11TH ST., N.W.
TEL 202/898-1200;
800/332-7898
morrisonclark.com
This stately Victorian mansion on Massachusetts Avenue was built as two townhomes in 1864. A grand expansion in 2014 into the church next door doubled the room count. Chefs of the Morrison-Clark restaurant have won many awards for their New American cuisine.
🛈 114 🅿 📶 🀰 All major cards 🚇 Mount Vernon Square

🏨 HOTEL HARRINGTON
$$$
436 11TH ST., N.W.
TEL 202/628-8140 OR
800/424-8532
hotel-harrington.com
Low prices, a prime location, and very plain, clean rooms, make the Hotel Harrington popular with bus groups of students and other travelers on a tight budget.
🛈 242 🀰 All major cards 🚇 Metro Center

RESTAURANTS

🍴 PROOF
$$$$
775 G ST., N.W.

TEL 202/737-7663
proofdc.com
Impeccably prepared nouveau American cuisine, along with artisanal cheeses and charcuterie selections, complements the vast wine selection in this sleek and intimate addition to Penn Quarter. A four-course tasting menu is available.
🪑 90 🅿 Valet 🕐 Closed Sat.–Mon. L 🀰 All major credit cards 🚇 Gallery Place–Chinatown

🍴 THE SOURCE
$$$$
575 PENNSYLVANIA AVE., N.W.
TEL 202/637-6100
wolfgangpuck.com
/restaurants
This three-level glass-enclosed restaurant in the Newseum, with Asian-inspired menus, is chef Wolfgang Puck's inaugural D.C. venture. The casual ground-floor lounge has a Japanese-style menu heavy on sushi, sashimi, and noodles, while the upstairs is for fine dining. A prix fixe menu is available at lunch.
🪑 175 🅿 Valet 🕐 Sat. L & all Sun. 🀰 All major cards 🚇 Archives–Navy Memorial

🍴 TOSCA
$$$$
1112 F ST., N.W.
TEL 202/367-1990
toscadc.com
Cesare Lanfranconi spent five years in the kitchen at Galileo before starting his own restaurant with a menu based on the food of his native Lake Como region. Now headed by chef Massimo Fabbri, the sophisticated modern setting with widely spaced tables is designed for privacy and conversation. A Tuscan-style tasting menu is available, as well as a pre-theater menu.
🪑 120 🅿 Valet 🕐 Closed Sat. L & all Sun. 🀰 AE, DC, MC, V 🚇 Metro Center

🍴 THALLY
$$$–$$$$

1316 9TH ST., N.W.

TEL 202/733-3849

thallydc.com

Situated on the revitalizing 9th Street corridor in D.C.'s Shaw neighborhood, Thally serves "simple, fresh, and flavorful" modern American cuisine such as crab roulette and roast duck breast created by executive chef and co-owner Ron Tanaka. A rotating list of wines, craft beers, and custom cocktails keeps the 14-seat bar buzzing.

🍴 70 🅿 Valet 🕓 Closed Mon. & L 🕹 All major cards 🚇 Mt. Vernon Square–Convention Center

🍴 BRASSERIE BECK
$$$

1101 K ST., N.W.

TEL 202/408-1717

beckdc.com

This popular new European-style brasserie allows Robert Wiedmaier, owner of the formal Marcel's (see pp. 246–247), to offer robust food from his native Belgium—such as beef carbonnade and *moules* and *frites*—in a casual setting. The spacious bar features a huge array of Belgian beers.

🍴 165 🅿 Valet 🕹 All major cards 🚇 Metro Center

🍴 JALEO
$$

480 7TH ST., N.W.

TEL 202/628-7949

jaleo.com/dc

There are main courses at Jaleo, but most diners choose to make a meal of the large selection of tapas—wonderful Spanish cheeses and cold cuts, eggplant flan, spicy octopus, sausages and beans. It's a great place for a light dinner before a performance at the nearby Shakespeare Theatre.

🍴 145 🅿 Valet 🕹 All major cards 🚇 Gallery Place–Chinatown

🍴 OYAMEL
$$

401 7TH ST., N.W.

TEL 202/628-1005

oyamel.com

Mexican food goes upscale on a menu that invites grazing. Selections include cactus paddle salad, stuffed poblano peppers, and hominy soup. For something really different, there's an Oaxacan speciality of sautéed grasshoppers.

🍴 120 🅿 Valet 🕹 All major credit cards 🚇 Gallery Place–Chinatown, Archives–Navy Memorial

🍴 RASIKA
$$

633 D ST., N.W.

TEL 202/637-1222

rasikarestaurant.com

This chic Indian restaurant, launched by the owner of the Bombay Club, has developed a loyal following for its modern takes on the classics, as well as inventive entrées such tandoori lamb chops with cashews, ginger, and herbs. Dinner options include pre-theater and tasting menus.

🍴 120 🅿 Valet 🕓 Closed L Sat. & all Sun. 🕹 AE, MC, V 🚇 Gallery Place–Chinatown, Archives–Navy Memorial

■ GEORGETOWN

HOTELS

SOMETHING SPECIAL

🏨 FOUR SEASONS
🍴 HOTEL
$$$$$

2800 PENNSYLVANIA AVE., N.W.

TEL 202/342-0444

FAX 202/944-2076

fourseasons.com/washington

Located on the very eastern edge of Georgetown, this luxurious hotel provides a nice link into the rest of the city. **Seasons** restaurant, overlooking the C & O Canal, is a favorite power breakfast spot. The three-level fitness center with an adjoining spa is one of the most opulent in town.

🛈 222 🅿 🏊 🕹 🕹 AE, DC, MC, V 🚇 Foggy Bottom–GWU

🏨 THE GRAHAM GEORGETOWN
$$$$$

1075 THOMAS JEFFERSON ST., N.W.

TEL 202/337-0900 OR 855/351-1292

FAX 202/333-6526

thegrahamgeorgetown.com

This newly revamped hotel (formerly the Hotel Monticello) is located in the center of Georgetown and is named for one-time neighborhood resident Alexander Graham Bell. It is close to the historic C & O Canal. The Observatory rooftop bar and lounge offers panoramic views of the D.C. skyline.

🛈 57 🕹 AE, D, MC, V 🚇 Foggy Bottom–GWU

🏨 RITZ-CARLTON
🍴 GEORGETOWN
$$$$$

3100 SOUTH ST., N.W.

TEL 202/912-4100

FAX 202/912-4199

ritzcarlton.com

Built on the former site of a historic brick incinerator building, complete with a 130-foot-high (40 m) smokestack, this hotel offers views of the Potomac waterfront. The rooms and suites offer luxury and soothing retreat. **Degrees** restaurant features innovative regional cuisine with international flavors, while the cozy **Living Room** lounge offers cocktails and free s'mores in front of the fireplace.

🛈 86 🅿 🕹 🕹 AE, DC, MC, V 🚇 Foggy Bottom–GWU

🔼 Elevator ❄ Air-conditioning 🏊 Indoor Pool 🏊 Outdoor Pool 🕹 Health Club 🕹 Credit Cards 🚇 Metro

⌂ THE GEORGETOWN
🍴 INN
$$$$

1310 WISCONSIN AVE., N.W.
TEL 202/333-8900 OR
866/308-8883
FAX 202/333-8308
georgetowninn.com
This pleasant redbrick hotel
has colonial decor, large rooms,
and marble bathrooms. It's
conveniently located for
Georgetown shopping and
entertainment. The **Daily Grill**
is reminiscent of the great
American grills of the 1920s.
🛏 96 🅿 🈳 ♿ AE, D, MC, V
🚇 Foggy Bottom–GWU

RESTAURANTS

🍴 1789
$$$$

1226 36TH ST., N.W.
TEL 202/965-1789
1789restaurant.com
One of Washington's
loveliest and most beloved
restaurants, housed in a
federal town house. Chef
Anthony Lombardo sources
ingredients from local farms
for dishes such as duck
prosciutto salad. Downstairs
is the **Tombs,** where generations of Georgetown stu-
dents have drunk countless
pitchers of beer.
🪑 300 🅿 Valet 🕐 Closed L
♿ All major cards 🚇 Foggy
Bottom–GWU

🍴 SEA CATCH
$$$$

1054 31ST ST., N.W.
TEL 202/337-8855
seacatchrestaurant.com
The Carrera marble oyster
bar at the entrance to this
dependable seafood restaurant overlooking the C & O
Canal hints at what to order
first—oysters and clams on
the half shell. The seafood
selection, always perfectly
fresh, is based on market
availability. Try the steamed
shellfish platter or grilled

rainbow trout with jumbo
lump crab.
🪑 200 🅿 🕐 Closed Sun.
♿ All major cards
🚇 Foggy Bottom-GWU

🍴 BISTRO FRANCAIS
$$

3124 M ST., N.W.
TEL 202/338-3830
bistrofrancaisdc.com
In a city where restaurants
close early, this lively French
bistro serves until 3 a.m.
on weekdays and 4 a.m. on
weekends. The bistro classics
are dependably done: roast
chicken with *pommes frites,*
a hearty cassoulet, rabbit in
mustard sauce. There's a good
choice of well-priced wines.
🪑 150 ♿ All major cards
🚇 Foggy Bottom–GWU

🍴 CLYDE'S
$$

3236 M ST., N.W.
TEL 202/333-9180
clydes.com/georgetown
The founder of the Clyde's
group of restaurants had the
idea that he'd "rather eat in
a bar than drink in a restaurant." This Georgetown
original of the chain is built
around a bar business, but
offers an impressive menu of
bar food, particularly in the
summer when Clyde's makes
a point of sending trucks to
local farms for fresh produce.
It's an excellent place for a
restorative drink and a light
meal while out shopping
in Georgetown.
🪑 188 🅿 Georgetown Park
Mall lot ♿ All major cards
🚇 Foggy Bottom–GWU

■ DUPONT CIRCLE
& BEYOND

HOTELS

⌂ PALOMAR HOTEL
🍴 $$$$$

2121 P ST., N.W.

PRICES

HOTELS
An indication of the cost of
a double room in the high
season is given by **$** signs.

$$$$$	Over $225
$$$$	$175–$225
$$$	$125–$175
$$	$85–$125
$	Under $85

RESTAURANTS
An indication of the cost of
a three-course meal without
drinks is given by **$** signs.

$$$$$	Over $75
$$$$	$50–$75
$$$	$35–$50
$$	$15–$35
$	Under $15

TEL 202/448-1800 OR
877/866-3070
FAX 202/448-1801
hotelpalomar-dc.com
Sophistication and personal-
ized service are the hallmarks
of this Kimpton hotel
inspired by 1930s French
moderne style. Exotic woods,
bold art, and geometric
touches abound. **Urbana**
restaurant serves Mediterranean cuisine.
🛏 335 🅿 ♿ 🈳 ♿ All major
cards 🚇 Dupont Circle

⌂ THE CHURCHILL
🍴 $$$$

1914 CONNECTICUT AVE., N.W.
TEL 202/797-2000
FAX 202/462-0944
thechurchillhotel.com
Located just north of the
vibrant Dupont Circle area,
a part of town known for its
stately residences and embassies, the Churchill offers a
variety of suites and rooms
with separate studies. The
Chartwell Grill offers
elegant dining.
🛏 173 🅿 🈳 ♿ All major
cards 🚇 Dupont Circle

COURTYARD MARRIOTT DUPONT CIRCLE
$$$$
1900 CONNECTICUT AVE., N.W.
TEL 202/332-9300
FAX 202/328-7039
marriott.com
Not far from Dupont Circle, this pleasant hotel is popular with business and vacation travelers. The **Bistro** restaurant serves American cuisine.
ⓘ 147 🅿 ☲ 🆈 🆂 All major cards 🄼 Dupont Circle

THE DUPONT CIRCLE HOTEL
$$$$
1500 NEW HAMPSHIRE AVE., N.W.
TEL 202/483-6000
FAX 202/328-3265
doylecollection.com
Owned and operated by Ireland's Jurys Doyle Hotels, this recently remodeled hotel on Dupont Circle is in one of the city's liveliest areas.
ⓘ 309 🅿 🆈 🆂 All major cards 🄼 Dupont Circle

FAIRFAX AT EMBASSY ROW
$$$$
2100 MASSACHUSETTS AVE., N.W.
TEL 202/293-2100
FAX 202/293-0641
fairfaxhotel.com
Formerly the Westin Embassy Row, the hotel dates to 1924 and has been for many years the residential hotel favored by members of Congress. Former Vice President Al Gore grew up here. Guest rooms are luxurious, as one would expect from a hotel on Massachusetts Avenue's Embassy Row. The **Fairfax Lounge** restaurant offers good bistro cuisine.
ⓘ 259 🅿 🆈 🆂 AE, D, MC, V 🄼 Dupont Circle

HOTEL HELIX
$$$$
1430 RHODE ISLAND AVE., N.W.
TEL 202/462-9001 OR 800/706-1202
FAX 202/521-2714
hotelhelix.com
Pop Art is the theme here, with a Magritte-like mural welcoming you and lots of bright colors inside. An example of the amenities designed to create an atmosphere of fun are "bunk beds" for grown-up slumber parties: a sofa cum twin bed that converts to a regular-size double bed. Helix Lounge features politically inspired cocktails.
ⓘ 178 🅿 🆈 🆂 AE, D, MC, V 🄼 Dupont Circle

HOTEL MADERA
$$$$
1310 NEW HAMPSHIRE AVE., N.W.
TEL 202/296-7600 OR 800/430-1202
FAX 202/293-2476
hotelmadera.com
This pampering hideaway is like a B&B tucked in a quiet location near downtown office buildings and embassies. Part of the Kimpton chain, it has a sophisticated decor and the amenities of a big hotel. **Firefly** restaurant offers American bistro fare.
ⓘ 82 🅿 🆂 All major cards 🄼 Dupont Circle

HOTEL ROUGE
$$$$
1315 16TH ST., N.W.
TEL 202/232-8000 OR 800/738-1202
FAX 202/667-9827
rougehotel.com
Quirky red accents—from bloody Marys to wax lips—dominate this hip Kimpton hotel within walking distance of Dupont Circle.
ⓘ 137 🆈 🆂 AE, D, MC, V 🄼 Dupont Circle, McPherson Square

TOPAZ HOTEL
$$$$
1733 N ST., N.W.
TEL 202/393-3000 OR 800/775-1202
FAX 202/785-9581
topazhotel.com
This Kimpton boutique hotel promises "cosmic energy and good karma." Complimentary yoga mats are provided in every room, and you can even get an energy drink on your way out in the morning. The Topaz Bar is open for meals and drinks.
ⓘ 99 🅿 🆂 AE, D, MC, V 🄼 Dupont Circle

TABARD INN
$$$
1739 N ST., N.W.
TEL 202/785-1277
FAX 202/785-6173
tabardinn.com
This small hotel is greatly loved by those who consider it quaint and adore the Victorian clutter. Locals love the hotel's restaurant (see p. 253), which has a charming outdoor garden and imaginative food. The rooms vary widely in size, so look before you commit.
ⓘ 40 🅿 🆂 AE, D, MC, V 🄼 Dupont Circle

RESTAURANTS

CASHION'S EAT PLACE
$$$$
1819 COLUMBIA RD., N.W.
TEL 202/797-1819
cashionseatplace.com
This Adams Morgan restaurant founded by chef Ann Cashion offers distinguished modern American cooking in a setting that's casual enough for a weeknight dinner and attractive enough for a special occasion. You'll usually find a perfectly roasted free-range chicken or roast leg of pork with creamed collard greens. Desserts are a treat, particularly the chocolate

cake and the frozen lemon tart.

🛏 100 🅿 Valet 🕐 Closed Mon. 🅢 MC, AE, V 🚇 Woodley Park–Zoo/Adams Morgan, Dupont Circle plus 15-minute walk

🍴 OBELISK
$$$$
2029 P ST., N.W.
TEL 202/872-1180
At Obelisk, everything is small in scale except flavor. This tiny Italian restaurant holds fewer than 40 people, which makes it one of the hardest-to-get reservations in town. The $75 fixed-price menu, which changes too often to recommend specific dishes, offers two or three choices of antipasto, pasta, main course, and dessert. Chef Peter Pastan's cooking is simple but never precious, and is based around fresh ingredients.

🛏 30 🕐 Closed L & all Sun.–Mon. 🅢 DC, MC, V 🚇 Dupont Circle

🍴 THE PALM
$$$$
1225 19TH ST., N.W.
TEL 202/293-9091
thepalm.com/washington-dc
The downtown branch of this steakhouse chain is the epicenter of Washington power dining. The main attractions are the Palm's steaks and five-pound lobsters, served by an efficient and irreverent crew of wise-cracking waiters. The Italian food is also very good.

🛏 185 🅿 Valet 🕐 Closed Fri.–Sun. L 🅢 AE, DC, MC, V 🚇 Dupont Circle

🍴 RESTAURANT NORA
$$$$
2132 FLORIDA AVE., N.W.
TEL 202/462-5143
noras.com
Chef Nora Pouillon was a pioneer advocate of organic farming, and her restaurant is

the first locally to be certified organic by Oregon Tilth. The menu changes daily, but you will find first-course salads, beautifully cooked organic chicken, fresh seafood, and spectacular desserts. The dining room gains warmth from brick walls and the display of museum-quality American quilts.

🛏 135 🅿 Valet 🕐 Closed L & all Sun. 🅢 AE, MC, V 🚇 Dupont Circle

🍴 VIDALIA
$$$$
1990 M ST., N.W.
TEL 202/659-1990
vidaliadc.com
Named after the sweet Georgia onion, Vidalia is one of the city's leading exponents of Southern cooking. In season, there's a large variety of Vidalia onion dishes. The shrimp and grits is a signature dish, as is gravy-smothered chicken-fried steak. For dessert, don't miss the lemon chess pie.

🛏 115 🅿 Valet 🕐 Closed Sat.–Sun. L 🅢 All major cards 🚇 Farragut West

🍴 1905
$$$–$$$$
1905 9TH ST., N.W.
TEL 202/332-1905
1905dc.com
Located in D.C.'s up-and-coming Shaw neighborhood just off the U Street corridor, this cozy, intimate bistro features soft lighting, warm-hued fabrics, and sparkling mirrors. Chef Joel Hatton serves up tasty dishes such as quinoa-crayfish hush puppies, cornmeal crusted catfish, and Coca-Cola baked beans. Sunday brunch offers bottomless mimosas and Bloody Marys. Seasonal roof deck.

🛏 100, including roof deck 🅿 Valet 🕐 Closed Mon. & Tues.–Sat. L 🅢 All major cards 🚇 U Street–Cardozo

🍴 BIRCH & BARLEY
$$$
1337 14TH ST., N.W.
TEL 202/567-2576
birchandbarley.com
Giant copper pipes dominating the brick-walled decor signal the focus of this hip new place in the Logan Circle area. On offer are more than 500 beer varieties from 30 countries, including 50 on tap. Snagging a table can be tough in the downstairs dining room, where the food tends toward hearty fare such as loin of venison and miso-marinated black cod. ChurchKey, the upstairs bar, is casual and crowded.

🛏 80 🕐 Closed L & all Mon. 🅢 All major credit cards 🚇 Dupont Circle

🍴 BISTROT DU COIN
$$$
1738 CONNECTICUT AVE., N.W.
TEL 202/234-6969
bistrotducoin.com
It's not a place for quiet conversation, but Bistrot du Coin is a lot of fun. Owner Michel Verdon and chef Yannis Felix strike a nice balance between good cheer and good cooking. Mussels are a tasty way to start a meal here. For a main course, it's hard to go wrong with steak *frites*, but the more adventurous can order tripes *à la Niçoise* or a delicious stew of rabbit and mushrooms. The house wines offer good value.

🛏 150 🅢 AE, D, MC, V 🚇 Dupont Circle

SOMETHING SPECIAL

🍴 IRON GATE
$$$
1734 N ST., N.W.
TEL 202/524-5202
There's no more charming spot in Washington for outdoor dining than the terrace at the Iron Gate Inn, a former stable built after the Civil War. The menu is

Mediterranean-inspired and the kitchen does a good job on Middle Eastern dishes—stuffed grape leaves, braised lamb shank, and grilled fish.

🍴 80 🕐 Closed Mon. L 🚇 Dupont Circle

🍴 PERRY'S

$$$

1811 COLUMBIA RD., N.W.

TEL 202/234-6218

perrysadamsmorgan.com

Despite its meat-and-potatoes name, Perry's serves sushi and new takes on familiar fare such as scallops and soft-shell crabs. The Sunday brunch, with lip-synched entertainment by glamorous drag queens, is an Adams Morgan institution. The roof deck is pleasant for dinner.

🍴 90 outdoors, 90 indoors 🅿 Valet 🕐 Closed Mon.–Fri. L 🚫 All major cards 🚇 Woodley Park–Zoo/Adams Morgan, Dupont Circle plus 15-minute walk

🍴 TABARD INN

$$$

1739 N ST., N.W.

TEL 202/331-8528

tabardinn.com/restaurant

The restaurant of this quaint hotel south of Dupont Circle serves new American cuisine in a well-worn dining room that's a popular lunch spot. Sunday brunch is a favorite, and the pleasant brick-walled garden is a good place for a drink and dinner on a spring evening. Similarly, the lounge, with fireplace and creaky wood floors, is cozy on winter evenings.

🍴 80 (30 summer patio) 🅿 Valet Fri.–Sat. 🚫 AE, MC, V 🚇 Dupont Circle

🍴 COMPASS ROSE

$$–$$$

1346 T ST., N.W.

TEL 202/506-4765

compassrosedc.com

Newly opened Compass Rose

offers international flavors in a chic neighborhood tavern setting, with exposed brick walls and wood accents. After traveling the world for three years, owner Rose Previte was inspired to share her culinary discoveries, transforming the first floor of her 125-year-old row house near hopping 14th Street into a bar and restaurant. Favorite dishes are sourced from Brazil, Turkey, Morocco, and Peru, while the extensive drinks list features craft beers, wine, and inventive cocktails. The small patio strung with lights provides delightful outdoor seating on warm summer nights.

🍴 65 🕐 Closed Mon. & Tues.–Sun. L 🚫 All major cards 🚇 U Street–Cardozo

🍴 CORK WINE BAR

$$

1720 14TH ST., N.W.

TEL 202/265-2675

corkdc.com

Conceived as a casual but elegant neighborhood tasting room, Cork offers some 50 wines by the glass and 160 bottles from small producers around the world. The menu consists of cheese and charcuterie selections, salads, and hot plates to share.

🍴 70 🕐 Closed L & all Mon. 🚫 All major credit cards 🚇 U Street–Cardozo, Dupont Circle

🍴 HANK'S OYSTER BAR

$$

1624 Q ST., N.W.

TEL 202/462-4265

hanksoysterbar.com

After laboring in several Washington restaurants, chef Jamie Leeds opened this restaurant in her own neighborhood near Dupont Circle to offer the kind of New England beach seafood cherished by her fisherman father, Hank. The crowded tables and eclectic decor were designed for joviality. Lobster

rolls, clam chowder, steamed mussels, fish and chips, oysters, and ceviche are on offer, along with signature dishes such as Leeds's molasses-braised short ribs.

🍴 65 🚫 AE, MC, V 🚇 Dupont Circle

🍴 LAURIOL PLAZA

$$

1835 18TH ST., N.W.

TEL 202/387-0035

lauriolplaza.com

There's almost always a wait to get into this well-run Tex-Mex restaurant that offers much more than the usual burritos and enchiladas. The roof deck is a wonderful place to spend a summer evening over a pitcher of sangria or a few bottles of Dos Equis.

🍴 330 🅿 🚫 All major cards 🚇 Dupont Circle

🍴 MASA 14

$$

1825 14TH ST., N.W.

TEL 202/328-1414

masa14.com

Two master chefs of Latin-Asian fusion food and sushi have teamed to create the small-plate menu of this new restaurant, north of Logan Circle. Recent offerings have included smoky octopus on pickled vegetables, hot oysters in cool lettuce wraps, and pork-belly tacos. With a 65-foot-long (20 m) bar and late-night hours through the week, this is a great place for hanging out.

🍴 100 🕐 Closed L 🚫 All major cards 🚇 U Street–Cardozo

🍴 SETTE OSTERIA

$$

1666 CONNECTICUT AVE., N.W.

TEL 202/483-3070

setteosteria.com

A companion restaurant of Washington's popular Café Milano, this casual eatery was fashioned on traditional trattorias of Naples. Pizzas from

---

🛗 Elevator ❄ Air-conditioning 🏊 Indoor Pool 🏊 Outdoor Pool 💪 Health Club 🚫 Credit Cards 🚇 Metro a wood-burning oven are the star attraction, along with homemade pastas, a range of appetizers, and a few grilled entrees. Patio dining in season

🍴 75 🅿 Valet
🚇 Dupont Circle

🍴 PIZZERIA PARADISO
$

2003 P ST., N.W.
TEL 202/223-1245
eatyourpizza.com
This small pizza parlor, with sister locations in Georgetown and Old Town Alexandria, makes the best pizzas in Washington. The crust, which tastes like good bread, is thin but supports the sparely applied toppings. If you don't want pizza, there are also superb panini, Italian sandwiches, and salads.

🍴 35 💳 DC, MC, V
🚇 Dupont Circle

▪ CLEVELAND PARK & BEYOND

HOTELS

🏨 MARRIOTT WARDMAN PARK HOTEL
$$$$

2660 WOODLEY RD., N.W.
TEL 202/328-2000 OR 800/228-9290
FAX 202/234-0015
marriott.com
Washington's largest hotel, the Wardman Park is set on 16 acres (6.4 ha) of flower-planted gardens within walking distance of the National Zoo. There are several on-site dining options.

🛏 1,152 🅿 🏊 🍴 💳 All major cards 🚇 Woodley Park–Zoo/Adams Morgan

🏨 OMNI SHOREHAM HOTEL
$$$$

2500 CALVERT ST., N.W.

TEL 202/234-0700
FAX 202/265-7972
omnishorehamhotel
.com
Opened in 1930 on 11 land-scaped acres (4.4 ha) near Rock Creek, the Shoreham is a frequent convention site and location for large events. Its location gives it convenient access to the jogging trails and paths of Rock Creek Park.

🛏 834 🏊 🍴 💳 All major cards 🚇 Woodley Park–Zoo/Adams Morgan

🏨 KALORAMA GUEST HOUSE
$$

2700 CATHEDRAL AVE., N.W.
TEL 202/588-8188
FAX 202/588-8858
kaloramaguesthouse
.com
This and a companion guest house in Adams Morgan offer B&B-style accommodation in the European tradition, with some shared baths and continental breakfast, afternoon lemonade, and sherry in the evening. The many repeat customers can help attest to its comfortable atmosphere.

🛏 19 💳 All major cards 🚇 Woodley Park–Zoo/Adams Morgan

RESTAURANTS

🍴 NEW HEIGHTS
$$$$

2317 CALVERT ST., N.W.
TEL 202/234-4110
newheightsrestaurant.com
A gracious second-floor dining room with large windows overlooking Rock Creek and a menu of creative new American cooking make this restaurant a perennial favorite.

🍴 92 🅿 Valet 🕐 Closed L 💳 All major cards 🚇 Woodley Park–Zoo/Adams Morgan

🍴 ARDEO & BARDEO
$$$

3311 CONNECTICUT AVE., N.W.
TEL 202/244-6750
ardeobardeo.com
This sophisticated neighborhood restaurant and wine bar is the creation of restaurateur Ashok Bajaj, who frequently pops in unexpectedly to make sure the food and service are up to snuff. The kitchen starts with top-quality ingredients. Order simple dishes, such as diver scallops, fresh fish, or braised lamb shanks, and you'll eat well. Brunch is served on weekends.

🍴 40 🅿 Valet 🕐 Closed Mon. L 💳 All major cards 🚇 Cleveland Park

🍴 MACON BISTRO
$$$

5520 CONNECTICUT AVE., N.W.
TEL 202/248-7807
maconbistro.com
Macon, Georgia, meets Mâcon, France, at this family-friendly restaurant that blends old-fashioned Southern cooking with European flair. The bistro, which features vintage fixtures, an open kitchen, and a 20-stool bar, is located in the historic 1925 Chevy Chase Arcade building. The dinner menu uses seasonal, local ingredients in classic dishes such as fried green tomatoes, short ribs, and hand-cut pommes frites. Pick up packaged house-made items like cheese coins and sea-salt caramels in the Macon Larder.

🍴 60 💳 All major cards 🕐 Closed Mon. & Tues.–Sat. L 🚇 Friendship Heights

🍴 CACTUS CANTINA
$$

3300 WISCONSIN AVE., N.W.
TEL 202/686-7222
cactuscantina.com
This many-chambered cantina, usually noisy and

crowded, serves very good Tex-Mex food, both large combination platters and specialties from its mesquite grill. The tamales are a terrific way to begin, but for a main course, order from the grill: crispy quail, great grilled shrimp, or full-flavored spareribs.

🍴 130 inside, 30 outside 🅿️
🅢 All major cards
🚇 Tenleytown–AU plus a 15-minute walk

SOMETHING SPECIAL

🍴 LEBANESE TAVERNA
$$

2641 CONNECTICUT AVE., N.W.
TEL 202/265-8681
lebanesetaverna.com
There's no better place in Washington to experience the legendary hospitality of the Middle East—and its wonderful cooking—than at this busy Lebanese restaurant. It's possible to order a traditional three-course meal here, but you'll get to try a larger variety of dishes if your party makes a meal from mezes, the small appetizer plates that precede a Middle Eastern meal: spicy beef sausages, stuffed vine leaves, tart hummus, baba ghanoush, Lebanese "pizzas"—count on about three dishes per person. The restaurant has several locations around town.

🍴 100 🅿️ 🅢 AE, DC, MC, V
🚇 Woodley Park–Zoo/ Adams Morgan

🍴 MEDIUM RARE
$$

3500 CONNECTICUT AVE. NW
TEL 202/237-1432
mediumrarerestaurant.com
Located just across the street from the Cleveland Park Metro station, Medium Rare adheres to the tradition of classic French steak-and-frites restaurants and its prix-fixe dinner menu serves up virtually one thing: delicious

culotte steak and hand-cut fries. The more expansive weekend brunch menu offers steak and eggs and the house eggs benedict, with sliced steak and portobello mushrooms.

🍴 120 including patio
🕐 Closed L 🅢 All major cards
🚇 Cleveland Park

■ ACROSS THE POTOMAC

HOTELS

ALEXANDRIA, VA

🏨 MORRISON HOUSE
🍴 $$$$$

116 S. ALFRED ST.
TEL 703/838-8000 OR
866/834-6628
FAX 703/684-6283
morrisonhouse.com
A Kimpton hotel designed to evoke the atmosphere of Old Alexandria, the Morrison resembles an 18th-century manor house. Guest rooms are furnished in federal-period reproductions. Dinner is offered at the hotel's very good **Grille** restaurant.
🛏️ 45 🅿️ 🅢 AE, MC, V
🚇 King Street, then bus to Old Town

🏨 HAMPTON INN OLD TOWN
$$$

1616 KING ST.
TEL 703/299-9900
FAX 703/299-9937
hamptoninn.com
Located in the heart of historic Old Town and near Metro, this well-run hotel combines comfort and value with convenience. Walk to many restaurants in the area.
🛏️ 80 🖥️ 🎽 🅢 AE, D, MC, V
🚇 King Street

ARLINGTON, VA

🏨 RITZ-CARLTON
🍴 PENTAGON CITY
$$$$$

1250 S. HAYES ST.
TEL 703/415-5000 OR
FAX 703/415-5061
ritzcarlton.com
A part of the Fashion Centre mall, this hotel offers luxury with the added advantage of shopping. It is minutes from Reagan National Airport. Modern American cuisine is offered in the **Fyve Restaurant Lounge**. Afternoon tea is popular.
🛏️ 366 🅿️ 🎽 🖥️ 🅢 All major cards 🚇 Pentagon City

🏨 CRYSTAL CITY MARRIOTT
$$$$

1999 JEFFERSON DAVIS HWY.
TEL 703/413-5500
FAX 703/413-0192
marriott.com
Located a mile (1.6 km) from Reagan National Airport, this hotel connects to the Crystal City Metro stop, so access to the memorials and Smithsonian museums is easy.
🛏️ 343 🎽 🖥️ 🅢 All major cards 🚇 Crystal City

🏨 HOLIDAY INN
🍴 ROSSLYN
$$$$

1900 N. FORT MYER DR.
TEL 703/807-2000 OR
800/368-3408
FAX 703/522-8864
hirosslyn.com
This hotel is located in Rosslyn, just across Key Bridge from Georgetown. Enjoy dinner in Rosslyn, Georgetown, or the hotel's **Vantage Point** restaurant.
🛏️ 306 🎽 🖥️ 🅢 All major cards 🚇 Rosslyn

🏨 **KEY BRIDGE**
🍴 **MARRIOTT**
$$$$
1401 LEE HWY.
TEL 703/524-6400
FAX 703/524-8964
marriott.com
Just across the river from Georgetown, the Key Bridge Marriott offers easy access by Metro to downtown and its sites. The recently renovated **Capital View Ballroom** offers an indulgent Sunday brunch with stunning views of Washington.
🛏 582 🖼 📺 🚭 AE, D, DC, MC, V 🚇 Rosslyn

🏨 **RESIDENCE INN**
BY MARRIOTT
PENTAGON CITY
$$$$
550 ARMY NAVY DR.
TEL 703/413-6630 OR
800/331-3131
FAX 703/418-1751
All rooms are suites with fully equipped kitchens and other amenities for extended stays.
🛏 299 📺 🚭 All major cards 🚇 Pentagon City

🏨 **BEST WESTERN**
🍴 **PENTAGON**
$$
2480 S. GLEBE RD.
TEL 703/979-4400;
866/561-7476
FAX 703/979-0189
pentagonhotel.com
This newly renovated Best Western provides a courtesy shuttle to Reagan National Airport, Pentagon City Metro station, and the Fashion Centre Mall. The restaurant **Monuments** serves dinner, and breakfast is served daily in the **Capital Ballroom**.
🛏 205 🅿 🖼 📺 🚭 All major cards 🚇 Pentagon City

🏨 **AMERICANA HOTEL**
$
1400 JEFFERSON DAVIS HWY.
TEL 703/979-3772 OR

800/548-6261
americanahotel.com
This modest, well-maintained hotel offers good value and a great location for easy access to Washington and many restaurants in Arlington.
🛏 102 🚭 AE, D, MC, V 🚇 Crystal City

RESTAURANTS

ALEXANDRIA, VA

🍴 **RESTAURANT EVE**
$$$$
110 SOUTH PITT ST.
TEL 703/706-0450
restauranteve.com
At this highly celebrated gastronomic restaurant in Old Town, chef Cathal Armstrong wins accolades for modern American cuisine based on seasonal, organic produce and sustainable meats from a handpicked network of suppliers. Choose between the Tasting Room, featuring five- and nine-course prix fixe menus, or the slightly more casual Bistro. Plan to make reservations well in advance of your desired date.
🪑 100 🕐 Closed Sat. L & all Sun. 🚭 All major credit cards 🚇 King Street

🍴 **BASTILLE**
$$$
1201 N. ROYAL ST.
TEL 703/519-3776
bastillerestaurant.com
At this hidden gem on Old Town's northern edge, chefs and owners Christophe and Michelle Poteaux accent French bistro food with Mediterranean and global influences. You'll find dishes such as black truffle and mushroom risotto and duck with spiced pineapple sauce. Michelle Poteaux's pastry and desserts are among the best in the area. The indoor decor is warm and inviting, but on a gorgeous day, opt for the charming patio.

🪑 50 🚭 All major credit cards 🚇 Braddock Road

🍴 **EVENING STAR CAFÉ**
$$$
2000 MT. VERNON AVE.
TEL 703/549-5051
eveningstarcafe.com
An ambitious American comfort-food menu and an impressive wine program raise this appealing eatery out of the neighborhood restaurant category. A new bar offers wines by the glass and small plates for snacking. In fair weather, there's outdoor seating.
🪑 70 🕐 Closed Mon.–Fri. L 🚭 All major cards 🚇 Braddock Road

🍴 **MAJESTIC CAFÉ**
$$$
911 KING ST.
TEL 703/837-9117
majesticcafe.com
First established in 1932, the Majestic Cafe opened on this King Street spot in 1949. After the building had been left vacant for many years, chef Susan Lindeborg reopened the historic restaurant in 2000, modernizing the interior while preserving its art deco elements. Now run by the owners of Restaurant Eve and headed by chef Shannon Overmiller, the local landmark serves simple American classics such as home-style meatloaf and Amish roast chicken. The family-style "Nana's Sunday Dinner," served Sunday nights, is a popular draw.
🪑 72 🚭 All major cards 🚇 King Street, then DASH bus or Metro shuttle

ARLINGTON, VA

🍴 **WATER & WALL**
$$$$–$$$$$
3811 N FAIRFAX DR.
TEL 703/294-4949
waterandwall.com
Traditional French fare such

as liver pâté and duck confit stars at this elegant restaurant in a quiet Arlington neighborhood. Chef Tim Ma trained at the French Culinary Institute in New York City, and his ingredients are responsibly sourced from local suppliers. Try the refreshing cucumber bellinis or pineapple mimosas during weekend brunch.

🍴 90 🅿 Public lot behind restaurant free on weekends & after 7 p.m. ⏱ Closed Mon.– Fri. L 🅢 All major cards 🚇 Virginia Square–GMU

🍴 EVENTIDE
$$$
3165 WILSON BLVD.
TEL 703/276-3165
eventiderestaurant.com
Dark blue drapes, antique mirrors, and an air of quiet elegance make this upscale neighborhood restaurant a place for savoring food and company. The chef elevates the basics and uses seasonal produce to great advantage in dishes such as creamy squash risotto and foie gras with rhubarb mustard. The popular rooftop bar (open seasonally) has a separate nibbling menu.

🍴 90 🅿 ⏱ Closed Sun.– Mon. & L 🅢 All major credit cards 🚇 Clarendon

🍴 CAVA MEZZE
$$–$$$
2940 CLARENDON BLVD.
TEL 703/276-9090
cavamezze.com
Chef Dimitri Moshovitis was born in D.C. to Greek immigrant parents and follows his family's philosophy of using fresh local ingredients and simple seasonings such as salt, pepper, oregano, olive oil, and lemon to enhance the flavor of his Greek small plates. First opened in 2006, the wildly successful restaurant now has three locations in Arlington, Capitol Hill, and Rockville, and a casual spin-off called Cava Grill in multiple spots in the

D.C. metro area.

🍴 190 🅿 ⏱ Closed Mon. L 🅢 All major cards 🚇 Courthouse

■ EXCURSIONS

RESTAURANTS

ANNAPOLIS, MD

🍴 WILD ORCHID CAFÉ
$$$
200 WESTGATE CR.
TEL 410/268-8009
thewildorchidcafe.com
Loyal patrons love the seasonal and creative American cuisine that's heavily influenced by Southern and French techniques. You can't go wrong with the many dishes that showcase seafood from the Chesapeake Bay.

🅢 All major credit cards

🍴 CANTLER'S RIVERSIDE INN
$$
458 FOREST BEACH RD.
TEL 410/757-1311
cantlers.com
A short drive from downtown Annapolis, Cantler's—owned by a family of watermen—is one of the city's most popular seafood restaurants. You eat at benches at communal tables, or at picnic tables on the deck, overlooking the docks and beautiful creek. Begin with a cup of she-crab soup. There are meat and chicken dishes, but the best main courses feature seafood from Maryland waters—crab cakes, softshell crabs, and rockfish.

🍴 318 🅿 🅢 AE, D, DC, MC, V

BALTIMORE, MD

🍴 THE BLACK OLIVE
$$$$–$$$$$
814 S. BOND ST.

TEL 410/276-7141
theblackolive.com
The cobblestoned streets of Baltimore's historic Fells Point neighborhood lend quiet charm and elegance to this recently opened, family-run restaurant. Whitewashed brick walls and wooden tables deliver the atmosphere of the Greek islands. The menu boasts seafood such as Dover sole and grilled octopus, organic produce from local farms, and an immense wine list with more than 3,000 bottles in the private wine cellar. Fresh fish is filleted tableside. Be sure to sample the succulent baklava ice cream. The accompanying Black Olive Inn offers spacious rooms with organic materials and views of the Inner Harbor.

🍴 90 🅿 Valet ⏱ Closed Sat.– Sun. L 🅢 All major cards

🍴 CHARLESTON
$$$$
1000 LANCASTER ST.
TEL 410/332-7373
Chef Cindy Wolf's Charleston in the Inner Harbor is Baltimore's most praised restaurant. As the name suggests, this is low-country Southern cooking. Starters have included Charleston she-crab soup, cornmeal-crusted oysters, and fried green tomatoes with lobster. Wolf frequently features traditional Carolina dishes such as seafood Perlau, or southern improvisations such as venison medallions with spoonbread or duck breasts with Madeira-poached pears and pecan rice. The wine selection is well chosen and well priced.

🍴 130 🅿 Valet ⏱ Closed Sun. & L 🅢 AE, D, DC, MC, V

Shopping

Washington is the place to pick up that perfect political souvenir—from campaign buttons to White House Easter eggs to presidential seal mouse pads. But just as there is more to the city than what goes on atop Capitol Hill, there is more to Washington shopping than political paraphernalia. The museum stores, for starters, have wonderful inventories of unique books, arts and crafts, jewelry, and artifact reproductions. It's natural that in such a highly educated city you'll find countless excellent bookstores. And local markets feature interesting bric-a-brac.

For a real shopping experience, however, wander into the neighborhoods, which harbor neat little one-of-a-kind shops and boutiques. Georgetown's two main arteries—M Street and Wisconsin Avenue—have many fashionable boutiques, bookstores, art galleries, antiques stores, and contemporary clothing stores. Dupont Circle is much funkier, with its eclectic boutiques, vintage clothing stores, and antique furniture shops. Adams Morgan resembles Berkeley, California, perhaps more than anyplace else on the East Coast, with its down-to-earth selection of African goods, items from India, and curious New Age paraphernalia. Across the river, Old Town Alexandria's historic core along King Street showcases a slew of antiques shops, art galleries, and carpet stores in charming 18th-century buildings.

This listing covers some of the more unique shopping experiences in the Washington, D.C., area.

Antiques

Georgetown overflows with antique shops, especially on Wisconsin Avenue between P and S Streets, and along M and O Streets. Store after store features gorgeous furniture and such accessories as grandfather clocks, 19th-century paintings, and sterling tableware. **Adams Morgan** and **Dupont Circle** also offer a good selection of antiques.

In **Kensington, Maryland,** Howard Avenue is one of the foremost antique districts in the mid-Atlantic, with prices being better than those in Georgetown. Head to the lower, warehouse end of the street for serious antiques shopping. The downtown Antique Row has cute, smaller shops full of collectibles.

Old Town Alexandria has dozens of antiques shops, purveying authentic Persian rugs, as well as French, English, and American period furniture.

Arts & Crafts Galleries

The best places to look for handmade works of art are Adams Morgan, Georgetown, Dupont Circle, and Old Town Alexandria. Seventh Street, N.W., between D Street and the Verizon Center, has become a mecca of galleries.

Addison/Ripley Fine Art, 1670 Wisconsin Ave., N.W. (Georgetown), tel 202/338-5180. One of Washington's foremost galleries, established in 1981, featuring painting, sculpture, photography, and fine arts prints.

Appalachian Spring, 1415 Wisconsin Ave., N.W. (Georgetown), tel 202/337-5780; & Union Station (Capitol Hill), tel 202/682-0505. Traditional and contemporary crafts, including jewelry, gorgeous pottery, quilts, and woodcarvings.

Canal Square, 31st & M Sts. (Georgetown). Art galleries galore.

Torpedo Factory Art Center, 105 N. Union St., Alexandria (Across the Potomac), tel 703/838-4565. More than 80 working artists' studios (each one selling their works) and six galleries showcase sculpture, pottery, paintings in watercolor, acrylic, and oil, plus much more.

Books

Government Printing Office Bookstore, 710 N. Capitol St., N.W., bet. G & H Sts. (Capitol Hill), tel 202/512-0132, closed weekends. The largest general printing plant in the world, the GPO serves the printing needs of Congress. With nearly 16,000 titles (books and pamphlets) covering every conceivable area, from "Cardiac Rehabilitation" to the "Dictionary of American Naval Fighting Ships," you should be able to find something that relates to any new hobby, interest, or activity. Also photography books, CD-ROMS and diskettes, prints, lithographs, and posters.

Kramerbooks & Afterwords Café, 1517 Connecticut Ave., N.W. (Dupont Circle & Beyond), tel 202/387-1400, kramers.com, open 24 hours on weekends. Small but good selection of books. Late-night dining and entertainment at the café.

**Politics and Prose Bookstore &
Coffeehouse,** 5015 Connecticut
Ave., N.W. (Cleveland Park &
Beyond), tel 202/364-1919,
politics-prose.com. Popular with
Washington's intelligentsia. Fre-
quent author readings and book
signings. Café downstairs.

Second Story Books, 2000 P St.,
N.W. (Dupont Circle & Beyond),
tel 202/659-8884. A large shop
with used and rare books, including first editions, fine bound volumes, and just plain secondhand.
Stays open late.

Department Stores
& Malls

Crystal City Shops, Crystal Dr.
bet. 15th & 23rd Sts., Arlington (Across the Potomac), tel
703/922-4636. More than 200
stores and eateries.

**Fashion Centre at Pentagon
City,** 1100 S. Hayes St., Arlington (Across the Potomac), tel
703/415-2401. Four-story mall
with 130 shops, including Macy's
and Nordstrom. Dining and cinema as well.

Mazza Gallerie, 5300 Wisconsin
Ave., N.W., tel 202/966-6114.
This complex of exclusive shops,
restaurants, and theaters show-
cases Neiman Marcus, Saks
Fifth Avenue Men's Store, and
Williams-Sonoma.

Potomac Mills Outlet Mall,
2700 Potomac Mills Circle,
Woodbridge, VA (Excursions),
703/496-9330. Off I-95 about
30 miles (48 km) south of
Washington. Said to be Virginia's
number one tourist attraction,
the 152-acre (61 ha) shoppers'
paradise has some 250 discount
and outlet stores, including
Nordstrom Rack, Coach, and Neiman Marcus. IKEA, the popular

Swedish furniture store, has
recently expanded to twice its
original enormous space.

**The Shops at Chevy Chase
Pavilion,** 5335 Wisconsin Ave.,
N.W. (Cleveland Park & Beyond),
tel 202/686-5335. Stores at this
newly renovated popular mall
include J. Crew, H & M, and
World Market.

Shops at Georgetown Park,
3222 M St., N.W. (Georgetown),
tel 202/342-8190. Several shops
and boutiques in a restored
tobacco warehouse, including
Anthropologie, J. Crew, H&M,
and Olivia Macaron's. Recent
openings include DSW and
Forever 21.

Tyson's Corner Center, 1961
Chain Bridge Rd., McLean, VA
(Excursions), 703/893-9400.
Washington's largest mall, with
more than 300 shops and bou-
tiques, including Nordstrom,
Bloomingdale's, and Lord &
Taylor. With many dining options.

Union Station, 50 Massachusetts Ave., N.E. (Capitol Hill), tel
202/289-1908. An interesting
mix of dozens of stores on three
levels, plus a food court, in an
active, historic train station.

Farmers &
Flea Markets

Alexandria Farmer's Market,
301 King St., Alexandria (Across
the Potomac), Sat. a.m. only.
Traditional farmers market with
the freshest fruits and vegetables,
preserves, just-baked breads and
pastries, and flowers. Opens at 5
a.m.; locals love to show up early.

Dupont Circle Farmers Market,
see p. 168.

Eastern Market, 225 7th St.,
S.E. (Capitol Hill), closed Mon.
Damaged by a major fire in 2007,
Washington's last remaining public market, dating from 1870, has
been beautifully renovated and
looks better than ever. The location also features a farmers market and flea market (Sat.–Sun.).
Popular breakfast and lunch grill
(Tues.–Sat.).

Georgetown Flea Market, 1819
35th St., N.W., at Hardy Middle
School (Georgetown), Sun.
Vendors offer a museum's worth
of antique musical instruments,
rugs, clothes, furniture, new jewelry and sunglasses, old cameras
and books, and much more.

Maine Avenue Fish Market,
Washington Channel, S.W.
Canopied dockside barges hold
beautiful, gleaming piles of
recently swimming rockfish,
bluefish, shad, catfish, swordfish,
pompano, crabs, clams, and just
about any other catch you can
name. A couple of stands sell hot
cooked crabs, for those who just
can't wait to get home or are
just visiting and hungry.

Gourmet Foods
& Wine

Balducci's, three locations in
the Washington area, including
600 Franklin St., Alexandria, VA,
tel 703/549-6611. Modeled on
European markets, featuring
specialty foods and wines.

**Calvert Woodley Fine Wines &
Spirits,** 4339 Connecticut Ave.,
N.W. (Cleveland Park & Beyond),
tel 202/966-4400, 202/966-
0445 (wine line), calvertwoodley
.com. This family-owned
emporium, in business for
over 30 years, offers deluxe
cheeses from beaufort to brie
and a vast selection of beer,

wines, and spirits. The expert wine staff assists customers in finding the perfect varietal.

Dean & Deluca, 3276 M St., N.W. (Georgetown), tel 202/342-2500. Tasty foods in the historic Markethouse building on Georgetown's main drag, plus kitchen accessories and gifts. Its café is a wonderful place to pick up a quick bite, including sandwiches, sushi, and salads.

Marvelous Market, 2424 Pennsylvania Ave., N.W. (Georgetown), tel 202/333-2591. Offers inventive sandwiches, small yet impressive selection of prepared foods, wonderfully crusty bread, and tempting cookies.

Museum Shops

Bureau of Engraving & Printing, 14th and C Sts., S.W. (The Mall), tel 800/456-3408, closed weekends. Engravings of Presidents, Washington landscapes, and government seals. Purchase sheets of uncut $1 and $2 bills.

Decatur House museum shop, 1610 H St., N.W. (White House & Around), tel 202/842-1856. Small and elegant, with reproductions of home accessories from the 18th and 19th centuries, including presidential china, books, and children's selections.

Hillwood Museum, 4155 Linnean Ave., N.W. (Cleveland Park & Be-Beyond), tel 202/686-8510. The former home of Marjorie Merriweather Post, cereal heiress, has a shop with French and Russian decorative arts and reproductions.

Hirshhorn Museum, 700 Independence Ave., S.W. (The Mall) tel 202/633-0126. Unusual items, including contemporary jewelry that's fun and quirky.

John F. Kennedy Center for the Performing Arts, Rock Creek and Potomac Pkwy. & New Hampshire Ave., N.W. (White House & Around), tel 800/444-1325. Good selection of gifts with music, dance, theater, and opera themes.

Mount Vernon Estate, George Washington Memorial Pkwy., Alexandria (Across the Potomac), 703/799-6301. Reproductions of the Washingtons' belongings, including china and silver, as well as toys and souvenirs.

National Air and Space Museum, 7th St. & Independence Ave., S.W. (The Mall), tel 202/633-1000. Freeze-dried ice cream (just like what the astronauts eat), kites, books, and videos for aspiring pilots and astronauts.

National Archives Museum Store, 7th St. & Constitution Ave., N.W. (Downtown), 202/ 357-5000. Copies of the Charters of Freedom, posters, and cards.

National Building Museum, 401 F St., N.W. (Downtown), tel 202/272-7706. Well-chosen architecture-related books, prints, posters, toys, and gifts.

National Gallery of Art, 600 Constitution Ave., N.W. (The Mall), tel 202/842-6002 or 800/697-9350. Several shops in the museum feature quality prints and posters, art reproductions, gifts, and art books.

National Geographic Society, 1145 17th St., N.W. (White House & Around), tel 202/857-7588. Wall maps, books, globes, and educational children's toys.

National Museum of African Art, 950 Independence Ave., S.W.

(The Mall), tel 202/633-0030. Books for adults and children on history, travel, culture, and the natural world. Also African crafts, posters, dolls, jewelry, and tapes.

National Museum of Women in the Arts, 1250 New York Ave., N.W. (Downtown), tel 202/783-7994 or 877/226-5294. Unique jewelry, decorative objects, books on the arts, and other gifts.

Phillips Collection, 1600 21st St., N.W. (Dupont Circle & Beyond), tel 202/387-2151. Jewelry, ceramics, glassware, and other objects by contemporary artists, plus hand-painted scarves, reproductions, books, stationery, and more.

Renwick Gallery, Pennsylvania Ave. at 17th St., N.W. (White House & Around). Features contemporary crafts of fiber, metal, ceramic, wood, and more. Currently under renovation; due to reopen in 2016.

Smithsonian American Art Museum & the National Portrait Gallery, 8th & G Sts. N.W. (Downtown), tel 202/633-5450, Portrait Gallery; 202/633-1589, American Art Museum. Souvenirs and gifts inspired by the collections in the museums.

Textile Museum, G & 21st Sts., N.W., George Washington University's Foggy Bottom Campus (White House & Around), tel 202/546-1210. Tapestries, clothing, gift items, and books related to fiber arts.

Other

Washington National Cathedral, 3101 Wisconsin Ave., N.W. (Cleveland Park & Beyond), tel 202/537-6267. Gothic- and medieval-inspired products, including window decorations, scarves, and stuffed gargoyles. Don't miss the Herb Cottage on the grounds.

Entertainment

After traipsing around all day from site to site, be sure to save some energy for Washington after dark. Your choices are many: theater, a movie, dancing, or just hanging out at one of the local bars. Check the Friday Weekend section of the *Washington Post* for goings-on; as well as the weekly *Washington City Paper. Washingtonian* magazine is another good source of information.

Dance

Dance Place, 3225 8th St., N.E., tel 202/269-1600. Metro: Brookland. Dance Place presents programs of modern and ethnic dance most weekends.

Washington Ballet, tel 202/362-3606. The nationally recognized Washington Ballet presents a full season between September and May at the Kennedy Center as well as *The Nutcracker* each Christmas at the Warner Theatre.

Film

American Film Institute Silver Theatre and Cultural Center, tel 301/495-6720, afi.com. The AFI screens hundreds of films every year at its AFI Silver Theatre and Cultural Center. Actors and directors often are present to discuss their work at these showings.

Filmfest DC, tel 202/274-5782, filmfestdc.org. The DC International Film Festival, held in late April and early May, screens American and international films in a variety of local theaters and auditoriums.

National Gallery of Art East Building, 4th St. & Constitution Ave., N.W., tel 202/842-6799, nga.gov. The National Gallery shows free classic films and films relating to exhibitions in the galleries. Programs in the Auditorium may be moved to other locations in the gallery while the museum is undergoing renovation. Check the website for info.

Reel Affirmations, realaffirmations.org. D.C.'s gay and lesbian

film festival, held in October each year, shows films of gay and lesbian interest at various Washington area theaters. Between festivals, films are screened at the E Street Cinema (*555 11th St., N.W.)* and other locations.

Music
Chamber Music

Corcoran Gallery of Art, 17th St. & New York Ave., N.W., tel 202/639-1700. Metro: Farragut West. Well-known groups appear in the musical evenings series from October to May.

Library of Congress, 1st St. & Independence Ave., S.E., tel 202/707-5502. Metro: Union Station, Capitol South. Broad range of classical music and modern performers, from the Danish String Quartet to Audra McDonald and Rosanne Cash.

Phillips Collection, 1600 21st St., N.W., tel 202/387-2151. Metro: Dupont Circle. Sunday concerts in the Phillips mansion's music room from October to May.

Choral Music

Choral Arts Society of Washington, tel 202/244-3669. Between September and May, this 200-voice ensemble, directed by Scott Tucker, presents frequent classical programs in the Kennedy Center Concert Hall.

Opera

Washington Opera, Kennedy Center Opera House, tel 202/467-4600, kennedy-center.org/wno. Metro: Foggy Bottom-

GWU. During its lengthy season, the Washington Opera, directed by Francesca Zambello, produces up to eight operas, sung in their original languages with English subtitles.

Orchestra

National Symphony Orchestra, Kennedy Center Concert Hall, tel 202/416-8100. Metro: Foggy Bottom–GWU. From September to June, the NSO performs at the Kennedy Center. In the summer, there are concerts at **Wolf Trap** *(tel 703/255-1900),* **Carter Barron Amphitheatre,** and other locations in and around town.

Nightlife

The Birchmere, 3701 Mount Vernon Ave., Alexandria, VA, tel 703/549-7500, birchmere.com. The Birchmere takes music very seriously—the club's no-talking policy is strictly enforced. But the performers and the sound are terrific; the food, from Alexandria's King Street Blues, is very good.

Blues Alley, 1073 Wisconsin Ave., N.W., tel 202/337-4141, bluesalley.com. Metro: Foggy Bottom–GWU, then walk or bus to Georgetown. All the legends of blues have played at this small club—Dizzy Gillespie, Wynton Marsalis, Nancy Wilson, Charlie Byrd. There are usually 8 p.m. and 10 p.m. shows, and sometimes on weekends a midnight set. Reservations are essential.

Bohemian Caverns, 2001 11th St., N.W., tel 202/299-0800, bohemiancaverns.com. Metro: U Street–Cardozo. Bohemian Caverns was once a Washington institution, hosting Duke Ellington, Billie Holiday, Louis Armstrong, Jelly Roll Morton, Thelonious Monk, and others.

HR-57 Center for the Preservation of Jazz and Blues, 1007 H St., N.E., tel 202/253-0044, hr57.org. Named for the House of Representatives resolution that honored jazz as a national treasure, this nonprofit music cultural center holds jazz jam sessions and performances several evenings a week.

IOTA Club & Cafe, 2832 Wilson Blvd., Arlington, VA, tel 703/522-8340. Metro: Clarendon. Iota consistently books some of the best folk, alternative country, and rock music in the area, and the food's good, too. Live music offered every night.

Kramerbooks & Afterwords Café, 1517 Connecticut Ave., N.W., tel 202/387-1462, kramers.com. Metro: Dupont Circle. Serving latte to the literati, this bookstore with attached café is the informal community center for the Dupont Circle neighborhood. It's open all night Friday and Saturday nights, and has live music Wednesday through Saturday.

Madam's Organ, 2461 18th St., N.W., tel 202/667-5370, madamsorgan.com. The popular Madam's Organ has a full schedule of bluegrass, R&B, and blues. Try to arrive before 10 p.m. Thursday through Saturday—after 11 p.m., be ready to wait in line.

9:30 Club, 815 V St., N.W., tel 202/265-0930, 930.com. Metro: U Street–Cardozo. A great sound system makes this crowded club the best place in town to hear top-tier rock, punk, hip-hop, and country performances.

Theater

Arena Stage, 1101 6th St., S.E., tel 202/488-3300, arena stage.com. Metro: Waterfront–SEU. This respected resident theater company presents a busy season on its three stages.

Ford's Theatre, 511 10th St., N.W., tel 202/426-6924, fordstheatre.org. Metro: Metro Center. See p. 140.

Howard Theatre, 620 T St., N.W., tel 202/588-5595, howardtheatre.org. Metro: Shaw–Howard University. See p. 177.

Lincoln Theatre, 1215 U St., N.W., tel 202/888-0050, thelincoln theatre.org. Metro: U Street–Cardozo. See p. 177.

National Theatre, 1321 Pennsylvania Ave., N.W., tel 202/628-6161, thenationaldc.org. Metro: Federal Triangle, Metro Center. See pp. 145–146.

Shakespeare Theatre, 450 7th St., N.W., tel 202/547-1122, shakespearetheatre.org. Metro: Archives–Navy Memorial, Gallery Place–Chinatown. See pp. 138–139.

Signature Theatre, 4200 Campbell Ave., Arlington, VA, signature-theatre.org, tel 703/820-9771. Especially known for its productions of modern musical theater.

Studio Theatre, 1501 14th St., N.W., studiotheatre.org, tel 202/332-3300. Metro: Dupont Circle. Presents the best of contemporary theater. It is the home of Studio Theatre Acting Conservatory, which runs a widely respected school for the theater arts.

Warner Theatre, 13th & E Sts., N.W., tel 202/783-4000, warnertheatredc.com. Metro: Metro Center. See p. 146.

Woolly Mammoth, 641 D St., N.W., tel 202/393-3939, woollymammoth.net. Metro: Gallery Place–Chinatown. *Variety* comments on Woolly Mammoth's "fierce dedication to the offbeat," a dedication that is pursued with genuine devotion and solid production values for more than 25 years. In 2005, this company moved into its first permanent home—a courtyard-style theater in the heart of downtown D.C. See p. 134.

Activities

From boating to golfing to ice skating, Washington offers an amazingly diverse selection of options for outdoor enthusiasts. If you're in the mood to watch others do the work instead, you have a number of big-name sports teams from which to choose, including the Capitals, Nationals, Wizards, Redskins, and D.C. United. For something a little different, join one of the many specialty tours— a chance to see the city from a different point of view, by walking, boating, or even by bike.

Outdoor

Boating

Key Bridge Boathouse, 3500 Water St., N.W., tel 202/337-9642, boatingindc.com. Open April–Oct. Located under Key Bridge in Georgetown, rents canoes and kayaks.

Thompson Boat Center, 2900 Virginia Ave., N.W., tel 202/333-9543, thompsonboatcenter.com. Open April–Oct. Canoes, rowing shells, and kayaks for rent. Lessons available. Also, all-terrain and cruiser bike rentals.

Golf

The National Park Service operates the following three public golf courses in Washington. Check the website (golfdc.com) for amenities and details.

East Potomac Park Golf Course, 972 Ohio Dr., S.W., tel 202/554-7660. This public course near the Mall consists of one 18-hole, par-72 course and two 9-hole courses.

Langston Golf Course, 26th St. & Benning Rd., N.E., tel 202/397-8638. The Langston Golf Course is an 18-hole, par-72 public course that also offers a golf school, golf shop, driving range, putting green, and snack bar.

Rock Creek Park Golf Course, 16th & Rittenhouse Sts., N.W., tel 202/882-7332. This 4,798-yard, par-65 public course has a hilly and challenging terrain. Amenities include a golf school,

golf shop, a putting green, and a snack bar. The course is open every day from dawn to dusk.

Ice Skating

National Gallery of Art Sculpture Garden Ice Skating Rink, 7th St. & Constitution Ave., N.W., tel 202/216-9397. Open mid-Nov.–mid-March. This charming rink right on the Mall affords skaters views of modern sculpture in the museum garden.

Tennis

East Potomac Tennis Center, 1090 Ohio Dr., S.W., tel 202/554-5962, eastpotomactennis.com. Indoor and outdoor courts, seasonal membership as well as walk-in court rental, tennis lessons, and racquet stringing.

Rock Creek Park Tennis Center, 16th & Kennedy Sts., N.W., tel 202/722-5949, rockcreektennis .com. The facility has 25 outdoor courts: 15 hard courts and 10 clay courts. Five indoor courts are heated and available for play in colder weather.

Spectator Sports

D.C. United, tel 202/587-5000, dcunited.com. Professional MLS soccer team at RFK Stadium.

Washington Capitals, tel 202/266-2277, capitals.nhl.com. Professional hockey right in D.C., at the Verizon Center.

Washington Mystics, tel 202/397-7328, wnba.com/ mystics. Professional women's

basketball played at the Verizon Center.

Washington Nationals, tel 202/675-6287, washington .nationals.mlb.com. The Nationals' new stadium is located near the Washington Navy Yard in Southeast (see p. 67).

Washington Redskins, tel 301-276-6050, redskins.com. NFL football at FedEx Field.

Washington Wizards, tel 202/661-5050, nba.com/ wizards. Professional men's basketball at the Verizon Center.

Specialty Tours

Bus & Trolley Tours

Take a spin around town to get your bearings and figure out just where you want to spend more time exploring.

Big Bus Tours, tel 877/332-8689, eng.bigbustours.com. The National Park Service authorizes these comprehensive tours. The **Patriot Tour** covers D.C. then heads across the river to Arlington Cemetery.

D.C. Tours, dctours.us. See the sights from the vantage of an open-top double-decker bus.

Old Town Trolley, tel 202/832-9800, historictours.com. Find out all the local history during a two-hour narrated tour.

Walking Tours

A number of self-guided walking heritage tours have been established around the city including **Roads to Diversity: Adams Morgan, City Within a City: Greater U Street,** and **River Farms to Urban Towers: Southwest** as well as the **African American Heritage Trail.** For information on these as well as many other biking and walking tours contact Cultural Tourism DC (*cultural tourismdc.org*) for their free brochures.

Anecdotal History Tours, tel 301/294-9514, dcsightseeing .com. Author Anthony Pitch leads tours of monuments and memorials with a special focus on anecdotal history of events such as the Lincoln assassination at Ford's Theatre and the burning of Washington in 1814. Private tours any day by appointment.

Bike the Sites, tel 202/842-2453, bikethesites.com. This venture offers family-oriented tours that combine bicycle riding and walking. Bike and stroller rentals are available. Bike the Sites has outlets in three downtown Washington locations (L'Enfant Plaza; Martin Luther King, Jr. Memorial Library; Union Station) and in Old Town Alexandria.

Washington Walks, tel 202/484-1565, washingtonwalks. com. Offered April–Oct. Among the walks to choose from are **The Most Haunted Houses,** which seeks out the ghosts that frequent the area around Lafayette Park and the White House; **Embassy Row,** Washington's grandest boulevard; **Georgetown**; and **Memorials by Moonlight,** which is as its name reflects a tour of Washington, D.C., at its most beautiful.

Boat Tours & Cruises

Dandy Restaurant Cruise Ship, Zero Prince St., Alexandria, VA, tel 703/683-6076, dandy dinnerboat.com. The *Dandy*, similar to a riverboat, cruises from Old Town Alexandria to Georgetown, heading under the Potomac River bridges and past the monuments and memorials. Breakfast, mid-day, and dinner cruises are offered.

D.C. Ducks, 855/323-8257, dcducks.com. By land and by sea! A former amphibious military personnel carrier used in World War II takes you around the city streets for a look at the Mall and a peek at museum facades and then splashes into the Potomac for a little water travel. You end up at Union Station.

Odyssey **Cruises,** Gangplank Marina, 600 Water St., S.W., tel 866/306-2469, odysseycruises .com. The two- to three-hour *Odyssey* cruises feature innovative meals, an excellent wine list, and live music, while taking in the sites of the nation's capital. A real treat is the full-moon cruise.

Spirit of Washington, Pier 4, 6th & Water Sts., S.W., tel 202/554-8000 or 866/302-2469, spiritofwashington.com. With three interior decks and roomy outdoor observation decks, the *Spirit of Washington* can comfortably accommodate up to 450 people for leisurely afternoon or evening cruises. Food, entertainment, and dancing are available. Themed cruises include a Saturday gospel buffet lunch trip along the Potomac River.

Potomac Riverboat Company, tel 703/684-0580, potomac riverboatco.com. This outfit provides water taxi service that will take you to National Harbor for a day of shopping or Nationals Park for an evening of baseball and hot dogs. Traditional cruises also available.

Other

Scandal Tours, tel 202/783-7212, gnpcomedy.com. This irreverent tour of Washington's infamous scandal sites is hosted by the critically acclaimed comedy group Gross National Product, which gives you an impudent commentary on some of Washington's most embarrassing moments. Find out the gossip while taking in the city's beauty. Reservations required. Offered from April Fool's Day through Labor Day. Pickup is at the Old Post Office Pavilion, 1100 Pennsylvania Ave., N.W.

Washington Photo Safari, tel 202/669-8468 or 877/512-5969, washingtonphotosafari .com. Professional photographer David Luria offers half- and full-day photography workshops in English, French, and Spanish designed to improve amateur photographers' shooting skills as well as showcase some of Washington's most photogenic subjects.

INDEX

ILLUSTRATIONS CREDITS